A SPECIAL MISSION

ALSO BY DAN KURZMAN

*No Greater Glory: The Four Immortal Chaplains and
the Sinking of the* Dorchester *in World War II*

Disaster! The Great San Francisco Earthquake and Fire of 1906

Soldier of Peace: The Life of Yitzhak Rabin

Blood and Water: Sabotaging Hitler's Bomb

Left to Die: The Tragedy of the USS Juneau

Fatal Voyage: The Sinking of the USS Indianapolis

A Killing Wind: Inside Union Carbide and the Bhopal Catastrophe

Day of the Bomb: Countdown to Hiroshima

Ben-Gurion: Prophet of Fire

Miracle of November: Madrid's Epic Stand, 1936

The Bravest Battle: The 28 Days of the Warsaw Ghetto Uprising

The Race for Rome

Genesis 1948: The First Arab-Israeli War

Santo Domingo: Revolt of the Damned

Subversion of the Innocents

Kishi and Japan: The Search for the Sun

A SPECIAL MISSION

Hitler's Secret Plot
to Seize the Vatican
and Kidnap Pope Pius XII

DAN KURZMAN

DA CAPO PRESS
A Member of the Perseus Books Group

Designed by Brent Wilcox
Set in 11 point Sabon by the Perseus Books Group

Library of Congress Cataloging-in-Publication Data
Kurzman, Dan.
    A special mission : Hitler's secret plot to seize the Vatican and kidnap
Pope Pius XII / Dan Kurzman.
        p.   cm.
    Includes bibliographical references and index.
    ISBN-13: 978-0-306-81468-6 (hbk. : alk. paper)
    ISBN-10: 0-306-81468-4 (hbk. : alk. paper)
    1. Germany—Foreign relations—Catholic Church.   2. Catholic
Church—Foreign relations—Germany.   3. Political kidnapping.
4. Pius XII, Pope, 1876–1958.   5. Holocaust, Jewish (1939–1945)
6. Vatican City—Strategic aspects.   I. Title.
DD256.8.K87 2007
940.54'87430945634—dc22

                                                            2007007454

Published by Da Capo Press
A Member of the Perseus Books Group
http://www.dacapopress.com

Da Capo Press books are available at special discounts for bulk purchases in the U.S. by corporations, institutions, and other organizations. For more information, please contact the Special Markets Department at the Perseus Books Group, 11 Cambridge Center, Cambridge, MA 02142, or call (800) 255-1514 or (617) 252-5298, or e-mail special.markets@perseusbooks.com.

10 9 8 7 6 5 4 3 2 1

For my dear wife, Florence,
whose serene presence is a
ray of light in a world
dark with war, greed,
and inhumanity

Contents

Contents

Preface

Adolf Hitler's plot to kidnap and perhaps kill Pope Pius XII and loot the Vatican after Italian dictator Benito Mussolini was ousted from power was a most important and intriguing episode of World War II. Yet, it has been barely mentioned in even the most comprehensive history books about the war. And what has been reported is treated as inconsequential rumor.

The plot, however, was real indeed, and all the more consequential because it was linked to a Nazi threat intended to keep Pius publicly silent when a planned roundup of the Jews of Rome occurred. Whatever he might have done without such pressure, German officials in Rome opposed to the kidnap plot warned that he had a choice: seal either his lips or his fate.

No official German documents referring to the plot apparently exist, since Hitler forbade any reference to it in writing, keeping it as secret as his plan for Jewish genocide. But my interviews with the Nazi general ordered to plan the plot, other involved Germans, and knowledgeable Vatican officials leave little doubt that the plot was serious with ramifications that wove through a critical segment of history like a red thread.

Though it was never implemented, awareness of it helped not only to determine what happened to the Roman Jews, whose ancestry in the Eternal City dated back to the time of Caesar, but to mold the policies and behavior of the pope, Hitler, and their subordinates in the months after Mussolini's overthrow in July 1943.

Pius and Hitler loathed each other. The pope, who, for his part, had been involved in a plot to oust or kill the Führer a few years earlier, feared that he intended to destroy the Church. And the Führer, viewing the pope as a potential rival in a postwar struggle for control of the minds and souls of much of mankind, feared that he might speak out publicly against the Jewish genocide, especially if it took place right under his window and turned Catholics against him, including those in the German army.

The coup against Mussolini brought to a head this bitter mutual hostility, with Hitler ordering his troops into Rome, where they would be in a position to carry out the plot against Pius. But some German officers and diplomats who felt a papal abduction would be ruinous to Germany, saw a window of salvation if the pope could be persuaded not to publicly protest the deportation of his Jewish neighbors. Perhaps then Hitler would cancel the kidnap plan.

Ironically, the man leading the conspiracy to save the pope, as well as the Jews, had been chosen by Hitler to prepare the abduction plot. He was SS General Karl Wolff, a little-known but powerful behind-the-scenes Nazi leader who became SS commander in Italy after having been chief of staff to Heinrich Himmler, orchestrator of the Holocaust, and then liaison between Himmler and Hitler.

But for his own reasons, Wolff, who once had to make sure that boxcars crammed with Jews reached the death camps on time, would now help to save, not only the pope, but most of the Roman Jews in an extraordinary confluence of events. Wolff's opportunistic talent was formidable. He would enjoy, simultaneously, the complete confidence of both the Vicar of Christ and the Antichrist.

I interviewed General Wolff for many hours after his release from a war criminal's cell about his role in the kidnap plot, which he claimed to have helped foil. Wolff was not always truthful; he surely lied when he said he had been kept in the dark about the mass killing of Jews, knowing that a confession of his role in that crime would doom him to the gallows if the Allies won the war.

But other key persons involved in the effort to thwart the kidnap plot offered me details that clearly support Wolff's account. They include Rudolph Rahn, German ambassador to Mussolini's rump state established in northern Italy after the Duce's ouster from Rome; Eitel Möllhausen, Rahn's deputy in the Italian capital; Albrecht von Kessel, deputy to Ernst von Weizsäcker, German ambassador to the Vatican; and SS Colonel Eugen Dollman, Wolff's liaison with Field Marshal Albert Kesselring, the supreme military commander in Italy.

Moreover, Father Peter Gumpel, who, as the Vatican's chief investigator of Pius's career to determine if he should be beatified, had unlimited access to documents and oral testimony, told me that the evidence showed Wolff had played the role he claimed to have performed. I gleaned information from hundreds of others who had participated in the drama or had relevant information. And I gathered material as well at archives in Rome, Washington, London, Berlin, Munich, and other German towns.

Nothing in this book is fictionalized, and all dialogue comes from memoirs, diaries, court testimony, or personal interviews, as indicated in the acknowledgments and notes.

Dan Kurzman
Rome 2006

Acknowledgments

I wish to express my deepest appreciation to my wife, Florence, who has played an indispensable role in the preparation of this book. She edited and rewrote with a flare for the colorful and humanistic that reflects her compassion and sense of fairness. And she participated in interviews and conducted research with professional expertise.

I am grateful as well to Robert Pigeon, my editor at Da Capo Press, for the excellent guidance and unremitting faith in this book that he demonstrated from the moment the idea was submitted to him.

My warmest thanks go also to those who spent much time helping me in various ways and offering me valuable insights and background for this book:

Father Peter Gumpel, the relater in charge of the investigation of Pope Pius XII's beatification for sainthood, was very cooperative in answering my questions.

Sister Margherita Marchione, a friend of Pius XII's family who has written many books on his life, presented her views with elegance and passion.

William Doino, Jr., an author and expert on religious matters, who had me constantly on the phone with new information.

Leading members of the Jewish community in Rome, who were eager to contribute their views on the Jewish role in this story.

Gary Krupp, president and founder of Pave the Way, a foundation dedicated to improving relations among all religions, who helped to arrange for invaluable interviews I had in Rome.

John Taylor, the venerable doyen of the National Archives and a dear friend, who, as with my past books, found seemingly unfindable documents hidden away amid millions of obscurely catalogued documents.

Elaine Markson, my agent, and Gladys Justin Carr, a literary adviser and former Harper/Collins vice president, who has been a friend since my reporting days at the *Washington Post,* encouraged me to keep going at those terrible moments of writer's cramp.

And Jeannette Kronick, who not only helped with my research but made sure that my computer worked at critical, exasperating moments when it balked and I was about to give up on the book.

Others deserving my deepest gratitude are:

David J. Alvarez—scholar and author

Silvia Haia Antonucci—archivist, Historical Archives, Jewish Community of Rome

Robert Armitage—humanities bibliographer, New York Public Library

Birgit Bernhard—translator, German to English

Robert Birschneider—chief archivist, Staatsarchiv, Munich

Jennifer Blakebrough-Raeburn—copy editor

Andrew Bolizi—translator, Italian to English

Richard Breitman—American historian

Giorgio Caputo—Italian historian

Rolando Clementoni—papal chamberlain

Renzo De Felice—Italian author and expert on the Roman Jewish community

Eugene Fisher—official, U.S. Conference of Catholic Bishops

Gerald Fogarty—historian on the Vatican

Father Robert L. Graham—Vatican historian

Bernhard Grau—archivist, Staatsarchiv, Munich
Leonidas Hill—biographer of Ambassador von Weizsäcker
Father Norbert Hofmann—Vatican official
Sally Hoult—archivist, British National Archives
Abi Husainy—records specialist, British National Archives
Father David Jaeger—canon lawyer, Vatican
Claire Knopf—helped with the research
David Kronick—helped in arranging contacts
Thaddeus Krupo—supervising librarian, Mid-Manhattan Library
Sally Kuisel—archivist, U.S. National Archives
Joseph Lichten—American Jewish expert on Pope Pius XII
Susanne Millet—archivist, Staatsarchiv, Munich
Jana Nazarro—translator, from Italian to English
Paul Polaczek—reader adviser, British National Archives
Claudio Procaccia—archivist, Historical Archives, Jewish Community of Rome
Aldo G. Ricci—superintendent, National Central Archives, Rome
Walter Ruby—writer on Jewish affairs
Msgr. Robert Sarno—Vatican official
Father Angelo Sodano—Vatican official
Laura Stine—project editor, Perseus Books Group
Risto K. Tahtinen—correspondent, *Torun Sanomat,* Berlin

I am indebted to the following characters involved in this book for agreeing to be interviewed:

Giovanni Agnelli—member of Italian industrial family
Susanna Agnelli—sister of Virginia Agnelli
Giorgio Amendola—communist chief in Rome
Richard Arvay—French Jew in Rome
Dietrich Beelitz—chief of operations under Field Marshal Kesselring
Father Benoit-Marie de Bourg d'Ire—French priest in Rome who helped Jews
Rosario Bentivegna—a communist leader in Rome

Yolanda Berardi—Virginia Agnelli's maid

Ottorino Borin—Italian Resistance officer

Carla Capponi—a communist leader in Rome

Maj. Gen. Giacomo Carboni—officer charged by Marshal Badoglio to defend Rome in September 1943

Gen. Filippo Caruso—commander of the carabinieri in Rome

Sophia Cavaletti—secretary to Chief Rabbi Zolli after his conversion

Felice Chilanti—Red Flag partisan

Gloria Chilanti—Felice's daughter

Viviana Chilanti—Felice's wife

Giovanni Cigognani—Vatican representative in Washington

Lilo Della Seta—a Jewish leader in Rome

Father Dezza—priest who knew Chief Rabbi Zolli

Col. Eugen Dollmann—SS officer in Rome

Donald Downes—American OSS agent

Aldo Garasci—Italian socialist partisan leader

Gerhard Gumpert—German diplomat in Rome

Wolfgang Hagemann—Field Marshal Kesselring's interpreter

Sister Katharine—French nun in Notre Dame de Sion Convent, Rome

Albrecht von Kessel—Ambassador von Weizsäcker's assistant

Renzo Levi—a Jewish leader in Rome

Franco Malfatti—Italian socialist partisan

Father Giovanni Battista Mocata—Roman priest

Robert Modigliani—acquaintance of Chief Rabbi Zolli

Eitel Möllhausen—German consul in Rome

Josef Müller—German Resistance official

Pietro Nenni—Italian left-wing socialist party leader

Pietro Palazzini—Vatican official in San Giovanni in Laterano

Princess Enza Pignatelli Aragona—friend of Pope Pius XII

Fernando Piperno—a Jewish leader in Rome

Donald Pryce-Jones—American OSS agent in Italy

Rudolf Rahn—German ambassador to Mussolini's Salo government

Alfredo Ravenna—Roman rabbi

Goffredo Roccas—Jewish leader in Rome

Marie Celeste Ruspoli—Col. Dollmann's secretary

Sesttimio Sorani—a Jewish leader in Rome

Harold Tittmann—U.S. representative to the Vatican

Peter Tompkins—American OSS agent in Rome

Adelheid von Weizsäcker—daughter of Ambassador von Weizsäcker

Marianne von Weizsäcker—wife of Ambassador von Weizsäcker

Richard von Weizsäcker—son of Ambassador von Weizsäcker

Lt. Gen. Siegfried Westphal—Field Marshal Kesselring's chief of staff

Gen. Karl Wolff—SS chief in Italy

Miriam Zolli (De Bernart)—Chief Rabbi Zolli's younger daughter

Prologue

In May 1945, as the war in Europe wound down, American troops were handed a prized catch. General Karl Wolff, the supreme SS commander in Italy, not only surrendered himself but the entire German army based in that country. Now he expected to be treated with the dignity and deference a man of his stature deserved; after all, he had acted even without the approval of his boss, Adolf Hitler—who had viewed him, he would proudly recall, as the ideal Aryan warrior.

Wolff looked the part, with his tightly combed blond hair that receded from a high forehead, piercing blue eyes with their hint of irony, and thin lips that were almost perpetually curled in a faintly mocking smile. He also exuded a personal charm that gave the SS a human face and even a touch of playboy glamour. Hitler, however, was attracted not just by Wolff's persona; more important, he was convinced of his unequivocal loyalty to him.

Although the general owed his meteoric career to the Führer, he had begun, more than a year earlier, to sense that Germany would lose the war, and had decided that at an opportune time he would abandon his patron and escape the vengeance that the enemy would surely wreak upon the vanquished.

But never in his wildest dreams did Wolff imagine that as a prisoner he would be savoring the peace and comfort he felt now that his lanky, slightly stooped body would be stretched out in a cane deck-chair as he inhaled the sweet scent of roses on a sunlit terrace of the Duke of Pistoia's palace in the Italian resort town of Bolzano. What a wonderful springtime in the Alps!

"It's really rather pleasant here, Eugenio," he mused with understated enjoyment to SS Colonel Eugen Dollmann, a Nazi intelligence officer and fellow prisoner, who had assisted him in the surrender negotiations.

It was the general's forty-fifth birthday, May 13, and what a welcome gift this was.

But to Dollmann, an aristocrat with more sensitive instincts, the day was not yet over. "I have a feeling," he warily responded, "that this is going to be your last birthday in sunny Italy, *Herr* General."

Wolff disagreed. The Americans he had negotiated with liked and trusted him. Just a day earlier, top American intelligence officials who had visited him seemed about to pin another medal on his SS jacket when he had driven them to a nearby village where he had stored art treasures from museums in Florence that he had kept out of the hands of partisan mobs—paintings by such great artists as Raphael and Rubens, sculptures by Michelangelo and Donatello.

And look at the "vacation" they had given him. At least it seemed like one, especially when his tall, blond, Teutonically reserved wife, Maria, the former Countess Bernstorff, called them for lunch while rounding up their four children playing and picking flowers in the garden.

Staff officers of his once-murderous SS, dressed in their newly pressed uniforms, then drove up to congratulate Wolff on his birthday and share in a feast of champagne and delicacies while saluting back to a squad of men who presented arms as they might at a parade. The cry—"Happy birthday, *Herr* General"—echoed across the fields that were, paradoxically, dotted with American army tents just beyond a hedge of roses.

What a party! Everyone was amazed. Had Germany really lost the war? Wolff had given the American Fifth Army's 38th Division "permission" to set up a command post, and GIs watched in amazement while their prisoners drove through the streets in powerful cars, fraternized with civilians, and dined in restaurants catering almost exclusively to German soldiers. Groups of fifteen or twenty members of the Hitler Youth goose-stepped down the main streets in the evening singing "Hitler Is My Führer" and the *Horst Wessel Lied*. Even a German newspaper was printed for several days.

And now this joyous birthday party the general's men were throwing for him.

But gradually the chants of "happy birthday" faded into the rumble of approaching tanks. And before the popping champagne bottles could be emptied, white-helmeted American military policemen broke into the dining room, pointing their machine-pistols at the celebrants, and shouting for them to pack a few things and get ready to leave.

Ten days earlier, an American commander had ordered his men to let Wolff and his troops behave without regulation—apparently in gratitude to Wolff for surrendering the troops in Italy to the Allies. After the surrender, Allen Dulles, chief of the Office of Strategic Services (OSS) in Switzerland, had guaranteed the safety of Wolff's family, according to an undated OSS document, and directed the general to have his family and their belongings brought from their home in Germany to Bolzano, which had been German headquarters. The Wolffs were to be "interned and later utilized in helping rebuild and reconstruct Germany."

Now, with the baffled GIs wondering who won the war, their leaders would finally make it clear to Wolff and his men: The war—and the party—was over!

The two high-ranking SS officers were jammed into a jeep, Wolff's family into another, and they were all taken to Modena camp, a mosquito-infested marshland where prisoners were forced to exercise in the nude. Wolff was shocked. He expected more of the Americans.

"The way the Americans are behaving is disgraceful," he later told Dollmann.

His disillusion grew when he was led into the courtyard of a school serving as a jail and "put into a gloomy wooden cubby hole" where "rats were squeaking excitedly and scampering around behind the rotting woodwork."

"This will very likely be our last night," Wolff observed, feeling betrayed by the Americans for apparently having forsaken him even though he himself had stooped to betrayal by serving their cause. "I have a feeling they're going to shoot us."

In desperation he approached an American officer and blurted: "You don't seem to realize who we are!"

It was perhaps fortunate for him that the officer—and his superiors—did not realize who Wolff was: the former top aide of Heinrich Himmler, the SS chief, the greatest mass murderer in history. But Wolff felt that his opportunistic abandonment of Hitler should have earned him a place in the enemy's good graces, even if they no longer gave him a rose garden.

Neither Wolff nor Dollmann was shot, but the general would later tell of "horrible incidents" and "even suicides of fellow prisoners" in the American camps: "I have myself seen one of my comrades go mad, really mad."

As he waited to die in a cell that would have seemed palatial to those whom Wolff "didn't see" die in the concentration camps he had helped to administer, he wondered whether he, too, might go mad. Did he deserve this? Had he not brought an end to the war in Italy, and even risked his life foiling a plot by the Führer to kidnap Pope Pius XII and plunder the Vatican?

CHAPTER 1

Prelude to Madness

The plot had germinated almost immediately after the Italian dictator Benito Mussolini was ousted from power on July 25, 1943, by King Victor Emmanuel III and a group of rival fascists. Hitler was furious, especially with the "Jew-loving" Pope Pius XII, whom he was sure had encouraged the revolt. He had been betrayed by all of them—and at a time when the Allies were threatening to invade Italy. The following day, he called for a meeting of his military leaders at his headquarters compound near Rastenburg, in East Prussia, to decide how to avenge this humiliation. Among them were Hitler's two top military advisers, Field Marshall Alfred Jodl and General Field Marshall Wilhelm Keitel.

The Führer's anger was reflected in the sparse furnishing of the conference room—a long table stretched across the middle, but no chairs. At a previous meeting, *Luftwaffe* Minister Hermann Göring had been caught napping during a fiery Hitler speech, and the Führer this time made sure that the participants had to stand. No one would sleep while Rome burned!

Mussolini must be liberated and returned to power, Hitler roared. And the king and prime minister must be found and arrested. Rome must be purged of its enemies, including the Jews. To do this, German troops must occupy Rome.

Someone asked about the Vatican, where many Jews were surely hiding. Should they close all roads leading there?

"I will go right into the Vatican," Hitler replied. "Do you think the Vatican disturbs me? We will take it immediately! It's all the same to me. That rabble is in there. We'll get that bunch of swine out of there. Later we can make apologies."

And he added: "We must destroy the Vatican's power, capture the pope, and deport him to Germany and say that we are protecting him."

How could the king, a cowardly weakling, overthrow the mighty Mussolini, Germany's closest collaborator and best friend, without the help and encouragement of a powerful figure like the pope, who hated the Duce?

The hatred ran deep, and was demonstrated earlier in the war when an anti-Hitler German conspirator, Josef Müller, told me he had given Pius documents detailing the SS crimes committed against the Jews and Poles in Poland. Pius showed these documents to the Italian ambassador to the Holy See and asked him to tell Mussolini about the crimes. The Duce would resent papal involvement in such matters, the ambassador warned.

Pius was not intimidated. He might be thrown into a concentration camp, he replied, but he would be responsible "before mankind" if such atrocities happened in Italy and he wanted Mussolini to know it. He was especially worried that Hitler was trying to persuade the Duce to send his fascist forces into the Vatican. Now the Führer was sure to learn of the pope's approach to the ambassador and further suspect that Pius had masterminded the coup—and planned to speak out about the Nazis' Jewish genocide. The pope would reveal to the world the most closely guarded SS secret, though even the German people might not understand why this policy was necessary.

Pius, Hitler suggested, might have to be killed. Meanwhile, he ordered his enforcers to find the king and his men and let them know what happened to traitors.

◆

Victor Emmanuel III had ascended the throne in 1900 and became the puppet of a long line of premiers, the last being Mussolini, whom he brought to power in 1922 to save his tottering, corrupt monarchy. From then on, the king never refused to sign a fascist decree, despite his usually more moderate political views.

In 1938, he even approved, if reluctantly, the fascist anti-Semitic laws and greeted Hitler with pomp and smiles on the Führer's visit to Rome. Only after the Fascist Grand Council, shaken by the Allied invasion of Sicily and the first bombing of Rome, had demanded Mussolini's resignation on July 25 did the king summon the courage to stand up to the Duce.

On that day, dressed in a dark blue suit, his face haggard after a sleepless night, Mussolini, though bitter, was guardedly optimistic upon entering the royal residence, Villa Savoia, for the encounter. He seemed less contemptuous than usual of the dwarfish little man with the large white mustache as he challenged the legality of the Grand Council's action. The king, his usually darting, indifferent blue eyes fixed relentlessly on the visitor, was blunt:

My dear Duce, it is no longer any good. Italy is in pieces. Army morale is at rock bottom. The soldiers don't want to fight any more. The Grand Council's vote is overwhelming. . . . At this moment, you are the most hated man in Italy. You can no longer count on more than one friend. But one you have left: I am he. That is why I tell you that you need have no fear for your personal safety, for which I will ensure protection. I have been thinking that the man for the job is Marshal Badoglio.

Mussolini was shocked. Only a few years earlier, in 1939, he had signed a pact of conquest with Hitler, dreaming of a new Roman Empire, and now he was being dismissed by what he considered a spineless, treacherous figurehead king.

Victor Emmanuel escorted the Duce to the entrance of the villa, smiled weakly, and shook hands with him. Minutes later, a group of policemen grabbed the dictator and propelled him into an ambulance. He was under arrest.

Marshal Pietro Badoglio, the conqueror of Ethiopia, was the king's next guest—not surprisingly, since he always managed to rebound from defeat. Even though his troops were crushed in World War I, a few years later he emerged as chief of staff. In December 1940, Mussolini forced him to resign from the army after a near military disaster in Greece, but again he bounced back—this time as premier.

With fascism all but swept away, at least formally, the same fear and opportunism that had once made the king and Badoglio grovel before Mussolini now made them hesitate to break away from the Axis. They assured the Germans that "the war continues" but at the same time disingenuously started to negotiate an armistice with the Allies.

They could not bolt the Axis, they said, until the Allies could guarantee that fifteen divisions would land to protect Rome—and themselves. The Allies eventually agreed to parachute just *one* airborne division into Rome. At the same time, they planned to land American forces at Salerno, in the south.

On September 7, 1943, the night before the scheduled air drop, Badoglio was visited in Rome by two Americans, Brigadier General Maxwell Taylor and another officer, who had daringly smuggled themselves ashore from an Italian naval craft and had been driven to the capital hidden in an ambulance. Their objective was to assess conditions for the airborne landing.

Badoglio, dressed in pajamas and bathrobe, was about to greet them in his study when Major General Giacomo Carboni, whose task would be to defend Rome against the Germans, expressed shock at the premier's appearance. He found him "a demoralizing sight, with his bald cranium, long wrinkled yellow neck, glassy eyebrowless eyes, . . . a weird featherless bird."

"Excellency," the general said, "you cannot show yourself thus to two unknown American officers. You are still a marshal of Italy. Please dress and freshen up."

Badoglio agreed, but elegant clothes could not cloak his fear. The Italian forces, he told the Americans, were not yet ready to guarantee the security of the three airfields where the division was to land. Nor, it seemed, would they ever be. To Badoglio and his subordinates, it would be tragic enough to turn their beloved Rome, the seat of their fortunes, the source of their power, the root of their culture, into a ravaged battleground. But worse, what reprisal would the Germans wreak on them if the operation failed?

"If I announce the armistice and the Americans don't send sufficient reinforcements and don't land near Rome," Badoglio said almost tearfully as he sat surrounded by the mementos of a glorious military career, "the Germans will seize the city and put in a puppet fascist government."

Drawing his hand across his neck, he added: "It is my throat the Germans will cut!"

Nevertheless, the Allies went ahead with the armistice announcement as planned since it had to coincide with the landing at Salerno to ensure that Italian troops would not help the Germans resist the invasion. Badoglio, after hesitating, delivered a radio address in a depressed, subdued voice; he confirmed that Italy had surrendered to the Allies and asked the people to cease resisting the victors but to resist "any attack which might come from another quarter."

In the early hours of September 9, Badoglio, afraid for his life, awakened the king and urged that both of them flee to the Allied lines in the south.

"I'm an old man," the monarch muttered. "What could they do to me?"

He did not wait to find out. Wearing a light raincoat over his uniform and carrying an old fiber suitcase, he climbed into his Fiat limousine and left the sleeping Romans to their fate.

A general then said to Badoglio: "I'm going to give some orders before I leave. You'll want to do the same, I presume."

Badoglio replied: "No, I'm going to leave right away."

And he, too, abandoned the Romans—hours before German troops marched into the eternally tormented Eternal City. Too late to catch the two renegade Italian leaders before they leaped into the arms of the Americans.

Hitler would rant in fury when he learned of their getaway. But at least he knew where to find the pope—when the time was ripe he would let him know who owned the future.

CHAPTER 2

Wolff in the Wolf's Lair

General Wolff was incensed, he told me, when the telephone rang in his lodging at Hitler's headquarters, the Wolf's Lair *(Wolfsschanze)* as it was called, near Rastenburg in East Prussia. It was early in the morning of September 13, 1943. Who would wake him up at this hour? A familiar voice let him know. His boss, SS Chief Heinrich Himmler, bellowed into the phone that the Führer wanted to see him urgently.

Wolff suspected why; Himmler had secretly given him advance notice. On September 10 German troops marched into Rome, climaxing the comic opera effort by the king and Badoglio to break away from the Axis and join the Allies. Everything had been in flux since July 25, when Mussolini was toppled from power and hidden in a ski resort in the Apennine Mountains, about a hundred miles from Rome.

German intelligence had discovered the location, and on September 12 German paratroopers snatched him away; two days later he was flown to the Führer's headquarters. After a warm greeting, Hitler promised to restore him to power—in a new rump republic comprising most of northern Italy.

Wolff knew that the Führer was enraged by the Duce's overthrow weeks earlier and that he still hungered for revenge on those he believed mainly responsible, including Pope Pius XII, even though there was no evidence of his involvement. He knew, too, that Hitler intended to send him, Karl Wolff, to Italy to make sure the liberated dictator remained a loyal puppet and that the leftist "rabble" didn't take over the streets of Rome and other occupied Italian cities.

Himmler had hinted that Hitler also had a secret special mission in mind for him, and that, Wolff surmised, was what the Führer wanted to talk to him about. It was understandable that his idol wanted to see him, but why so early? After all, he was just recovering from a serious illness.

Now, on the day Mussolini was to arrive, Wolff hurriedly dressed and then threaded his way through a nest of fir trees partly concealing Hitler's bunker from view. He was greeted in the Führer's office by a figure who, though cordial, was trembling with impatience. According to notes that Wolff took during and following the meeting, Hitler, after fulminating against the "treacherous" king and the pope and discussing the general's new job in Italy, gave Wolff an order:

"I have a special mission for you, Wolff. It will be your duty not to discuss it with anyone before I give you permission to do so. Only the *Reichsführer* [Himmler] knows about it. Do you understand?"

"Of course, my Führer."

"I want you and your troops," Hitler went on, "to occupy Vatican City as soon as possible, secure its files and art treasures, and take the pope and the curia to the north. I do not want him to fall into the hands of the Allies or to be under their political pressure and influence. The Vatican is already a nest of spies and a center of anti-National Socialist propaganda.

"I shall arrange for the pope to be brought either to Germany or to neutral Liechtenstein, depending on political and military developments. When is the soonest you think you'll be able to fulfill this mission?"

Stunned, Wolff replied that he was unable to offer a firm schedule because the operation would take time. He must transfer additional SS and police units to Italy, including some from southern Tyrol. And to secure the files and precious art treasures, he would have to find translators well-versed in Latin and Greek as well as

Italian and other modern languages. The earliest he could start the operation, Wolff concluded, would be in four to six weeks.

Hitler's eyes bore more deeply into Wolff's. The kidnapping had to take place while the Germans still occupied Rome, and they might be forced to leave shortly.

"That's too long for me," Hitler growled. "Rush the most important preparations and report developments to me approximately every two weeks."

Wolff agreed and departed in a state of turmoil. Until now, he would have willingly, and proudly, committed almost any act for the Führer—but abduct the pope? Madness! That could turn all of Italy and the whole Catholic world against Germany.

The general apprehensively prepared to leave for the northern Italian town of Fasano in the shadow of the Alps, sprawled along the banks of Lake Garda southeast of neighboring Salò. That's where the Duce would set up a rump government. Being his political nanny did not exactly fit into Wolff's career plan. Yet he was confident he could turn what seemed like a setback into a triumph. And if he had to, he would betray the Führer.

◆

Wolff knew that Hitler trusted him completely, in part because Himmler had so highly recommended him for the task. Besides, the general's anti-Semitic credentials seemed gilt-edged. He had been, after all, Himmler's chief aide and had not shirked his responsibility for helping his boss do his emotionally draining but necessary chore of dealing with the Jews.

So valued was Wolff that he was given the unique title of "Highest SS and Police Leader" *(Hochster SS und Polizeiführer)*, placing him just under Himmler in the SS hierarchy and on an equal level with Ernst Kaltenbrunner, head of the Reich's security office. The general seemed just the man to rein in Mussolini, who would surely seek greater independence than Nazi policy permitted.

The Führer was especially irritated by what had been the Duce's growing reluctance to crack down on the Jews. When Foreign Minister Joachim von Ribbentrop visited him in Rome several months before his ouster from power, Mussolini daringly refused to discuss the "Jewish problem" with him. Nor would he support SS actions taken against the Jews either in Italy or in the Italian-occupied zone of France.

◆

Wolff's initial reaction to Hitler's blunt kidnap order was to think of a way to avoid carrying it out. He was worried not only about the violent reaction of the Italians to such an operation but also about his reputation.

Though Wolff hardly seemed disturbed that his name would be linked with the deportation and death of millions of Jews, he dreaded the prospect of being associated for posterity with the abduction of the pope, and possibly his murder.

Wolff had abandoned his Protestant religion after joining the SS, feeling that the Nazi Party was a good enough substitute, at least if he wished to advance to the top. And he knew little more about Catholicism than what he had learned from the anti-Church ravings of Himmler. But he worshipped power, and Pope Pius XII, like Adolf Hitler, was one of the world's most powerful leaders, having the ability to capture people's souls and to mold their minds. The two men were to the calculating general like earthly gods. And now he was ordered by one of them to destroy the other.

Still, his mission might be useful to him—if he could sabotage it and win the pope's gratitude. Useful indeed should the worst happen and Germany lose the war. A blessing from His Holiness for saving his life could perhaps save his own. Having reached a high position in a criminal world with no regard for human life, Wolff had begun to feel that only the supremely opportunistic could in the end escape accountability in the hands of a vengeful enemy. And how many were in greater need of an opportunity to cheat the noose than the chief aide to history's most notorious practitioner of genocide? Now, in his special mission to kidnap the pope, he perceived a unique opportunity.

Wolff would try to delay, or even sabotage, the kidnap plan. But he would have to walk a possibly fatal tightrope. If Hitler suspected him of disobedience, he would exact a vengeance that would make an enemy noose almost seem a pleasant way to die. Yet this fear of the Führer melded with a sense of guilt for disobeying him and the awe he felt in the man's presence, reflected in a letter the general wrote to his mother in 1939 saying it was "so wonderful [to work] in such close contact with the Führer."

Though only Wolff, Himmler, and probably Martin Bormann, Hitler's powerful secretary and confidant, apparently knew of the Führer's order, other top Nazis knew what Hitler had in mind, especially after the meeting with his military chiefs on July 26.

The day after the meeting, Joseph Goebbels, who, as propaganda minister, personally believed that kidnapping the pope would be bad publicity both at home and abroad, wrote in his diary that he and Ribbentrop had helped to convince the Führer that he should give up the plan. But Wolff now knew that Hitler hadn't, in fact, done so.

The general's main problem was that Hitler had given him little time to stall the plot. Why was Hitler in such a hurry to carry it out? Was it, at least in part, because he wanted to rid Rome of the pope before Pius could see from his window the Jews of Rome being fatally piled into trucks and finally feel compelled to speak out against the mass killings? And even if the pope remained silent during the roundup, did Hitler fear he might protest if the Allies reached Rome and exerted sufficient "pressure and influence" on him to do so?

When I asked these questions, Wolff was clearly perturbed. Hitler, of course, hated the Jews, he replied. And he sent them to concentration camps, always fearing the pope would protest.

But the general quickly added: "You must understand that I just did administrative work for Himmler and did not know the Jews were being killed. I only learned about that after the war."

◆

In 1947, on appearing as a witness at the Nuremberg trials, Wolff made a similar statement to a prosecutor: "I regret to have to confirm to you that today I am of the opinion that exterminations were actually carried out without our knowledge."

He was referring to the "great majority" of SS men, who, he said, were really the "elite" of the German army. And he clung to this claim even after the prosecutor read letters exchanged by Wolff and the state secretary of the Reich ministry of transportation. In replying to the secretary's report about the transport of Jews to the death camp of Treblinka, Wolff wrote:

"Thank you very much, also in the name of the Reichsführer SS, for your letter of 28 July 1942. I was especially pleased to learn from you that already for a fortnight a daily train, taking five thousand members of the Chosen People every time, had gone to Treblinka . . . I have contacted the departments concerned myself, so that the smooth carrying out of all these measures seems to be guaranteed."

Wolff admitted, after his "memory had been refreshed in this way" that he was "connected with these things." But he added that "it is completely impossible after many years have passed to precisely remember every letter which ever passed through my office, and may I also point out that this was the usual procedure . . . [The letter] only referred to the actual transportation movement, the actual movement of the people. . . . I really can't find anything which might be considered criminal." As for his reference to "the Chosen People," "the Jews themselves proudly call themselves" that.

Why were five thousand Jews a day being sent to Treblinka? the prosecutor persisted.

"I don't know," Wolff responded, "but it was done by order of the *Reichsführer* [Himmler]."

"Well, you don't claim today," the prosecutor asked, "that Himmler was among those elite people who represented the best of Germankind, do you?"

The question seemed to startle Wolff, perhaps because he had never asked it himself for fear the answer might shatter the depraved illusion of glory and greatness that shielded his conscience from recognizing evil.

"No," Wolff nervously responded, "I cannot maintain that today, much as I would like to."

CHAPTER 3

The Plotters

It is not surprising that Wolff would have liked to, for he and Himmler had been close for years. Both were born in 1900, but the general had served the SS chief almost like a son, having been appointed his adjutant shortly after the Nazis came to power. With his easygoing charm, Wolff was more the diplomat than the enforcer and thus did not threaten Himmler's position. Although the two men shared many traits, especially a burning ambition, with each drawing on the other's strength in furthering his own career, their personalities could hardly have been more disparate.

From childhood, Himmler, the son of a school teacher with social-climbing illusions of grandeur because he once tutored a provincial prince, was a sullen loner, sickly, homely, with a weak chin and marble-like grey-blue eyes that peered through thick pince-nez glasses, a social misfit who was despised by his classmates for informing on them for any unruliness.

Himmler was an ultranationalist fanatic who lusted for power to meet psychological needs at whatever cost, even at the moral cost of genocide. He heartily embraced Hitler's ideology, which called for a pure-blooded Germany and Europe purged of a Jewish taint, but preferred to expel the Jews through forced emigration.

Himmler acted, however, with cold-blooded opportunism when Hitler required him to practice genocide. Hoping one day to replace the Führer and rule a huge empire stretching to the far reaches of

Asia, Himmler thus became the reluctant murderer of millions. And the equally opportunistic Wolff went along for a demonic ride he thought might catapult him to the zenith of power. Indeed, when Germany seemed to be losing the war, both men would dicker with the possibility of a coup to hasten their ascent.

Pressed by his father to mount the social ladder as he himself had done, Himmler tried to compensate for his physical and personal defects. But he was more eager to take revenge on society than to win its approval, viewing it as a massive aggregate of hostile humanity that had humiliated him in the past and would likely do so in the future.

By contrast, Wolff, living a prosaic life after heroically serving in World War I, yearned to strut once more through the halls of power and glory in shiny black boots, his chest ablaze with medals and the ladies agape with admiration. In any event, to understand Wolff and his role in history, one must understand Himmler.

◆

In the early 1920s, Himmler tried to join the army so he could demonstrate his macho potential to his family, to all who knew him, and to himself. He also wanted to confront enemies who had humiliated Germany in World War I, as he would confront his domestic enemies, especially the Jews, who personified for him all those who had debased him in the past (though he did not know any Jews personally). But his awkward, unhealthy appearance and inane conversation drew only the familiar contemptuous looks and comment of "unfit" in the numerous recruiting offices he haunted. In 1925, however, when Hitler accepted Himmler into his banned Nazi Party, the new member savored the thought of engaging in street fights with rival gangs or simply of throwing rocks at Jews.

Himmler was apparently encouraged in this aggressive attitude after studying the life of Thomas Torquemada, who was the inquisitor-general of Spain in the fifteenth century. Torquemada expelled the Jews and confiscated their wealth, acting in the name of the Church.

A fine example to follow—in the name of a living god, Adolf Hitler, one of the few people who ever tolerated his repelling presence.

He seemed like the ideal choice to head the *Schutzstaffel,* or SS, originally a select group of bodyguards chosen to protect Hitler and other Nazi leaders. On taking it over in 1929, Himmler transformed it into a racially elite formation. He set up the *Sicherheitsdienst,* or SD, as the SS's exclusive intelligence service, which eventually would be united under the SS with the secret state police, or Gestapo, to form a security office of the Reich.

When the Führer came to power in 1933, the ugly loner became the modern "inquisitor-general" commanding an elite "death's head" order of black-uniformed thugs who made up Germany's new ruling class. Millions of Jews and other "enemies of the state" were at Himmler's mercy.

Would he show them mercy? He perhaps noted that while Torquemada expelled the Jews from his country, he did not resort to genocide. And neither would Himmler. He would rob them of their wealth and throw them out of Germany, but mass murder? He wasn't a madman.

According to Himmler's Finnish doctor, Felix Kersten, who became a confidant while treating the SS chief for chronic headaches and stomach pain, the patient told him:

"Ach, Kersten, I never wanted to destroy the Jews. . . . Extermination was a dirty business. . . . [But]some years ago the Führer gave me orders to get rid of (them) . . . I made a start and even punished excesses committed by my people. . . . In 1938 Roosevelt had enquiries made about our intentions with regard to the Jews. We let him know what our intentions were: to remove all Jews from Germany. . . . We asked for Roosevelt's support in executing the entire project. We never received an answer. . . . In 1934 I had proposed to the Führer that he should give the Jews a large piece of territory and let them set up an independent state in it. I wanted to help them. We made enquiries in a number of different quarters, but no one wanted to have the Jews."

Was he thinking of Palestine? Kersten asked.

"No, Madagascar. It's an island which has good soil and a climate which suits the Jews. . . . We could have had an international conference and arranged matters with France (which possessed the island), but things turned out differently. Then finally the war came and brought with it circumstances which sealed the fate of the Jews."

And, it seems, Franklin D. Roosevelt received and considered the request, which was also made to Winston Churchill. A British official cabled Secretary of State Cordell Hull on February 20, 1943, in reference to possible ways to rescue the Jews: "I recalled that some thought had once been given before the war to finding a home for oppressed Jews in Madagascar, . . . [but] the area did not seem climatically well suited, that it was planned to send other refugee groups there, if possible, and that transport presented outstanding difficulties."

It is not clear that Hitler ever really intended to send the Jews to Madagascar, but after the war started he ordered Himmler to arrange for their extermination. And the SS chief could no longer resist the order if he wished to rise in the Nazi hierarchy. It didn't make sense to jeopardize his own future, and possibly his neck, to save people he despised anyway.

Besides, he rationalized, there was a certain logic in the decision to kill them all. The Führer demanded that Germany and all German-controlled areas had to be cleansed of Jews in order to ensure the purity and dominance of the Aryan race, but if no other country would take them, what option was left but genocide? Try as he might, however, he could not rationalize his way out of his depression over Hitler's order.

Kersten would later say that he gave Himmler some sound advice: "He still had a chance to stand well with history by showing humanity to the Jews and other victims of the concentration camp— if he really disagreed with Hitler's orders to exterminate them. He could simply forget certain of the Führer's orders and not carry them out."

"Perhaps you're right, *Herr* Kersten," Himmler responded, but added that "the Führer would never forgive him and would immediately have him hanged."

This response suggested not only a self-serving brand of loyalty to Hitler, but a sense of fear as well, an emotion not generally felt by those Nazi fanatics ready to die for or with their leader if necessary—though at another time he would claim that he would obey every order from Hitler, even if it was to kill himself. So now he had to kill the Jews. When Kersten "begged Himmler to give up this idea," the shaken SS chief desperately noted a precedent. Hadn't the Americans exterminated the Indians?

"It is the curse of greatness," he said, "that we must step over dead bodies to create new life. Yet we must create new life, we must cleanse the soil or it will never bear fruit. It will be a great burden for me to bear."

Thus, with Wolff at his side sharing his boss's opportunistic resort to the most criminally rationalized decision in history, Himmler made his deal with the devil. He could not place his loyalty in question by seeking any more moral compromises. He must either withdraw into obscurity, perhaps into his grave, or obey to the letter every order his master issued. The Führer would permit no compromise. How could he more effectively prove his loyalty— and pave his path to the summit—than to proceed with a program to murder all the Jews he could grab in Germany and, perhaps one day, in Europe?

With this decision, Himmler would find that the more people he massacred the easier his task. For the transformation of humans into subhumans who could be squashed like vermin soon became a normal phenomenon in his mind, if not in his conscience, which apparently generated the almost unbearable physical pain that plagued him constantly.

◆

Karl Wolff apparently never felt such pain, assuring himself that his responsibility was not to initiate orders but to follow them and sometimes offer recommendations on appointments and other mundane matters. Why think about what might have happened when the boxcars he scheduled to carry cargoes of some three hundred thousand human beings arrived at their destination?

Or about what might have happened to the hundreds of Czech civilians whose arrest he had organized after Reinhard Heydrich, Himmler's chief deputy, was assassinated near Prague in June 1942—an operation that included the murder of all male residents of Lidice and the deportation of all the women and children of that village?

He did not know about the killing of any of these people, Wolff would claim, though at least once he accompanied Himmler to witness a massacre. In July 1941, he watched as more than a hundred Jews were gunned down after the Germans captured Minsk in their invasion of the Soviet Union. Since a German officer, Erich von dem Back-Zelewsky, who was present, testified after the war that Wolff had also viewed the massacre, the general, under oath, was forced to admit this was true, though he played down his role. As a witness in 1958 at the trial of the operation's commander, he would give this testimony:

Even though I was only a viewer, this execution was a shocking experience, which I will most likely never forget. The persons being executed were transported by truck to the execution site from a nearby forest. At the execution site two holes were dug out upon our arrival. . . . The delinquents were led in groups of eight to ten to the hole. They had to climb in the hole and lie on their belly. An executioner fired, and then the next group was brought over. . . . This group also had to climb into the hole and lie on their belly.

The dead bodies of the previous group were not buried or covered in any way, but the persons now being executed had to lie directly on the dead bodies. This repeated itself until one hole was nearly full and the remaining delinquents were executed in the same manner in the other hole. Today I can only say that I got sick to my stomach, and I had to turn away to avoid looking at this gruesome execution.

Wolff neglected to say that the "delinquents" he referred to were innocent Jews, arguing that Himmler had told him they were partisans, who could legally be executed.

If Wolff had been in Himmler's position and was trying to please the Führer as he, Wolff, was trying to please Himmler, would he have issued the same orders? It was a question Wolff apparently never asked himself. Who knew how the war would develop and the political climate might change? Why torment himself over a hypothetical situation?

◆

Sometimes pressed by Wolff, Himmler took the risk of showing some mercy in defiance of ideology, either at the requests of friends or apparently to prove to himself that, for all the horror, he was really a compassionate man and hardly a symbol of evil. And indeed, placed outside a genocidal context, stripped of his intimidating SS uniform, he appeared to be a retiring, even sentimental family man who, like his father, could be taken for a small-town school teacher, unnoticeable in a crowd.

Himmler was happiest when, as a dedicated agriculturist, he experimented with plants and flowers and tinkered with ways to breed the finest livestock. He could sometimes make Wolff gratefully forget that he was the devil's apprentice, so kind and courteous was he to many people, including some select Jews, even as the monster in him sent millions of others to a grisly death. And although many of them were children, he doted on one favored child, Wolff's young son, Bubi. A letter he received in 1937 from the general's first wife, Frieda, read: "You made me so happy when you congratulated my Bubi on his birthday. The teddy bear is a true beauty and Bubi had a smile all over his face when I gave him this beautiful toy. Please accept my heartful 'thank you.' With kind regards also to your dear wife. 'Heil Hitler,' Yours gratefully, Frieda Wolff."

At times, Wolff found Himmler thoughtful of others to a fault. Once, the SS chief turned down an offer to be war minister, a job that would make him Field Marshall Keitel's superior. Why reject so important a post? Wolff asked him.

"He was always so decent," Himmler is said to have replied. "I would have taken his position away!"

Didn't that show, Wolff asked, that Himmler was a decent man?

Another beneficiary of Himmler's perceived compassion was his mother's doctor, who, though partly Jewish, was permitted to remain by her side at all times. As a botanist, he was even given large sums of SS money to conduct agricultural experiments. Ironically, in view of his race, the doctor was to develop a formula for exterminating all field pests, an effort that, no doubt to Himmler's amusement, brutally mocked the SS leader's larger genocidal enterprise.

At another time, Himmler, with Wolff's support, approved the request of an SS doctor to use concentration camp "criminals" in experiments on high-altitude flying and human freezing. On November 13, 1942, Himmler would write to a high official dealing with medical matters:

> You will recall that through General Wolff I particularly recommended for your consideration the work of a certain SS Führer. . . . These researches which deal with the behavior of the human organism at great heights, as well as with manifestations caused by prolonged cooling of the human body in cold water and similar problems, which are of vital importance to the air force in particular, can be performed by us with particular efficiency because I personally assumed the responsibility for supplying asocial individuals and criminals, who deserve only to die, from concentration camps for these experiments.

After all, they would soon die in the gas chambers anyway.

One experiment had simulated the conditions of a parachute descent "without oxygen at a height of ten miles conducted on a thirty-seven-year-old Jew in good general condition," the doctor's report stated. "After four minutes the [man] began to perspire and to wriggle his head; after five minutes, cramps occurred; between six and ten minutes, breathing increased in speed and the [man] became unconscious; from eleven to thirty minutes, breathing slowed down to three breaths per minute, finally stopping altogether."

Other scientists protested that these experiments were unscientific. Said one professor: "If a second-term student dared to submit a treatise of that kind, I would throw him out!" And *Luftwaffe* Field Marshal Erhard Milch wrote to Wolff on May 20, 1942:

> *Dear Wolffy,*
> Our medical inspector reports to me that any continuation of these experiments seems essentially unreasonable.

Himmler and Wolff could now salve their conscience. The SS leader wrote to the experimenting doctor: "Considering the long-continued action of the heart, the experiments should be specifically exploited in such a manner as to determine whether these men could be recalled to life. Should such an experiment succeed, then, of course, the person condemned to death shall be pardoned to concentration camp for life."

A true act of mercy.

◆

Nor did Himmler or Wolff lack sympathy for at least some SS men who discovered to their horror that they had Jewish blood. Himmler wrote to one such man:

> I can so well imagine your position and your feelings. So far as our blood is concerned, I have stipulated that the end of the Thirty

Years War (1648) is to be the day to which each of us is obliged to make sure of his ancestry. Should there be some Jewish blood after that date a man must leave the SS. . . . In telling you all this I hope that you will understand the great sacrifice I have to impose on you. . . . In your heart of hearts you still belong to us, you can still feel you are an SS man.

In other words, a man who would massacre his fellow Jews.

Another such man was luckier; he would have the opportunity to do so. Indeed, Himmler and Wolff were more than happy to show this man mercy. He was Reinhard Heydrich, the deputy SS commander who was assassinated in Czechoslovakia. His grandmother was Jewish. (Heydrich was said to have carved her a new tombstone omitting her name, Sarah.) In a secretly recorded conversation with fellow inmates in a British prison after the war, Wolff stated that "the Wolff-Heydrich friendship was one of the pillars of the original SS." In an effort to prove his loyalty to Hitler despite his "bad blood," Heydrich supervised the death camps with even greater zeal and efficiency than his boss. He was a Jew worth keeping and after his assassination, worth honoring—with the horrific massacres in the village of Lidice that followed the arrests of hundreds that were vengefully supervised by Wolff.

◆

If Wolff sought to make moments of mercy, staged or not, humanize his boss—and himself—such deception was sometimes unmasked. Once, for example, they were reviewing a line of female prisoners in Dachau concentration camp when Himmler stopped in front of a young woman and remarked to his aide:

"Look, Wolff, she has blond hair—an Aryan type." And he addressed the girl: "I will order your release immediately if you sign a document saying that you have recognized your Aryan heritage."

Whether she was really an Aryan didn't seem to matter.

She looked Aryan, didn't she? When the woman remained silent, Himmler shouted, "Take her away!" A Jew never appreciated one's generosity! And as Himmler and Wolff continued their review, the girl was dragged away to her execution, though Wolff apparently never asked what happened to her. He didn't want to know.

In any event, as Himmler's closest confidant, Wolff clearly knew of his boss's moral dilemma and could identify with it. Yes, the man could be mean, even savage, but didn't his boss's proposal to simply send the Jews to live elsewhere demonstrate his benevolent side? As for the "forced" alternative, why think about what happened when the flesh-filled boxcars reached their destination?

Unlike his boss, Wolff was not a fanatical anti-Semite. In fact, at great risk to himself, he helped save many individual Jews earmarked for the concentration camp. Such incidents of mercy apparently stemmed from a feeling that occasional good deeds, whether involving Jews or others, would help compensate morally for his pragmatic engagement in far more consequential evil deeds, and thus ease the stress on his calculatedly bridled conscience.

On one occasion, when Adolf Eichmann, who headed the Nazi Jewish Unit, refused an order by Wolff to rescue two Jewish doctors, the general pulled rank and commanded him to obey, brusquely asking him, "Do you realize with whom you are speaking?"

Eichmann then dared challenge Wolff to a duel, but Himmler, who ruled that he alone had the right to dispense mercy, forbade a duel and presumably refused Wolff's request for mercy in this case—while leaving him exposed as a "Jew-lover."

On another occasion, Gestapo Chief Heinrich Müller accused Wolff of "having a relationship with a Jewess"—a charge that might have landed a lesser figure in prison. Actually, the "Jewess" referred to had been a longtime friend of the Wolff family, whom Wolff abandoned only when his future appeared to be in jeopardy.

Wolff also helped save one especially notable Jew. When he and Himmler followed their troops into Vienna during the Nazi takeover of Austria, they watched from their car as SS men rounded up Jews and put them to work scrubbing the streets and washing cars and trucks with acid that severely burned their hands, a prelude to deportation. But in one hotel, they found a Jew they treated differently—Baron Louis von Rothschild, whom Hitler considered one of the super-wealthy elitist Jews most fervently seeking to control the world.

The SS had already humiliated him by refusing to let him shave and then publishing his picture to show his "criminal appearance." But on arriving, Himmler, apparently urged by Wolff, treated him well, even asking him whether he had any complaints. Rothschild had none, nor did Himmler. Instead of being deported, this prisoner was released—after agreeing to turn over enough money to finance, according to Wolff, the transfer of thousands of Jews to other countries.

◆

The general, like many Germans, felt the Jews had played too prominent a role in the economy of Germany and the world—conventional thinking and envy that clearly played a role in his attitude toward them. Being only of upper-middle-class heritage himself, he aspired to reach the social summit, having been captivated by the good life of the elitists with their wine, women, and royal companions in his hometown of Darmstadt. He saw himself as superior in both a racial and class sense to those either rotting in the ghettos or ranting in the boardrooms. But because he had climbed to great heights himself, thanks to the Nazi Party, he did not, like most of his associates, feel threatened by the Jews.

The problem was that to reach the top he would have to follow the Nazi racial rules. He was not a racist when he joined the party, but had been attracted by its glitter and nationalist fervor and the unique opportunity for achieving power and prestige. Gradually, however, the elite SS doctrine of racial superiority melded with his view of class distinction, replacing the now-powerless communists as a perceived threat to his class values. In any event, racism was an absolute requirement for Nazi leadership.

Still, if race was important, it didn't mean the Jews should be killed. All right, if he had to, he would help throw them out of the country. But kill them? Instinct and the military sense of honor in him rebelled. But did he have a choice? Like Himmler, he asked himself if he could sacrifice his future for the Jews, though, unlike his boss, he did not hate them; he even associated with some. He would try not to watch them die or even to believe what he knew was happening.

Had Wolff been a rabid, blood-seeking anti-Semite, he would have found his job incalculably easier. Just kill every one of them without a twinge of conscience. But Wolff managed to computerize his brain to react to the "Jewish problem" in two contradictory ways, apparently as an intellectual and psychological means of diminishing his sense of guilt. Yes, Hitler was going too far, if indeed he ever did give the order to destroy the Jews. As far as he knew—and he didn't want to know more—the Jews were being concentrated in camps similar to the Indian reservations in America, as he would claim at a postwar trial. He obviously knew this wasn't true, having witnessed at least one massacre, but apparently drove any such episode from his mind.

He would, on the one hand, save individual Jews from deportation if he could, and even befriend them despite the risk. For each one had a face, with eyes hauntingly reflecting a tortured soul; they were creatures suddenly springing from his neatly kept transport sheets, almost surprisingly, as human beings like himself, if intrinsically inferior in quality.

But Jews when packed in the cattle cars lost their human identity and were suddenly reduced to faceless subhumans, mere statistics to be filed away, just like the cattle that in earlier days had also been shipped in these cars to the slaughterhouse. He didn't hate them, any more than he hated the cattle. How could he justify mass murder without turning the victims into cattle? This aptitude for self-deception gave him an enormous sense of power, especially the power to decide who would live and who would die.

Wolff's boss, Himmler, played this savage, psychodynamic game, too, though each cheated Hitler of dead Jews with different priorities in mind. Wolff largely chose for survival Jewish acquaintances and friends of friends, but Himmler more superficially favored those with blue eyes and blond hair who could pass ideological scrutiny. Moreover, the SS chief carried out the murder of all but the lucky few with an incredible zeal, born of an ambition that was even stronger than ideology, that simply overwhelmed conscience.

But whatever conflicts between the two SS men would evolve in the future, they would be forever bound together by the soul-poisoning glue of guilt for that massive crime against humanity, each adapting to Hitler's extremist Nazi philosophy. In fact, Wolff grew depressed when his two sons were found to have non-Aryan features that would automatically exclude them from membership in the SS. In 1939, before the Final Solution was introduced, he thus wrote to his wife from Sicily:

Fate made me one of the closest colleagues of a unique man, the *Reichsführer* SS (Himmler), whom I not only immensely admire for his quite extraordinary qualities, but in whose historical mission I deeply believe. Our common and my endlessly satisfying work . . . [is] rooted in thoughts of race. My entire being and effort is for the SS and its future goals.

It is, therefore, no surprise that the thought that my sons will not fulfill the SS selection conditions that, according to human expectations, will be valid for the next fifteen to twenty years, pains me greatly, especially because I could theoretically give my people children who are racially better qualified. I do not need to discuss with you the absence of children having absolutely complete SS qualities.

An esteemed army officer in World War I, Wolff had spent the 1920s studying law and political economics, working as a bank clerk, and operating an advertising agency, prosaic activities that made him long for those heroic days fighting, however futilely, for a nationalist cause. And adding to his malaise was the postwar Weimar economic chaos that threatened his tottering business, and a feeling that his socially elite pretensions might succumb to the creeping slime of communism. Had he not mingled with the cream of Darmstadt society, taking dancing lessons from a ballet star, and even dating the daughter of a baron?

As with Himmler, Wolff saw that hitching onto Adolf Hitler's rising star could lead him to heavenly heights. Unlike Himmler, he had no need to prove his manhood, but he did need to find an environment in which he could exploit his charisma in achieving new success in a patriotic setting.

Wolff himself would explain how he ended up in the infant Nazi Party in a secretly recorded conversation with fellow prisoners in a British prison:

> The world collapse after the last war was terrible. I remained a regular [army officer] till 1920 because I had been assured that I should be given a vacant post, but when my former commanders could not retain me any longer, I came out, because I was the youngest, and my mother was in a position to give me an education or allow me to study. It was years before I stopped wanting to listen to the German national anthem. . . . [Finally] the time had come for a clear decision, either communism or National socialism— something would have to happen.

Something did. In 1931, Wolff joined the Nazi Party. He assured his comrades:

> I can honestly say that I volunteered again for service for Germany because I believed that every decent available man ought to serve

this new Germany that was being born, and as I had been [an offi-
cer] in the last war, I was glad to be serving this time too in the elite
of the movement, the SS.

All my activities were for that end, and if there is anyone who
happens to know me and my work as chief of personal staff of
[Himmler], he will know that my work was of a positive nature,
and thank God, had nothing to do with police matters; on the contrary, I was in the fortunate position, in my capacity as constant
and trusted adviser to [Himmler], to settle all cases of injustice or
unfair treatment.

His listeners, all of whom were involved in the Final Solution, remained silent. Didn't they take orders from him?

Party chiefs were delighted to welcome a distinguished army officer into their rowdy, racist ranks who could inspire greater army cooperation with them and thus help to ease Hitler into power. They
bestowed upon him honorary membership in the elite SS, and he
soon struck up a friendship with Himmler, who viewed him as a potential alter ego, a man who could bring to his office with its
macabre activities the prestige of a sterling military record. Also the
warmth and smooth manners he himself lacked—not to mention the
nobility stemming from Wolff's aristocratic associations.

When Hitler intrigued his way to power in 1933, Himmler became chief of police, and he chose Wolff as his personal adjutant,
and eventually as his chief of staff. The SS leader, who knew more
about policing than about business administration or public relations, found his aide the best choice to keep SS finances honest,
guest dignitaries happily entertained, and, most important, the Jew-
filled boxcars running on time.

Wolff's career started to soar one day in 1937 when he was chosen one of the officers to greet Mussolini, who had come to Munich
to meet with Hitler. As Wolff stood watching a band marching past
a balcony where the two dictators were preening for the huge
crowd, the drum major's staff flew out of his hand and was about to

fall on the marchers when Wolff suddenly leaped up and caught it just in time to save any number of people from injury. Gasping with relief, the crowd applauded, and Hitler and Mussolini rushed to shake his hand. The incident solidified the Führer's impression that Wolff was indeed the ideal SS man.

Thus, no one was surprised when in 1939 he was appointed SS liaison officer between Hitler and the SS, based in the Führer's headquarters, where he would be Himmler's eyes and ears in the heart of Nazi power. Now he had rare access to Hitler himself. Before breakfasting together, they would walk along the rocky paths through the shimmering forest that hid the Führer's bunker from view. During these strolls, Wolff was able to offer frank opinions without giving anyone the impression that he was challenging Hitler's authority. Who could hear them amid the rustle of the tall trees?

Also, to his satisfaction, he could now claim that he had less time to accompany Himmler to the concentration camps, where he had to endure the putrid smell of decay and the sight of living skeletons—the remains of the detestable Chosen People.

Even so, as the years rolled by, the ties between Wolff and Himmler grew stronger, and there were few open differences, at least until 1943, shortly before the general was assigned to Rome. At times, however, their relationship resembled the waspish ties between a quarreling married couple that always ended in reconciliation. But Wolff was only too glad to remain in the background most of the time, not only to keep his boss from suspecting his aspirations, but to avoid being identified too closely with Himmler's criminal activities. Who, after all, could be sure that Germany would win the war?

At the same time, Himmler encouraged Wolff to keep from knowing too much about "the matters" that weighed upon him. Once in 1942, after Himmler had had an argument with his wife, he told Wolff in a moment of depression, according to the general, that it wasn't a family problem that worried him.

"That, dear Wolffchen," Himmler said affectionately, "I could deal with. But you cannot even imagine all that I must silently take on for the Führer so that he, the Messiah for the next two thousand years, can remain absolutely free from sin. You know very well . . . that if I should pass away or if I am unable to continue in my position, only you could be my successor. It is then better for you and for Germany if you neither have anything to do with nor know about these matters that weigh upon me."

Himmler didn't have to tell Wolff to distance himself as much as possible from the horrors he was helping facilitate. Thus, Wolff would assure me long after the war, he "had no idea" that the boxcars he had sent to Treblinka were carrying Jews to their death.

Wolff claimed later that he sometimes openly opposed Himmler's view on some matter. He appeared especially outraged when, after the collapse of Poland, his boss recommended mass executions and turning that country into a nation of slaves. Himmler commended his aide's "endearingly humane characteristics," but called him a hopeless "idealist and optimist" who didn't know how to treat a defeated enemy.

After this dispute, Wolff threatened in a huff to quit the SS and join the less-ideological *Wehrmacht,* the regular German army. But he soon changed his mind. Yes, he wouldn't have to deal with the Jewish horrors any more, but how could he ever reach the summit as a regular army officer in competition with all its entrenched and equally ambitious leaders?

Besides, whatever his differences with Himmler, Wolff felt obliged to reciprocate his boss's sense of loyalty to him that was so dramatically reflected in the SS chief's fatherly advice that he cover his tracks. When German officials met after their victory in Poland to consider allowing some Poles to become German citizens if they met certain Aryan standards, Himmler objected that too much Polish blood was staining the German nation. One official then remarked:

"If I looked like Himmler, I wouldn't talk about race!"

Infuriated by this "racial slur," the SS chief, whose physical appearance hardly met the required standards, wanted to take action against the "slanderer," but backed down apparently for fear that his enemies would support the awful truth. Wolff appeared to be deeply disappointed by Himmler's timidity. His boss, he felt, should have taken the matter to the party High Court.

Wolff simply shrugged off with a rueful smile some of Himmler's quirky rules, which, it seemed, were largely aimed at impressing the Führer with his ideological perfectionism.

One such rule was that an SS man had to be at least six feet tall; because, as Himmler explained to a group of army generals, "I know that only men of a certain size have the necessary quality of blood." Candidates also could not have a Slavic or Mongolian bone structure (though many had it), and officers had to prove Aryan ancestry back to the year 1750, enlisted men to 1800. Himmler, for his part, viewed his popular aide as a man who could win him support among the various figures vying for Hitler's favor.

But more than mutual ambition drew Himmler and Wolff together; they developed close personal ties. Once, in 1941, when Himmler prevailed upon the Reich treasurer to lend Wolff money to pay for a house, the SS leader wrote the treasurer a note of thanks, expressing his warm feelings toward his aide in a rare moment of self-revelation:

"You actually helped me with a tremendous favor. I have gotten to know SS *Gruppenführer* Wolff's honorable and irreproachable character on a daily and hourly basis in the last eight years, and consider him one of my most valuable colleagues and have personally grown very fond of him as a friend."

Wolff was equally caring about Himmler's interests. When the SS chief, who called his aide "Wolffchen," wanted to impress his men with his athletic ability despite his scrawny physique, Wolff, with stopwatch and tape measure in hand, made sure his boss passed all his tests. When Himmler opened an office in Berlin, Wolff went house-hunting for him. And when the doting aide saw his boss— who mistrusted orthodox doctors—slumped over his desk writhing in pain with his hands tightly clamped around his head, he found

Dr. Kersten, the nature healer, whose nimble fingers would ease Himmler's severe headaches and stomach cramps.

These afflictions were apparently psychological byproducts of Himmler's relentless, guilt-breeding effort to commit a perfect genocide. And they seemed to be exacerbated by Hitler's increasingly violent explosions of rage that hinted at a serious deterioration of the Führer's health. Could a sick man lead Germany to its glorious destiny? Was the time near for Heinrich Himmler to replace him on the throne? Was this very thought consistent with his oath of loyalty to Hitler? The cramps kept coming back.

◆

In mid-1943, with the Allies pounding Germany from all sides, Hitler, between outbursts of frustration, appointed Himmler minister of the interior with orders to tighten up the home front against "traitors" and "defeatists," whom he held partly responsible for critical enemy successes. The Afrika Korps had been crushed in Tunisia, and Italy turned into a tumultuous battleground; the best panzer divisions were being demolished in the Soviet Union; and German cities were crumbling under the blows of Allied bombers. Germany could indeed lose the war, Himmler and Wolff realized.

They perceived some hope for victory in repelling an expected cross-channel Allied attack and in producing a "secret weapon" promised by Hitler. But the best hope, they felt, lay in persuading Britain—which Himmler regarded as Germanic ethnically—that it was fighting the wrong war. That it should, together with the Americans if possible, join Germany in fighting the Red Army hurtling westward and threatening to communize all of Europe.

Wolff also favored such an outcome, but he could not abide the fantasy of Himmler's end dream. When the Russians were crushed and either enslaved or killed, Himmler imagined he would one day follow in the footsteps of Heinrich I, king of Saxony, who conquered the Slavs in the tenth century and first united the lands that would constitute the Reich. Dr. Kersten would report that a high Nazi official close to Himmler had informed him "that he knew for a fact" that his powerful patient "regarded himself as a reincarnation" of Heinrich I.

How would he adapt the king's dream of empire to present-day circumstances? Another historic figure, this one a terrible enemy, came to mind: Genghis Khan. In the thirteenth century his Mongol hordes demolished entire cities and exterminated whole enemy populations while storming through Russia, China, Korea, Persia, Asia Minor, and eastern Europe almost to the gates of the Reich. Why not follow the example of this military genius, who came close to nullifying the conquests of Heinrich I, reverse his path of attack, and in the process wipe out thirty million Russians and Poles to make space for German settlement?

This apparent anticipation of an almost mystical future glory probably contributed not only to Himmler's internal conflict and physical pain but also to the planting of doubt in Wolff's mind about Himmler's mental stability.

CHAPTER 4

Flirting with Treason

Although General Wolff shared Himmler's less fanciful geopolitical aspirations, in 1943, after ten years of intimate cooperation, relations between the two men cooled with the suddenness of a winter wind. The rift occurred when Himmler found that his subordinate, who served as a link between central headquarters and the SS and had routine access to Hitler, had worked his charm on the Führer to bypass Himmler and the powerful chain of command.

Since no SS man could marry or divorce without Himmler's approval, Wolff had asked him, if without success, to approve a divorce from his wife so he could marry another woman, a countess. His wife and their son did not have Germanic features, and as a top SS leader hoping to go higher, he wanted to impress Hitler with a family that more closely resembled the ideal Aryan image—as he viewed himself. Wolff would later explain: "When there were state receptions, the *Reichsführer* [Himmler] would lead with his wife— light blond hair and blue eyes, but her cheek bones and her hips were anything but Germanic. And then I would come, and if then the perfect specimen had a beautiful Frisian at his side, there would be even more obvious a difference."

Wolff met Countess Ingeborg Maria von Bernstorff, a young, beautiful blond widow, in 1934 at a charity party arranged by Himmler, who apparently had designs on her himself. Wolff fell in love with her even though he learned that she was not a real countess (her husband

had been an influential businessman), that she had spent a night at
the home of Hermann Göring, the *Luftwaffe* minister (he had kidnapped her), and that she had Jewish friends.

Did he view his adultery as immoral? Well, that was why he
wanted a divorce.

Divorce! Himmler seemed shocked. Didn't Wolff know that SS
men were forbidden to sully their personal lives with this immoral
act? He should keep the countess as his mistress, have children with
her—as well as with his wife—and leave them in the care of the
Lebensborn, an organization he had formed to encourage more
births. These babies would eventually replace the German soldiers
dying in war.

Himmler himself, Wolff knew, was estranged from his wife, apparently because Hitler disapproved of her, and he was living with a mistress who had given birth to two children whom he had turned over
to the *Lebensborn*. The SS chief, who was almost as anti-Catholic as
he was anti-Semitic, would opine to Dr. Kersten on marriage:

> It would be a natural development for us to break with monogamy.
> Marriage in its existing form is the Catholic Church's satanic achieve-
> ment; marriage laws are in themselves immoral. . . . With bigamy
> each wife would act as a stimulus to the other so that both would try
> to be their husband's dream-woman—no more untidy hair, no more
> slovenliness. Their models, which will intensify these reflections, will
> be the ideals of beauty projected by art and the cinema.

But Inge, as she was known, would not consider competing with
Wolff's wife for his affection, and the general, who was deeply captivated by her, would not give Inge up. He had long pegged his career
to complete harmony with Himmler, much as Himmler pegged his
own to total subservience to Hitler; but now, in a reckless moment of
politically calamitous passion, Wolff appealed directly to Hitler.

The Führer overruled Himmler after receiving a letter from
Wolff's wife saying she agreed, even though she still loved her hus-

band after twenty years of marriage. She did not wish, she wrote, to stand in the way of his happiness. It seems that Hitler was impressed by Wolff's daring, almost unheard-of breach of SS discipline. The general might warrant punishment, but his courage reflected the special audacious quality of a potential top SS commander.

Besides, the Führer felt, Himmler was a man of limited intelligence (though, ironically, every candidate for his SS had to submit to a rigorous mental examination before he could join) and did not deserve undue respect despite his unstinting willingness to undertake horrific tasks that might drive another man mad. In any event, Wolff got his divorce. He fathered a son with Inge and placed the boy in a *Lebensborn* home, though a few months later he reclaimed him as a foster child.

Wolff's personal problems didn't end there. Inge demanded that her previous husband will his fortune to their son. When the count refused, Wolff had the Gestapo arrest him, and an agreement was finally reached. The man, however, was soon rearrested and shot to death by the SS. Now Wolff not only had a count in his family, but a very rich one.

When Hitler overruled Himmler's attempt to block Wolff's request to divorce, both Himmler and Wolff wondered whether Wolff had not effectively been thrust to the top of the SS hierarchy. But Himmler still had the power to avenge his humiliation. He thus urged Hitler to transfer Wolff to Italy—far from the power center at home—to help manage the crisis there. He could be tough on the leftist rebels and, since he got along well with Mussolini, could, when the Duce was liberated, make sure he remained loyal to Hitler.

The Führer agreed, but the transfer was postponed when Wolff became gravely ill with a kidney stone. According to Wolff, he may never have departed because Himmler, he believed, had instructed his doctor at the time to hide the gravity of his condition from him and advised a dangerous operation that might have killed him— deliberately. The doctor, in any event, did not operate on him.

Wolff's accusation apparently grew out of anger after an explosive confrontation that had taken place earlier. According to Wolff, he leaped at Himmler after crouching in fright behind his desk.

"For God's sake," Himmler cried. "Don't ruin things for yourself! A physical attack on a superior could cost you your head!"

"After beating you," Wolff snapped in reply, "I will go to the Führer and report to him what I've done. I think that he'll reward me!"

Neither man would risk taking any action against the other, for each could not be sure how Hitler would react to his story. Also, they were linked together by a secret, which could be disastrous for both if the Führer learned of it from one of them. Ever since the Nazi rout in Russia during the summer of 1943, he and Himmler, doubtful that Germany could win the war, had been planning for the future. They had therefore made contacts that could serve them if the worst should happen.

◆

One day in March 1943, Himmler suggested to Walter Schellenberg, his chief of foreign intelligence, that he get in touch with a certain contact whom he knew was in the Resistance. Like Karl Wolff, Schellenberg was a scheming opportunist who, convinced the war was lost, was seeking a way to survive after an Allied victory. He wanted to conclude a peace deal with the enemy and knew that Hitler had to be ousted to get it. Who would have the power to take over the reins? Only Himmler in his view, for he had the SS formations behind him.

Karl Wolff agreed. Both somehow convinced themselves that the Allies would accept a man who personified the most horrendous crime in history as the new Führer, at least until the end of the war. This incredible notion reflected how the murder of millions of innocents had become so routine in their minds that the enormity of the evil was reduced to just another atrocity that the enemy, with blood on its own hands, would overlook as the unfortunate but inevitable result of war.

Nor did Himmler himself believe that the gas chambers and flesh-filled ovens would be held against him personally. Like any soldier, he was just following orders. But though his long-running dream of ruling the country intrigued him, he balked at the idea for various reasons. (Himmler's dream would not have materialized even if he had pursued it, for the army generals supporting the plot planned to liquidate Himmler and his SS once they had seized power.)

Finally, the SS chief, driven by his dreams, uncharacteristically tempted fate and decided to explore the possibility of a coup. His contact was Frauline Hanfstaengl, the sister of Putzi Hanfstaengl, a former intimate of Hitler. The Führer had met the woman through her brother and they soon grew close enough to stir gossip of possible marriage.

At a meeting with Schellenberg, Frauline Hanfstaengl, whose relationship with Hitler had apparently ended unhappily, told him of a "peace plan" she had developed with a few other conspirators. Himmler would forcibly abduct Hitler with the aid of the *Waffen* SS, the SS armed force, to Obersalzberg, where the Führer would be held secretly though ostensibly remaining in control of the government. The real government would be run by a Council of Twelve, led by Himmler.

When the council was in place, Frauline Hanfstaengl would go to Paris, where she would open an art shop as cover and make contact with important connections in France and England, including Randolph Churchill, who, she claimed, was a friend.

Himmler agreed, if with misgivings, to let Schellenberg advance the woman a loan of five hundred thousand French francs so she could open the shop. But the SS chief wasn't sure he would involve himself further in the plot. Yes, this might be a chance to realize his dream—but at what moral cost? Could he so cruelly betray the man who had stood behind him from the early days of the Nazi Party and entrusted him with grand, historic responsibilities? He had meticulously honored his vow to protect the Führer around the clock, even when the death screams from the gas chamber echoed loudest through his mind. And now he was weighing the possibility of doing what he might kill another man for doing! What would history say of him? But did it matter? Was he not the reincarnation of Heinrich I?

◆

While Schellenberg and Hanfstaengl met frequently in Paris and Berlin brewing the conspiracy, Wolff recovered from his illness and finally left in July 1943 for Italy, where he waited to learn whether the plot would materialize. Though he felt "exiled," he began to see certain advantages to his banishment from the Führer's headquarters. Having visited Rome several times with Himmler, and now, after his quarrel with his boss over a personal matter and the man's alleged effort to kill him, he felt he could afford to take a more independent view on weighty political matters, especially when Karl Wolff's interests were at stake.

And they were seriously at stake in Rome, for that was the home of the Vatican, and Himmler had made clear what he thought of the Church. But he claimed that his bias against the Church didn't mean he wasn't religious. He mused aloud to Dr. Kersten: "Some higher Being—whether you call it God or Providence or anything else you like—is behind nature and the marvelous order in the world of man and animals and plants. If we refused to recognize that we should be no better than the Marxists. . . . I insist that members of the SS must believe in God."

Organized religion, however, was another matter; it represented a threat to the dream of a great Germanic empire that would redesign the political and moral structure of the world. At a ceremony honoring the memory of Heinrich I, Himmler, wearing a black steel helmet and clutching a sword in a white-gloved hand, spoke emotionally of his hero's problems with the Church: "Open wounds testify to the radical and bloody introduction of Christianity. The Reich was weakened by the perpetual aspirations to power of the spiritual princes and the Church's interference in temporal affairs." But when Heinrich became king, he courageously refused to be anointed by the Church or to let it interfere in his government.

After one trip to Rome, Himmler elaborated on his opinion of the Church in a talk with Dr. Kersten:

"Have you seen these priests with their red robes in the streets of Rome? . . . Outwardly they seem to be perfecting themselves in their religious exercises, but in reality they're a highly efficient intelligence service. . . . We have to be on our guard against a world power which makes use of Christianity and its organization to oppose our own national resurrection. . . . In every crisis you'll trace the influence of two great world powers, the Catholic Church and the Jews. They're both striving for world leadership, basically hostile to each other, only united in their struggle against the Germanic peoples.

"We've already removed one of these powers, at least from Germany; the time will come to settle accounts with the other after the war. At the moment, unfortunately, our hands are tied; diplomatic caution demands that we should mask our real feelings, but it won't always be the same. Then we'll unfrock these priests—neither their God nor their Virgin Mary will be able to do a thing for them then."

◆

Wolff had listened passively to such talk from his SS superior, regarding it as churning the wind. He was not religious, though he came from an observant Protestant family and attended services with them. But in 1936, he abandoned his religious affiliations, apparently because he couldn't easily advance in the Nazi Party as a member of an organized religion. The Protestants, it was noted, were divided into two factions: One worshipped Jesus as a Nordic figure racially, and the other viewed him as a Jew in the context of the Old as well as the New Testament. Jesus a Jew? Who could tell where a Protestant stood?

To allay suspicion, Wolff, together with Himmler, adopted an old German pseudoreligion from the Middle Ages known as GOT, which was based on a mystical belief in an undefined monotheistic being. It became the SS religion. Wolff felt comfortable at a birth ceremony for his first son when an SS officer he chose held a ring over the child and said: "This ring, the SS family ring of the house of Wolff, shall you wear one day when you have proven yourself worthy of the SS and your lineage."

Unlike most of his colleagues, Wolff converted not for ideological but for practical reasons. He did not oppose any religion and was not determined to rid the world of any. Too bad about the Jews. Individual ones could be good people. But how could the good ones be separated from the others? And should even the bad ones be killed? He didn't approve of killing the Jews as a people, but he would have to live with the Nazi reality if he was to help create a better world for his son—and perhaps one day to rule that world.

For Himmler, too, killing Jews was simply a duty he had to perform, if he wanted to keep his job. His real passion was to kill a far more powerful and threatening force—the Church. He would destroy it from within by sending many SS young men to college to prepare them for ordination as priests. They would then revolt against the Church and throw it into chaos, paving the way for its demolition.

◆

When the Germans marched into Rome after Mussolini's ouster, Himmler saw a unique opportunity to honor the spirit of King Heinrich I. And with the Allies attacking up the Italian boot toward Rome, would history ever forgive the Third Reich for letting this window close?

Germany would have to act promptly to keep the pope from condemning the Final Solution and possibly turning Catholics in Germany and around the world against the Nazis, a danger that could affect morale in the German army—especially the 40 percent that was Catholic—at a critical time on the battlefield. Pius XII had so far refrained from publicly condemning the deportation of Jews in other German-occupied areas. But would he remain silent when the Jews of Rome—*his* Jews—were rounded up?

Hitler was only too ready to act. He was still in a vengeful mood, persuaded that the pope had helped engineer the coup against the Duce. And if Catholics or others condemned the kidnap plot, he would have a rational explanation: He wanted to save the pope from the "anti-Catholic" Allies, who were bombing Rome and would destroy the Vatican and take the pontiff prisoner—the plot that was actually being hatched in Berlin!

Karl Wolff would prepare and implement the plot—under Himmler's supervision. But the two SS men, who had worked together so closely for so many years, now found themselves embroiled in their most profound conflict. Himmler hoped to "defrock" the pope, but Wolff wanted to *use* him. And though both men hoped for a peace based on a united German-Allied force to fight the Soviet Union, the kidnap order lent a new dimension to Wolff's concept of Germany's possible destiny as his country seemed headed toward defeat: the support of the Catholic Church in building that alliance before the Red Army could overrun all of Europe. For who was more fearful of such a cataclysm than the powerful, zealously anti-communist world leader he was supposed to kidnap—Pope Pius XII?

CHAPTER 5

Fighting for Hitler's Ear

As he flew from Germany to Rome en route to his new base in northern Italy, General Wolff could not forget the rabid look in Hitler's eyes as the Führer rasped his demand for an almost immediate plan to attack the Vatican and abduct the pope. If the general could not somehow thwart Hitler's order with a counterplan, he would have to obey it; failure to do so would almost surely end his dream of power, if not his life. And so, as a precaution, he must now prepare a kidnap plan—just in case he had to execute it.

In late September 1943, Wolff arrived in a Rome seething with the chaos of anarchy, a city still without a government to replace the fascist regime abandoned when King Victor Emmanuel III and Premier Badoglio fled to Allied lines. German troops were now pouring into the metropolis after Italian forces, supported by ten thousand civilians armed by the leftist underground, were compelled after bloody battle to agree to a truce and German occupation of four-fifths of Italy, including Rome.

On numerous hoardings, Wolff was greeted by a newly posted proclamation signed by Field Marshal Albert Kesselring, the German army commander of occupied Italy. It read:

Rome is under my command and is war territory, subject to martial law. Those organizing strikes or sabotage as well as snipers will be shot immediately. . . . Private correspondence is suspended. All telephone conversations should be as brief as possible. They will be strictly monitored. . . . Italian civil authorities and organizations are responsible to me for the maintenance of public order. They will prevent all acts of sabotage and of passive resistance to German measures.

Kesselring had good reason to be worried about a popular uprising against his forces. According to Colonel Eugen Dollmann, who had become Wolff's liaison with Kesselring, the field marshal told him that he expected an Allied landing near Rome and "openly admitted that if this occurred and the Italians reacted, he was lost."

But the Italians did not react, at least strongly enough to resist a Nazi attack. "If the Italians had wished to they could have disposed of all the Germans in the Rome area very easily," Dollmann said. "It was only the complete failure on their part to do anything that enabled the Germans to regain control. When on September 9, 1943, some German parachutists were nearly cut off near the Coliseum, [I] was sent forward to find out what the Italians intended doing . . . and was told they were 'waiting to see who would win.'"

But however ineffectual the Resistance was at this stage of the drama, the turmoil swirling in the streets and the tension reflected in the proclamation only hardened Wolff's vow to sabotage Hitler's plot against the Vatican. If carried out, he felt, the plot would surely spark popular violence throughout the country immeasurably more threatening to Nazi control than the current fighting in Rome. And since his job would be not only to keep Mussolini and his rump northern republic loyal to Hitler but also to keep order in Italy and thwart a communist takeover, the plot, if triggered, could make this task almost impossible. Yet, he had to prepare to carry it out even as he sought means to impede it.

Wolff soon left for Fasano, where he would set up his new command. Once established there, Wolff ordered SS General Wilhelm Harster, the Gestapo chief in Italy, to recruit men from southern Tyrol who could speak and write Latin, Greek, French, and English, and he drew up a plan to carry out Hitler's order. The plot was to be executed with precision. About two thousand of his men would seal off all exits from the Vatican, then occupy the Vatican radio station, arrest the pope and the cardinals, and whisk them off in cars and police trucks to the north before the Italians or the Allies could intervene. The papal column would speed via Bozen and Munich into Liechtenstein, unless another destination was chosen.

Meanwhile, troops would search the Vatican for political refugees, German deserters, and Jews, and those who could not be found would be starved out. A special group of about fifty men would, at the same time, collect and pack the Vatican's treasures—paintings, sculptures, gold, foreign currency, and records—including some five hundred thousand books, sixty thousand pictures, and seven thousand incunabula, the Western world's first printed books.

Martin Bormann, whose colleagues often described as "Hitler's Mephistopheles," the devil in the Faust legend, had always wanted to find in particular the age-old runic papers, or scriptures, and other cultural documents showing that Christians had used violence against the ancient inhabitants of Germany. He was also eager to find recent documents "proving" that the Vatican, in league with the monarchy, had plotted Mussolini's ouster. With such "evidence," the large Catholic population of Germany, though already loyal to Hitler the political leader, could also be persuaded that the Führer was their only true spiritual leader.

While reluctantly preparing the kidnap plan—and seeking another scheme to thwart it if he could—Wolff felt that carrying out either one would be easier if he could enhance his power in Italy. He now was responsible for the security of the Italian interior, including air defense and the fight against the partisans, but did not wield such power farther south, within the zone occupied by the army, an area he wanted under his command as well. Such an extension of his power could perhaps permit him—if Germany's defeat seemed inevitable—to use his top position in Italy to take measures that might save him from the gallows that were surely being prepared for captured Nazi leaders.

Wolff therefore met with Field Marshal Kesselring and suggested that the SS take over every administrative function in the occupied zone in addition to its police duties. Kesselring, to Wolff's pleasant surprise, replied: "I consider this an ideal solution."

The field marshal felt that he was a soldier, not a bureaucrat, and was willing to let Wolff rule from behind a desk. Let the SS deal with Hitler. The Führer, he sensed, had lost trust in him anyway—after he had assured him that the king and Badoglio would remain loyal to Berlin even though Mussolini had been overthrown. Kesselring would later write that Hitler "once said of me in a long-suffering way, 'That fellow Kesselring is too honest for those born traitors down there.'"

In any event, Kesselring's chief of staff and other top officers objected to an administrative transfer of authority, fearful that acceptance would diminish their own power. So the field marshal eventually rejected it, too. Wolff would have to betray Hitler with fewer means than he had hoped to have.

◆

Meanwhile, Wolff, despite his pledge of secrecy to Hitler, described the kidnap plot to Rudolf Rahn, the ambassador to Italy, who would be transferred from Rome to Fasano as the emissary to Mussolini's new republic. The paunchy, bushy-browed diplomat was shocked by the idea. He belonged to the Nazi Party, but apparently had joined it automatically, unmotivated by ideology, to advance his career.

Ambassador Rahn was "not an independent thinker," Eitu Friedrich Möllhausen, his consul, told me. "He did things mechanically and had no personal ideal." But when it struck home that he was working for a genocidal government, Rahn was repulsed and grew to detest Hitler. Although he followed the Führer's orders, he gravely doubted that Germany could win the war.

Both Rahn and Möllhausen had previously been based in Tunis, where they helped to save the Jews there from deportation by persuading the air force quartermaster to report that not enough planes were available to fly them to Europe.

Rahn's enthusiasm for Nazism cooled even more as Germany faced defeat. A diplomat's job was to win diplomatic victories, the ambassador told me, but Hitler's rash and harebrained decisions had made this impossible. And now with the kidnap scheme, the Führer had reached another foolish one. But Rahn proved clever at hiding his true feelings, leading his superiors to think he was a "good Nazi." They could not know that he would ask Möllhausen to remove a dashing portrait of Hitler from a wall of the embassy in Rome. "I cannot bear to see that adventurer's face," Rahn said, according to the consul.

But after Wolff revealed to him the mission he had been given, the ambassador could hardly wait to stare once more at that face, the real one, so he could explain the folly of an anti-pope adventure. Was he to be the ambassador to a country in chaos, ripe for a communist takeover, which could very well happen should the Vatican be attacked? But he had to be careful not to let Hitler suspect that Wolff had revealed the plot to him, or the general could pay a heavy price for violating the pledge to secrecy.

Rahn might pay a price, too, the ambassador realized, if Hitler thought he opposed taking action against the pope for "sentimental" rather than practical reasons. To avoid this possibility, Rahn had always deliberately refrained from seeking an audience with the pontiff so that he didn't appear too friendly with the object of Hitler's distrust.

"I always wanted to be in a position to tell Hitler I didn't know the pope," he said to me, explaining that the plot "was a psychological problem" for him: "To influence Hitler, I had to play the role cleverly and make him believe that I was speaking not out of sentimentality but only from a practical viewpoint. Hitler appreciated toughness, and I decided to talk toughly to him when I had the opportunity."

Wolff supported Rahn's attempt to find this opportunity as part of an informal conspiracy he was forming with a few officials of like

mind, including Baron Ernst von Weizsäcker, the new German ambassador to the Vatican; Albrecht von Kessel, Weizsäcker's deputy
and secretary; Colonel Dollmann, Wolff's liaison with Kesselring;
and Consul Möllhausen. They all generally agreed that the plot
against the pope must be stalled, and then cancelled—with the cooperation of the pope himself. In his Nuremburg testimony, Wolff,
in reflecting this accord, said: "Since Weizsäcker and I were in
agreement that this plan should not be executed, I assured him of
my support."

◆

Pius, the conspirators knew, was under great pressure from the Allies
to speak out publicly and specifically against the genocide. And
though he had so far refrained from doing so elsewhere in Europe,
he would, the conspirators calculated, feel compelled to condemn it
publicly if it took place in Rome, figuratively right under his window.

But it was essential to persuade the pope to remain silent in public. If he did not, they were sure, Hitler would carry out the plot. If
he cooperated, however, the Führer could perhaps be persuaded to
cancel it. In any event, the pope would have to be told of the plot so
that he could, in a sense, be blackmailed, if for his own good; he
could choose either silence or seizure. And to increase the pressure
on him, Vatican officials must be made aware that if the pope spoke
out, not only would he jeopardize the papacy and the Church as an
institution, but he would also drive Hitler to drag more people out
of the monasteries and other Church-run hiding places, priests as
well as Jews.

Meanwhile, Rahn would try to persuade Hitler that his plot
would not serve German interests. He telephoned Berlin, Rahn told
me, and arranged to see the Führer the next day in his East Prussian
bunker to discuss the "general situation in Italy," including the
question whether Rome should be declared an open city. He was
careful not to mention anything about the kidnap scheme.

He then flew to Hitler's headquarters and was greeted politely by the Führer and his top lieutenants—Bormann, Himmler, Göring, Goebbels, Ribbentrop, Keitel, and Jodl. But tension pervaded the room. Why, they wondered, did Rahn call for an urgent meeting? More bad news from Italy?

There could be, the ambassador said he made clear after discussing the general situation. He had heard a rumor that "our soldiers" would soon invade the Vatican and kidnap the pope.

"This is the most stupid thing that could happen," he asserted with a slight laugh, as if to dismiss the rumor as ridiculous.

Of course, he didn't believe it, Rahn said, but perception could be as dangerous as reality. If the people thought their pope would be abducted, they might take to the streets and create enormous problems for the occupying forces.

"The Vatican," Rahn added, "is our best ally. With the pope's help, we could calm the spirit of the Italian population and prevent actions hostile to us."

When he had finished talking, Rahn told me, the room echoed for several moments with a thunderous silence. Most of those present were shocked that a mere ambassador would broach such a delicate, controversial subject. And since Hitler himself did not react, most had little inclination to express an opinion that might rile him. As for Himmler and Bormann, who had helped craft the plot against the Vatican, they knew the Führer wanted it to be kept secret (though Hitler apparently had not mentioned Bormann's name to Wolff earlier when he ordered him to prepare a plan).

◆

It was no secret how each of the participants felt about the Vatican and Christianity in general, indeed, how the Führer himself felt. At a lunch on December 13, 1941, he confided in some of his ministers:

"The war will be over one day. I shall consider that my life's final task will be to solve the religious problem. . . . I don't interfere in matters of belief. Therefore I can't allow churchmen to interfere with temporal affairs. . . . The final state must be in St. Peter's Church, a senile officiant, facing [the pope], a few sinister old women, as gaga and as poor in spirit as anyone could wish. The young and healthy are on our side."

If Hitler saw little reason to delay an attack on the Vatican, he had a parallel, more far-reaching plan for destroying the very concept of Christianity, if with deception rather than violence. He thus told one intimate:

"We should trap the priests by their notorious greed and self-indulgence. We shall be able to settle everything with them in perfect peace and harmony. I shall give them a few years reprieve. Why should we quarrel? They will swallow anything in order to keep their material advantages. Matters will never come to a head. They will recognize a firm will, and we need only show them once or twice who is master. They will know which way the wind blows."

Hitler had, in fact, begun his campaign of deception almost as soon as he came to power. He told the new Reichstag that "the government of the Reich, which regards Christianity as the unshakable foundation of the morals and the moral code of the nation, attaches the greatest value to friendly relations with the Holy See and is endeavoring to develop them."

This deceit was soon embedded in the Concordat that Pius XII, as Cardinal Pacelli, wishfully believed would save the Church. Meanwhile, it seemed, Hitler was prepared to pave the way to his long-range goal with a blow that would condition priests everywhere to the futility of paying homage to any god but himself.

◆

Not everyone in the room agreed with the Führer's tactical strategy. Goebbels, though equally anti-Christian, felt as propaganda minister that a strike against the Vatican, which he quoted the Führer in his diary as favoring, would hand the Allies a powerful tool in their propaganda campaign against Germany. Ribbentrop as foreign minister thought that such a move would complicate his effort to tighten ties with Spain and other nations leaning toward the Axis. Field Marshal Keitel feared that it would stir up a national maelstrom of communist rabble-rousing.

Colonel General Jodl apparently supported the attack, though he did not realize that Hitler also backed it. If the Germans had to flee Rome and planned to destroy buildings on their way out, Jodl had recommended that the Vatican be destroyed. He scribbled this answer on a note from a subordinate who suggested that it be spared: "This is not to be considered. Such an order creates instantly the supposition that even the top leadership doubts the ability of the [Germans] to resist."

Himmler, who, of course, knew about Hitler's decision, appeared to have had mixed feelings, even though his long-held dream of annihilating the Catholic Church could be near fulfillment. He had so far supported the abduction plan, and even tried to manufacture an excuse for it in Hitler's eyes by ordering a special terror campaign against the Italian Jews—torturing them, burning their property, and desecrating their cemeteries—to provoke the pope into publicly speaking out and thereby detonating the plan.

◆

Only weeks before this meeting of top Nazis, Himmler, accompanied by Wolff, had met with Professor Johannes Popitz, who was to be a leader in the Council of Twelve that would take over the government under Frauline Hanfstaengl's coup plan. Popitz, a former minister in the Prussian cabinet, wanted Himmler to head the council if it was formed.

Germany's position was hopeless, Popitz argued, and Berlin must try to make a separate peace with the West. America and Britain might well agree to shore up Germany as a bulwark against communism—if Hitler and Ribbentrop were ousted from power. And who would be the Führer's most suitable successor? Heinrich Himmler, who was strong, humane, and reasonable. Or, unsaid, at least a malleable man in command of an armed force.

Himmler was noncommittal. An intriguing idea—especially to Wolff. If Himmler became the new Führer, Wolff would probably be his deputy, a heartbeat away from the top. But Himmler was inhibited by a greater sense of loyalty to Hitler than was Wolff. He needed more time to think about it.

He thought more about it, and was soon consulting with a lawyer and personal friend, another important Nazi who, he had learned, had joined the opposition. Apparently Frauline Hanfstaengl had so far been unable to make the proper contacts in France and Britain. So Himmler sent Dr. Karl Langbehn to Switzerland to learn from his contacts there how the two enemy countries might react to the proposal. But when Langbehn returned with a negative response and word of his mission leaked out, Himmler ordered his arrest, then the execution of both Resistance leaders to make sure Hitler wouldn't suspect *him* of treason. The idea, however, did not die with them, at least not in the SS chief's mind. Heinrich Himmler, the new Führer?

His stabbing sense of guilt for such thoughts of betrayal exceeded even that which was causing him to reel in pain as he watched the slaughter of faceless millions. But if he was to succeed his master— in the interest of Germany, of course—he would be off to a good start with the pope and Vatican out of the way.

The question was, though, would the Allies be less inclined to accept him as the new Führer if they learned that he was involved in the kidnap scheme? In any case, he owed it to Hitler to remain loyal to him—at least until events required a contrary decision.

Nor was the Führer unaware, or unappreciative, of Himmler's worthy wish to finish his most important task with a flourish—ridding the world of the Roman Jews, the only living descendants of the ancient Roman people. And this meant ridding Rome of the pope before he could open his mouth and turn the world against a man who—if he recovered his strength—could purify it with godly efficiency.

Some knowledgeable Germans, Himmler knew, quietly criticized him for his genocidal operation, but none liked the Jews or really cared about what happened to them. Besides, he had tried to save them until circumstances intervened. Why was he being blamed for simply obeying orders, even if his job was disagreeable? Perhaps Britain and America would understand this and eventually embrace him, should he find their embrace necessary.

He would soon have to choose: Should he appease his hatred of the Church while continuing to appease Hitler's hatred of the Jews? Or should he deal with the Allies—who would surely insist that he stop the killings—and perhaps as a reincarnated Heinrich I realize his ancient hero's glorious vision of even greater conquest than Hitler foresaw?

Martin Bormann was caught in no such romantic dilemma. His loathing of the Church and its pope was even more venomous than that of Himmler and more intense than his feeling toward the Jews; he hardly mentioned them. Still, they alone, being hated for racial rather than for political reasons, deserved the gas chamber. In trying to impress Hitler, he signed numerous decrees condemning the Jews to destitution or death, but he let Himmler focus on getting rid of them. They were a problem, but a relatively peripheral one. As for Christianity, Bormann wrote his wife, Gerda, it was "a poison that is almost impossible to get rid of."

Nor did Bormann ardently study Nazi ideology. His all-consuming aim was to help Hitler become the most powerful man in the world and in history. He himself would work the wheels of that power from behind the scenes—until the time came to emerge into the open and reveal to the public his name and possible new role as successor to the Führer.

Bormann, who, like Wolff, had abandoned his Protestant faith in the mid-1930s, believed that the only way to realize this scenario was to crush not only the Vatican but Christianity itself, which he viewed as a deadly competitor of Hitler for the hearts and minds of mankind. In fact, the plot against the pope and the Vatican that the Führer ordered Wolff to prepare was apparently based on "Operation Pontiff," a plan drawn up by Bormann in 1940, with Hitler's approval, but was shelved until a more propitious time.

Simultaneously, Bormann proclaimed Nazism the New Church and said it would outlast "the Roman edifice of hypocrisy." To lay the foundation for this new church, he formed an office, with the enthusiastic support of the Führer, to conduct a relentless anticlerical campaign. It included an effort to promote "the expeditious transfer of priests to other professions" and a decree that "every cleric who resigned his office and, preferably, withdrew from the Church" could have a government job.

The following year, in June 1941, Bormann would further explain in a memorandum to top Nazis and provincial leaders:

> The ideas of National Socialism and of Christianity are irreconcilable. The Christian churches are built on the ignorance of their believers. . . . National Socialism rests on scientific foundations. . . . That is why the German emperors' struggles against the popes always failed. . . . Now, for the first time in German history, it is the Führer who holds the spiritual reins firmly in his hands [and] the people must be progressively alienated from the churches and the clergy. The churches must never recover the least influence over the national destiny. Their power must be broken forever.

In pressing for this ultimate goal of ecclesiastical cleansing, Bormann was fully supported by Hitler, who was himself quoted by Alfred Rosenberg, another Nazi leader, in his diary: "After the war . . . every Catholic State will have to elect its own pope, and the Christian-Jewish past is now approaching its end."

Bormann appeared to have rendered even *his* pope, Hitler, more extreme, though he knew that, unlike his own visceral malice toward

Christianity, the Führer opposed religion itself less vigorously than he did the religious establishment, especially the pontiff, if only because it opposed *him*.

Pius often challenged his policies, however subtly, and had developed what had been a loosely organized Church into a worldwide, tightly controlled institution that threatened to dilute the loyalty of German Catholics toward their only true master, the Führer. How satisfying it would be to whisk this demon in white robes from his throne and replace him with someone who knew who his superior was.

Bormann indeed made Himmler, who reviled Christian leaders but embraced their religion, seem almost like a devout man of faith. The two leaders had been good friends until, some months earlier, Hitler appointed Himmler his minister of interior. Before then, the SS chief often visited Bormann's home, where he was greeted as "Uncle Heinrich" by the Bormann children.

The pair had much in common, especially a desire to absorb all of Asia, though Himmler envisaged victory as a return to the glory of old German imperialism, while Bormann viewed it as an advance to the glory of a new uniquely powerful one untainted by memories of the old. But with Himmler adding a key ministry to his sphere of power, they inevitably had a falling out.

As head of the Nazi party, Bormann also wielded enormous power, and it was enhanced by Hitler's absolute trust in him. Although his name was unknown even to most of his own countrymen, he exerted in the shadows more influence over Hitler than any of his well-publicized cronies. He was, in fact, regarded as the secret ruler of Germany during the war years by some analysts. None had access to Hitler without going through him—though Goebbels, some observers believe, could have had direct access if he had pressed for it, since he was a closer personal friend of the Führer.

Bormann had come a long way since dropping out of secondary school in his sophomore year. He eventually managed an estate, then found relief from his boredom and felt an ego-boosting thrill with a job as a fancily uniformed junior press officer in the Nazi

Party. After writing crisply worded propaganda leaflets, he began reading prolifically in an attempt to polish his prose. He delved especially into the lives of influential leaders like Vladimir Lenin and his boss, Adolf Hitler, less to learn about ideology than about how to achieve and use power.

While building up a large personal library, Bormann learned that extraordinary charisma was an essential ingredient of greatness. And though he was eager to rise in the party, he realized that his lack of that attribute, accentuated by a distinctly non-Aryan appearance, with his fleshy face, stocky build, and black hair, did not bode well for the future—unless he could obscurely scratch his way upward in the shadow of greatness.

Thus, he hid in the background for many years while Hitler played one ambitious leader against another to make sure none grew dominant enough to threaten him. Since Bormann had played no role in this political game, Hitler brought him into his office, where his unscrupulousness, passion for intrigue, and bureaucratic genius—exercised from about midday to 5:00 A.M. to coincide with his master's working hours—compensated for his lack of creativity and earned him a high secret niche in the Nazi power structure.

With Himmler heading the SS and Bormann the Nazi Party, each in charge of a separate arm of government, they could at first ease into a warm relationship. But Himmler's appointment to the ministry of interior seemed to overturn the balance: "To our surprise, it did not take [Bormann] long to stalemate Himmler as minister of the interior," noted Albert Speer, a top Nazi official. And when Himmler, in his new post, sought greater power in the provinces, Bormann strengthened his own position by reporting this "illegal" action to Hitler.

◆

The two antagonists quietly agreed on the plot against the Vatican, though Bormann, unlike Himmler, had no second thoughts. After making his case against such action at the meeting of the Nazi leaders,

Ambassador Rahn, hopeful that his aggressively delivered plea would prevail, had only to glance at Bormann to know that it would be difficult winning over Hitler, who placed great weight on the view of his Mephistopheles in reaching many of his decisions.

"Bormann's face turned very red," Rahn told me, "red with excitement and anger. But he didn't have the courage to reply to my arguments."

Nor did the other sycophants. Hitler himself did not comment, clearly reluctant to discuss a secret decision already made and to listen to dissidents whom he had not consulted about the plot. He would let them know about it at the proper time. But everyone, probably even Hitler, knew that Bormann would be less tongue-tied once he was alone with his master behind a door barred to everyone else—except perhaps Goebbels.

And even Goebbels's record was stained and to some degree had cooled his relations with Hitler. In 1938, according to the diary of Ulrich von Hassell, one of Hitler's top diplomats, "Goebbels was [at that time] pretty much in disfavor because of his affairs with actresses and other women who are dependent upon the propaganda ministry for jobs." This was developing into too much of a scandal. Hitler was in a rage, especially because Goebbels wanted to divorce his wife—an indication of Hitler's strong affinity to General Wolff, whom he permitted to divorce despite Himmler's objection.

In any event, the Führer was aware and indeed appreciative of Himmler's worthy wish to finish his most important task with a flourish—ridding the world of the Roman Jews. And this meant purging these Jews before the pope could open his mouth and turn the world against the Führer who—if he recovered his strength—could purify humanity more efficiently than any papal messenger of God.

Hitler's legendary determination to act on any obsession that seized him did not offer much hope to those who feared he would carry out his kidnap plan.

CHAPTER 6

The Only Way
to Save Germany

Shortly after convening with Hitler and his chief lieutenants, Rahn flew back to Rome, where he met with Wolff and Weizsäcker, the tall, white-haired German ambassador to the Vatican, whom Wolff had also entrusted with Hitler's "secret" decision. Now, as Rahn reported on his mission, Weizsäcker had the depressed look of a man facing a firing squad, though a grim, unyielding glint in his eyes attested to his will to survive.

For it seemed that Hitler was serious about attacking the Vatican, especially with Bormann egging him on. And if it really took place, Weizsäcker's own secret plan would be doomed—a plan he thought was the only answer to the catastrophe looming for his beloved Germany. Like Wolff and Pius XII himself, Weizsäcker wanted a negotiated peace, using the pope as the mediator. His abduction would kill that last chance for rescuing Germany from utter destruction and, perhaps in the chaos, a communist takeover.

This was not to mention saving the magnificent metropolis of Rome from the same fate. The Allies had already started bombing Rome; they had hit some historic churches and might well escalate their operations to rescue Pius, if necessary. After all, on September 9, the day before the Nazis occupied Rome and four days before Hitler ordered Wolff to prepare the kidnap plot, President Franklin

D. Roosevelt remarked at a White House meeting, with Prime Minister Winston Churchill and the combined chiefs of staff present, that a new Allied slogan should be adopted:

"Save the Pope!"

That was Weizsäcker's personal slogan as well, but how could he act upon it? One thing he must do was to thwart what he knew was Hitler's intention to deport the Roman Jews. Not only did the deliberate killing of Jews horrify him, but such action might force the pope to condemn the Nazis, triggering the order to carry out the kidnap plot and ending any chance of a Vatican-mediated negotiated peace that could save Germany from destruction, his most desperate concern.

◆

Weizsäcker's brand of anti-Semitism, nonviolent and probably milder than that infecting most Germans at the time, was perhaps reflected in an observation he made in his memoirs about *Krystalnacht,* a horrific attack on Jewish shops and synagogues in Germany after Hitler came to power:

> Intelligent Jews had admitted before 1933 that with the great opportunities they had had in the Weimar Republic they had overdrawn their account. But nevertheless, the danger which now threatened them could not have been foreseen. Anti-Semitism was really not a German characteristic; but now it had become a weapon of revolutionary agitation, however little the middle classes and the state officials might like it. . . .
>
> All the immense human misery and injustice of the war years found their culmination in the fate which befell the Jews. Their only protection was the conscience of the world; and no trace of this could be found in Hitler's mentality. . . . There was no direct way of bringing about any change by means of arguments based on simple human feelings of compassion.

The ambassador would also claim that he "appealed to Ribben-trop . . . to take energetic actions against these atrocities in general."

And he would write his mother that "Hitler's persecution of the Jews is a violation of all the rules and laws of Christianity." At the same time, however, he signed a number of anti-Semitic documents and voiced approval of others:

- He sent Ribbentrop—it is not clear whether on request—the first proposal to get the Italian fascist regime to "bring about a final solution . . . also on their part."
- When Sweden offered to absorb the Jews deported from Nor-way to Auschwitz, he told Ribbentrop that he had refused even to discuss the question.
- He pressed Hungary to "resettle" in eastern Europe the Hun-garian Jews who might "stir panic."
- When the Slovakian Nazis complained about the lack of trans-portation to deport Jews, he sent the German mission in Slo-vakia this message: "The suspension of transportation of Jews was a surprise in Germany, especially because Slovakia's coop-eration regarding the Jewish problem has been estimated highly here."

Weizsäcker would say after the war that if he had refused to ap-prove such documents, he would not have saved any Jews but would have been expelled from the government, imprisoned, or even executed. He would tell a court in Nuremberg:

Of course, it was always clear to me that these [anti-Semitic] mea-sures were most repugnant to the greatest degree possible. . . . [But] in the interest of resistance I retained my office, and in remaining in office it was not possible for me to prevent such documents passing over my desk under such a state of government. . . . I had to accept this and bear it for the very reason that I proposed to put an end to these measures.

In the final analysis, he would assert, the Jews could be saved only by the overthrow of Nazism, and his central goal to promote a negotiated peace would achieve this end. Whatever the moral, or practical, aspects of his argument, he was prepared to sign—or do— almost anything to reach this goal.

Perhaps because he knew that he couldn't thwart Hitler's policies but could try only to limit their effect, Weizsäcker pursued diplomacy in an almost robotic manner, without a sign of emotion. After British Ambassador Sir Neville Henderson met with State Secretary Weizsäcker in Berlin in August 1939, shortly before the Germans invaded Poland, the ambassador would report:

"I was impressed by one thing, namely, Baron von Weizsäcker's detachment and calm. He seemed very confident. . . . My insistence on the inevitability of British intervention [did not] seem to move him."

◆

The need for peace at almost any price was an obsession with Weizsäcker, but not because he disagreed with Hitler's vengeful motives for war. Like the Führer, he had been psychologically crushed by the provisions of the Versailles Treaty that deprived Germany after World War I of much of its territory and national pride. In fact, though he hated Hitler for his barbarism, he was willing to accept him as long as he didn't resort to war to achieve his ends. He would revealingly write after the war:

> Peace with Hitler? Is that what the opposition within Germany wanted? To preserve Hitler—and in addition to let him have the glory of a victorious war? To me all this presented no problem, and I had no hesitations. I was for peace, no matter on what basis it was concluded. . . . My view was that both must be made an end of, the war as well as Hitler's rule, but Hitler must not be removed by means of war and by the incalculable sacrifices which war would

demand. . . . I should never have approved—I should have found it absolutely inexcusable—to promote the catastrophe, to bring on war, in order to lose it, and thus to get rid of Hitler.

The son of a minister-president in the old Kingdom of Württemberg, Weizsäcker, like most other members of a prominent family, had deplored the chaos and liberal permissiveness that wreaked havoc on the economy and social structure of the democratic Weimar Republic produced by World War I. He favored a monarchist system, but would have settled for some form of Prussian authoritarianism, though not the brutal, rabble-led kind offered by Nazism. Weizsäcker felt, however, that Germany should not give up its struggle to win back the territory it lost at Versailles, and to annex Austria as well, but to do so by diplomacy, not by war.

Why would Weizsäcker serve a man he despised both as a human being and as the Führer? Because he had a choice: retreat to the sidelines and helplessly watch the decline and fall of Germany, or remain in the inner circle and perhaps move events in the right direction. And he chose to remain and live a lie, pretending to support Hitler's policies while unobtrusively working to undermine them. He was a realist, not a moralist. Others serving Hitler—diplomats, bureaucrats, military officers—had chosen to tread the same path as Weizsäcker, but few possessed his skills, influence, and subtlety so necessary for survival.

He served as a naval officer in World War I, then joined the foreign service in 1920. He was quickly promoted to higher rank, filling posts in Switzerland before being called to Berlin in 1936 to head the foreign office political department. Two years later, Ribbentrop became foreign minister and was told by Erich Kordt, the head of his ministerial bureau, who was a leading conspirator against Hitler, that Weizsäcker would be an ideal state secretary. As a former naval officer, he "would know how to obey."

"So he can obey," Ribbentrop replied condescendingly. "Then please ask him to have lunch with me today."

Weizsäcker took the job with deep reservations. While he would be in a position to influence foreign policy, he viewed Ribbentrop as an arrogant, repulsive man who was even more war-minded than Hitler. A moral dilemma now chipped away for the first time at the rock of realism embedded in his character. He would, as a powerful government adviser, have to sabotage the government's policies. But where was the dividing line between sabotage and treason?

Shortly after taking office, Weizsäcker tested the answer when he and Kordt warned British Prime Minister Neville Chamberlain that Hitler intended to seize the Czechoslovakian province of Sudetenland. The British, they said, should press for a peaceful settlement, but make clear they would resist German aggression by force. Then Weizsäcker himself helped to draft a discussion plan for a meeting in Munich between Hitler and Chamberlain, and on the basis of this draft Sudetenland was swallowed up by Germany.

Exactly what Weizsäcker wanted—German hegemony by peaceful means. It was not morality that was important but what one could get away with.

"The Munich Agreement," he later crowed, "was one of the rare examples in modern history of important territorial changes being brought about by negotiation."

But in August 1939, Weizsäcker would learn, appeasement had its consequences. He warned Britain that Hitler would soon sign a pact with the Soviet Union dividing up Poland between the two dictatorships, hoping that London would make a deal with Joseph Stalin first. This time, however, Britain didn't listen and Poland was invaded by Germany and then the USSR, setting off World War II. On August 25, Weizsäcker recorded in his diary:

"It is an appalling idea that my name should be associated with this event, to say nothing of the unforeseeable results for the existence of Germany and of my own family."

On August 30, after appealing frantically but in vain to Hitler and Ribbentrop to reverse course, Weizsäcker, in a nervous sweat, claimed he was about to pull from his pocket a pistol loaded with two bullets but somehow couldn't kill the pair. On September 5, he wrote in his diary:

> And now the struggle has begun. God grant that not everything that is good and valuable will be utterly destroyed in it. The shorter it lasts, the better. But one must remember that the enemy will never conclude peace with Adolf Hitler and *Herr* von Ribbentrop. What does that mean? As if anyone could fail to see what that means!

In an agonizingly personal way, Weizsäcker soon learned what it meant. His son Heinrich had been killed in Poland on the second day of the war.

◆

Before the conflict, Weizsäcker had written that although he wanted to get rid of Hitler, it would be "absolutely inexcusable to . . . bring on war in order to . . . get rid of him." But now that Hitler had brought on war, a war that had already claimed his son, Weizsäcker felt, the Führer must indeed be gotten rid of. Although he would play only a diplomatic role, he threw his support to a military plot to accomplish that aim.

In particular, the plotters wanted to find what terms the British would offer if the German opposition brought Hitler down. And to convince London, which was then fighting without America at its side, that if the war did not end soon, Russia could devour much of Europe, unless stopped by a free Germany.

It seemed that the plot might succeed—with the help of Pope Pius XII, who, while loving Germany, loathed Hitler. (Curiously, at about the time the pope became involved in this plot against Hitler, the Führer was plotting Operation Pontiff against the pope.)

Shortly after the outbreak of war, Sir Francis D'Arcy Godolphin Osborne, the British minister to the Holy See, cabled the foreign office:

> If the German generals could be assured of a peace with Great Britain . . . they were prepared to replace the present German government by a . . . government with which it was possible to negotiate—and then to reach a settlement in eastern Europe with the British government. . . . [The pope felt that] his conscience would not be quite easy unless he sent for me. He wished to pass the communication on to me purely for information. He did not wish in the slightest degree to endorse or recommend it.

Actually, more than the easing of the pope's conscience was at stake. The pontiff may have placed his life on the line. According to one expert: "It was a step so daring as to seem akin to foolhardiness. The risks to both the pope personally and the Church were incalculable. The Nazis, had they learned of it, would . . . have been furnished every excuse they needed for as broad-gauged an assault on the Catholic Church in Germany and wherever else the SS might tread as would have suited their convenience."

The military conspirators against Hitler needed the pope to verbally exchange secret information with the British government because only he, they felt, had the prestige and authority to convince London that they were sincere opponents of the Führer. And without the help of an enemy power, they thought, the German people, whose support they needed for a coup, would be too nationalistic to back one.

The pope, who had always dealt cautiously and correctly with national leaders, including Hitler, now suddenly—and quietly—metamorphosed from an almost fanatical neutralist into a conspirator himself in a temporary, chameleonic switch of role. He enthusiastically agreed to the proposal, even to transmit secret military information to the British and, a high Vatican source told me, to support a decision to kill Hitler if the plan to take him prisoner failed.

The pope felt that resort to such an extreme measure, the source said, would be justified because it could save countless lives that would be lost if a catastrophic war engulfed Europe—a war that might also destroy the Church that God, in his view, had put in his charge.

The rebels now, through Pius, exchanged countless notes with British leaders dealing with Nazi troop movements as well as the kind of government the Germans would set up after the coup and what its role would be in a peaceful postwar Europe. Yes, the risk was worth it—and the Holy See could be in a position to mediate peace in a world rid of both Hitler and Stalin. But in the end, to the chagrin of Pius and Weizsäcker, the British couldn't fully trust the German conspirators and insisted on knowing their names—a demand the pope rejected for fear that Hitler would learn their identities.

Didn't he personally vouch for them? the pope might have asked himself. Now he could only pray that Hitler wouldn't learn of his own role in the plot and find the excuse he needed to annihilate the sacred kingdom he had helped to build. The chilling experience helped shape his cautious reaction to Hitler's future policies.

As fate would have it, the same conspirators would be involved in the plot of July 20, 1944, when Hitler escaped death. Many of the plotters were hanged, some from slaughterhouse hooks with the use of piano strings to prolong their suffering.

◆

Weizsäcker had glimpsed a flash of light in the first failure. Had not the pope agreed then to cooperate with the opposition? He was still, it seemed, the only man in the world who could bring about a ne-gotiated peace that would produce a German-Allied alliance against the Soviet Union.

Was Weizsäcker sincere in his portrayal of himself as a true anti-Nazi who wished to revise the Versailles Treaty through ne-gotiation, but served under Hitler so he could sabotage or soften his extremist policies? Professor Leonidas Hill, an expert on the subject, wrote:

> Ernst von Weizsäcker had striven for what he considered Ger-many's legitimate aims, and these aims were directed mainly against the Versailles Treaty. . . . Although not a fervent propo-nent of claims on the Sudetenland, he supported them and wel-comed the humbling of Czechoslovakia to vassal status without war, . . . but he did not favor the partition of Poland, and after the outbreak of the war wanted the establishment of a rump-Poland. . . .
>
> In each of the major crises his aims were precisely limited, as much because he was not a fanatical nationalist as because he feared war. . . . An appeaser, . . . he wanted concessions to Ger-many, but sufficient firmness toward Germany that would compel her to act in a more measured way. . . . He was a man of strong character who did what he believed was right and feasible.

Weizsäcker now once more felt he must do what he believed was right and feasible. To facilitate the peace he had found so elusive, he must get himself transferred to the Vatican. And with the current ambassador there being called home, the time was now ripe to ask Ribbentrop for this move—especially with the Allies pressing Pius to speak out publicly against the mass killing of Jews.

Didn't they realize, Weizsäcker asked, that if the pope agreed, Hitler would surely retaliate ruthlessly . . . perhaps even attack the Vatican, the key to Germany's salvation? (The Führer had not yet given his order to Wolff.)

The foreign minister, for his part, needed a seasoned diplomat to make sure that Pius, whom he distrusted, was not lured by the Allies to their side. Being uncertain of Weizsäcker's loyalty to him, he was glad to "exile" him to some far off, "less important" post where the man could presumably exercise his diplomatic brilliance without jeopardizing Nazi aims.

And so, in mid-1943 Weizsäcker flew to Rome, where he would serve as ambassador to the Holy See and seek to save the only man he believed might be able to save Germany.

CHAPTER 7

Closer to Himmler
than to *Himmel*

Hardly had Pius XII settled his slim form upon the papal throne after succeeding Pius XI in 1939 when he suspected that the Vatican and the papacy were in danger. Pius XI had already set the stage for a Nazi attack by boldly condemning Hitler's anti-Semitic atrocities. Bormann's initial plot against the Vatican, Project Pontiff, soon followed in 1940, eliciting the papal comment from the new pope:

"Come what may, even if they arrest me one day and send me to a concentration camp, we have no fear. Each one of us has to answer for his deeds one day before God."

But Pius XII's fear grew when on April 25, 1941, he heard that Ribbentrop had asked his Italian counterpart, Foreign Minister Count Galeazzo Ciano, to oust the pope from Rome. Ciano reportedly replied that he favored simply isolating and controlling the pontiff within the Vatican.

When Vatican officials inquired about that report, the Italian government denied it. They were so worried, however, that on May 8, 1941, at a meeting of cardinals, Secretary of State Cardinal Luigi Maglione revealed that special powers would be given to papal representatives abroad in case the pope would "not be able to communicate" with them.

When Mussolini was overthrown, the Vatican's fears became more urgent. At a special meeting of the curia on August 4, 1943, Maglione said that "the Italian government fears there will be a German strike against Rome. In such a case, they foresee also an invasion of the Vatican. This cannot be excluded, as German threats against the Vatican have been growing for the last few years."

Adding to the heightened tension were remarks by Monsignor Domenico Tardini, the Vatican's assistant secretary of state, who told the cardinals, according to a person who was present, "to keep a suitcase ready because we might be deported at any time. All of us had the feeling that the Germans at least would take the Holy Father. We lived in a very immediate expectation of it."

The pope himself was so alarmed by the danger that he called a meeting of cardinals to choose a possible successor—apparently Cardinal Maglione—in case he was kidnapped. When Weizsäcker arrived at the Vatican to take over as ambassador to the Holy See, he urged Cardinal Maglione to give him a sign the moment he saw a chance for peace—peace without Hitler. But the new envoy knew that unless the ousted Mussolini was quickly restored to *full* power, Hitler would send troops into Rome, where they could easily move against the Vatican to avenge its role in the ouster.

Thus, in one of his first moves, Weizsäcker guilefully sought to disabuse Hitler of his belief that the pope had helped to engineer the coup and perhaps diminish the possibility of so great a catastrophe. On August 4 he cabled the raving Führer that the pope wanted good relations with Germany, that "to the Church, the archenemy at home and abroad is communism and so it will remain." In other words, Hitler had no need to take aggressive steps against the pope.

Reflecting the Vatican's still greater fear when Nazi troops began pouring into Rome on September 10, Weizsäcker that day cabled Berlin that Maglione had asked him to ensure that the forces of the Reich respected the Vatican and its subsidiary buildings.

Later that evening, Weizsäcker and his deputy, Kessel, met to discuss the general situation in Rome. At the same time, Kessel, with

Weizsäcker's knowledge but not his active assistance, was involved in his own anti-Hitler scheme—he was plotting, along with some military officers, another attempt to assassinate the Führer. But more urgent now, with the Germans occupying Rome, was the need to foil any likely plot to attack the Vatican and abduct the pope.

Although Hitler had not yet ordered Wolff to prepare such a plan, both men knew that with the Germans occupying Rome it was just a matter of time before Hitler would order the deportation of the Jews in the city. And the pope, with the lives of his own Jewish neighbors at stake, might be pressured by conscience, the Italian populace, and the Allies to speak out against the action. As a result, Hitler might be incited to retaliate violently against the Vatican, and Pius then could never serve as the mediator for a negotiated peace. There was also the humanitarian question; both the ambassador and his deputy abhorred Hitler's murderous anti-Jewish policies.

◆

It was in the fall of 1942 that the Vatican first learned that the Nazis were exterminating Jews. According to American diplomat Harold Tittmann, his superior and President Roosevelt's special representative to the Vatican, Myron Taylor, "forwarded to Cardinal Maglione information regarding the liquidation of the Warsaw ghetto and massacres of Jews by the Nazis contained in a letter dated August 30, 1942, from the Geneva office of the Jewish Agency for Palestine."

The letter alleged that corpses of Jews were being used for making fats for manufacturing fertilizer. Maglione replied on October 10 that unverified reports of several measures taken against non-Aryans had also reached the Holy See from other sources, and that the Holy See was "taking every opportunity in order to mitigate the sufferings of non-Aryans."

But now, a year later, with the Vatican apparently unaware that an order for a roundup of Roman Jews was near, it was left to

Weizsäcker, Kessel, and other anti-Hitler German officials, who knew Hitler's intentions but not yet the timing, to warn them to leave their homes immediately and seek shelter elsewhere.

Kessel reported to Weizsäcker that he had visited his friend, Alfred Fahrener, the Swiss general secretary of the Institute of International Law, who knew some of the Jewish leaders, and asked him to spread word that the Jews should flee.

Kessel said he went home convinced that he had prevented a catastrophe. Both the Jews and the Vatican, it seemed, would be saved. He did not know that Himmler, apparently bypassing Wolff, whom he didn't entirely trust, had already cabled SS Colonel Herbert Kappler, head of the Gestapo in Rome:

> Recent events in Italy make it necessary that a final solution is found to the Jewish problem in the territories occupied by the armed forces of the Reich. The *Reichsführer* [Himmler] requests *Obersturmbhnführer* Kappler to put into operation immediately all necessary preliminary measures to ensure that operations [against the Jews] can be carried out quickly and secretly within the city of Rome. Further orders will follow.

◆

On September 13, three days after the invasion of Rome, German soldiers in full battledress and armed with antitank and submachine guns suddenly jumped out of military trucks and took up positions at Saint Peter's Square along the border of Vatican City. Just hours before the soldiers arrived, a secret advance SS report enthused:

"With satisfaction it was learned that the protection of the Vatican City State was taken over by German troops, and that, under the protection of Adolf Hitler's own lifeguards, the Vatican will now stop serving as an espionage center."

An officer summed up matters in the report: "Now the pope is closer to Himmler than to *Himmel* [heaven]."

And a few days later, Berlin Radio warned of "severe measures unless the pope accepts the policies of Hitler and Italian fascism." All food stocks were seized, with Vatican rations halved; postal facilities from the Vatican were cut off; and telephone trunk lines to Rome were tapped—all taking place even as Weizsäcker was told to assure the Vatican that the Germans would "protect the Vatican City from the fighting."

The ambassador, who by now knew of Wolff's mission, was more apprehensive than ever. He understood Hitler's mentality and recalled an earlier incident. While mulling over war plans with Göring, the Führer had ranted:

"Let's drop the all-or-nothing game. All my life I have played for all-or-nothing."

Hitler was playing the "all-or-nothing game," Weizsäcker was certain, when he issued his order to Wolff, and was now engaged in deception. Following instructions, the ambassador cabled Berlin in subtle language calculated to make it seem that he had convinced the pope there was no reason to worry about an attack on the Vatican and that he "is not our prisoner."

Berlin's mixed signals apparently confused the Vatican. While the tough measures warned the pope that if he spoke out when the Jews of Rome were rounded up he and the Vatican would be in real danger, the assurances that he was *not* in danger encouraged him to keep his guard down.

Meanwhile, anxiety over a possible Allied rescue effort shrouded the Nazi leadership after President Roosevelt declared on October 1 that "the Allied march northwards aims at freeing Rome, the Vatican and the pope much in the manner of a crusade." Three days later, Ribbentrop wired Weizsäcker:

Now that Roosevelt has picked up the contention that pope is a prisoner and the Vatican sealed off, and has attempted at the same time to hold us responsible, as of now, for any possible destruction to Rome and the Vatican area, it seems appropriate to make clear the German decision to respect the Vatican state in every way. . . . I therefore request you to seek an audience with the pope to draw his attention in emphatic terms to the malicious campaign of our opponents. In doing so, you may make the following oral statement:

As the curia is aware, enemy propaganda has been endeavoring by fabrications of all kinds, since the German troops moved into Rome, to represent the Vatican as the victim of German violence. The behavior of the German troops already has given the lie unequivocally to these assertions. Despite this, the calumnies of our opponents against Germany are continuing. Thus, for example, these have been taken up by the chief of state of the United States (Roosevelt). In the face of this, the Reich government affirms that Germany respects the sovereignty and integrity of the Vatican State to the full and that members of the German Armed Forces in Rome are conducting themselves accordingly.

The Reich government would welcome it if the curia, on its part, could publish an unambiguous account of the situation and so ensure dissemination of the truth. You may further inform the pope that the Reich government would be particularly gratified if this rectification could come from the pope's own mouth.

Ribbentrop then authorized Weizsäcker to hand Cardinal Maglione a declaration:

On the German side, it is reaffirmed that the sovereignty and territorial integrity of the Vatican will be respected and that the German troops in Rome will behave accordingly. It is further promised on the German side that everything possible will be done to ensure that Vatican City does not become involved in combat.

And so, as instructed, Weizsäcker requested a meeting with the man he was trying to save from a fate that would shake the world.

◆

Earlier, soon after Rahn returned from his Berlin meeting and consulted with Weizsäcker and Wolff, Weizsäcker had apparently renewed his contacts with British intelligence officers. The slogan for action, "Save the Pope!" that Roosevelt had suggested at his White House meeting with Churchill after the Nazis occupied Rome, took on new meaning.

Weizsäcker grew even more concerned when he learned that, on September 25, Himmler had sent a second highly secret "get-ready" message to Kappler, the Gestapo chief in Rome, telling him to arrest the Jews there. And though Kappler thought a roundup would be impractical and possibly stir public disorder, he was not a man to disobey orders, whether he approved of them or not.

Hardly had he read the order when Möllhausen advised him of a discreet way to evade it. The consul had learned of Himmler's second "get-ready" message earlier that day from General Rainer Stahel, the German commandant of Rome, who supported the conspirators' view. Although the message was intended for Kappler's eyes only, Stahel had surreptitiously scanned it and was chilled by what he read:

It is known that this nucleus of Jews has actively collaborated with the Badoglio movement and therefore its swift removal will represent, among other things, a necessary security measure guaranteeing the indispensable tranquillity of the immediate rear of the southern front. The success of this effort will be assured by means of a surprise action, and for this reason it is absolutely essential to suspend the application of any anti-Jewish measures in the way of individual acts in order not to arouse any suspicions among the population of an imminent 'Judenaktion.'

After reading this message, Möllhausen, as dismayed as Stahel, sent a telegram on October 6 classified "Urgent, Most Secret" to Ribbentrop:

Kappler has been instructed by Berlin to seize the eight thousand Jews living in Rome and to take them to Upper Italy where they are to be liquidated. General Stahel, city commandant of Rome, informs me that he will permit this action only if it is in accordance with the wishes of the Reich Minister for Foreign Affairs [Ribbentrop]. I personally am of the opinion that it would be better business to draft the Jews, as in Tunis, for fortification work and shall put this view, in conjunction with Kappler, to Field Marshal Kesselring.

The order to round up the Jews, though expected, also alarmed Weizsäcker. Now he would *have* to convince the pope that he must remain silent when it happened or almost certainly trigger a Nazi retaliation.

CHAPTER 8

A Wandering Dog

Israel Zolli, the chief rabbi of Rome, knew nothing of the kidnap plot, but he suspected that the Nazis would round up the Jews and counted on the pope to help save them from what he felt was almost certain deportation. On September 9, Zolli relates in his memoirs that he telephoned Dante Almansi, the president of the Union of Italian Jewish Communities, from the city's great temple and warned: "They are about to enter! Let us meet with [Ugo] Foa [president of the Jewish Community of Rome]. Invite him to be at your office tomorrow at seven. I shall tell you what I think must be done to protect the Jewish population. If you follow me, I will take upon myself the greater part of the responsibility for the transformation and the adaptation. If only you agree and act at once."

According to Zolli, Almansi, who had been a regional prefect, or governor, under Mussolini, laughed and replied: "How can a mind as clear as yours think of interrupting the regular functioning of offices and the regular conduct of Hebrew life? As recently as yesterday, I went to the minister and received quite reassuring information. Do not worry."

"But you see . . . "

"No, I repeat that you can keep quite calm. And, moreover, you must communicate absolute confidence to the people. Don't worry, and have a good night. Good night."

Zolli hung up and said to Gemma Contardi, an usher in the synagogue who was standing nearby: "Remember, in Rome there will be a bloodbath. Who knows how many Jews will pay with their life!"

The next afternoon, September 10, as the Germans were marching into Rome, Zolli rushed to see the regional commissioner of police, whom he knew was a secret antifascist. He anxiously asked him what he should do.

"If I have understood right," the commissioner replied, "one hour after entering Prague they killed off the chief rabbi of that city. In my opinion, you ought to leave your house for three or four days, until you see what system they will adopt here. After that you will be able to judge for yourself."

Returning home, Zolli had hardly shut the door when he heard cries from the street: "The Germans! The Germans!"

His daughter Miriam ran outside and returned pale and trembling. "Away at once!" she exclaimed. "Here we are at the entrance of the ghetto and everyone is fleeing."

She quickly packed some linen, then said, "Let us leave everything and go!"

"But I would like to take with me . . . "

"You will take nothing, Father. We must survive. Here we shall die!"

Zolli and his wife and daughter hurried out into the rainy evening and fearfully walked the deserted streets. The stout, white-goateed rabbi looked up as they passed the Palace of Justice and asked himself: "Justice, where was justice? Would it not have been just for the Jewish leaders to meet and coordinate their plans as I had suggested? Why were they leaving the people in ignorance, without directions? Why have they summarily rejected my ideas and shown me so little respect?"

Zolli's wife and daughter stayed in the home of Christian friends, but the rabbi, not wishing to overburden these people, sought shelter elsewhere with another gentile acquaintance.

"Let me spend the night here, I beg you!" he pleaded.

"It's impossible!" he was told by the frightened man, who then scribbled out a note to someone who might be able to accommodate him.

"Thank you, that's fine."

Zolli rushed to the designated address, but soon realized that a telephone call had preceded him.

"A chair is enough for me even in a dark corridor," he told his new potential savior. "I have some cigarettes with me and everything else I need."

But this man's expression, like that of the others, spoke for itself. Hide the chief rabbi and court death?

And so Zolli found himself on the deserted streets, now dangerously after curfew. He had no choice; he would have to go home. But how ridiculous! He had no home, only an empty house. He was a "wandering dog—Jew or dog, it was the same."

When he finally arrived there, he was unable to turn the key in the lock. Terror gripped him as a figure approached in the dark.

"Give me the key a moment. The Lord help you, Professor."

Zolli breathed a sigh of relief. It was the night guard.

"And you also; may He help us all!"

The rabbi, wet with perspiration, washed and changed his clothes in the dark and lay on his bed. His memoirs reflect his state of mind at that moment. . . . He was regarded as a foreigner, having been born in Austria. He was a Jew. He was the chief rabbi of Rome. What a great catch!

Zolli began to pray. Perhaps God would save him. Perhaps . . . even Jesus, whom he had seen, strangely enough, in several visions. He waited for the ring of the bell, the knock on the door.

Three days later, on September 13, the rabbi uneasily strode to the synagogue hoping, after his failed talk with Almansi, to persuade Foa to spread the word to members that they must leave their homes. It would not be easy, for Foa, who came from a renowned

Jewish family and had won a medal for military valor in World War I, was a proud and tough man, and the very idea of running like a scared cat, for whatever reason, was contrary to his nature. Besides, he and Almansi, as former fascist officials, had friends in high places who would surely protect them from Nazi arrest.

Foa had studied law; then, like most of his countrymen, he joined the Fascist Party in 1932 to advance his career. The ministry of justice appointed him a magistrate in 1936, and for two years—until anti-Jewish laws forced him out of the government—he administered fascist justice without harboring the least suspicion that one day this justice would be fused with a Nazi attempt to obliterate his community.

Foa felt it was impractical for people to leave their homes. In these hard times, only the relatively wealthy could afford so drastic a solution, which he considered unnecessary anyway. And how could one burden the Catholic institutions with thousands of refugees on the basis of questionable fears? Besides, Jews had to show they were a brave people.

Though Foa's feelings, and those of Almansi, reflected the sentiment of many Jews, they were tinted by a personal antagonism. For Zolli constantly reminded the community that both men had been high officials in the fascist hierarchy before they were ignominiously dismissed under the racial laws. How, the rabbi asked, could they have risen to such high positions within the government without compromising themselves completely with fascism?

And in this question lay the poisoned root of a conflict that had torn the community apart—a conflict that was aggravated because Zolli was not a native Roman and was not thought to have a deep understanding of the Italian culture or mentality.

"Listen, Mr. President," Zolli would claim he urged his white-haired listener, "give orders that the temple and all the oratories be closed. Send all the employees home and close the offices. Let the secretary . . . draw one million lire, or even two, from the bank; and give all the employees three months' advance pay.

"All this will give a little alarm to these thousands of people who are going about the streets of the ghetto ignorant of the danger. Give to a committee of three whom you trust a large sum of money to subsidize the exodus of the poorest. You will see that the first ten families will be a good example to the others."

With barely a pause, Zolli continued: "Solemn funerals must be handed over to Aryans of the city. The prayers can be said at home; the same for other functions. Let everyone pray where he is; after all, God is everywhere. All this is absolutely necessary, especially now in the fall, when there are so many great solemnities. We have thousands of Roman Jews and thousands from other cities who have taken refuge here. The Germans can surround the synagogue and the oratories with their cannons and guns exactly at the hour when those places are jammed with people."

As Zolli took a breath, he searched Foa's wrinkled face for a response until the president rang a little bell summoning the secretary of the temple. By some miracle, the chief rabbi concluded, he had convinced Foa.

But Foa responded by asking the secretary whether a particular employee was in the office.

"No, she is afraid."

"Notify her that she is fired!"

"Yes, sir."

The secretary then left, and the president growled to Zolli: "You should be giving courage instead of spreading discouragement. I have received assurances. As to your proposal, I shall keep the temple and all the oratories open."

◆

Most Italian Jews, like their Catholic countrymen, found Mussolini and his fascist system acceptable when he came to power in 1922. After all, since the unification of Italy in 1870, no government had demonstrated a significant degree of anti-Semitism, and there was little reason to believe the fascists would be different. The official fascist attitude up to about 1937 was expressed in an oft-used phrase: "The Jewish problem does not exist in Italy."

Since many of the Jews were strong nationalists precisely because they had been treated without prejudice for so long, they were attracted by the Duce's promise of a great and powerful Italian empire. Many thus followed in the tradition of their fathers who, like Foa, had fought bravely in World War I and were among the most enthusiastic soldiers to invade Ethiopia in 1936.

Mussolini himself had no special feelings toward the Jews and supported them as long as they proved useful—even after Hitler came to power in 1933. At that time, wishing to show the world that "humanistic" Italian fascism was superior to Nazi "barbarism," he authorized the Italian Jews to render aid to their persecuted brothers in Germany. But when he wanted to reduce Nazi influence in Austria, he advised Chancellor Engelbert Dollfus to add "a dash of anti-Semitism" to his program so that Dollfus could compete for popularity with Hitler.

Therefore, when the Duce decided to throw in his lot with the Führer, he had few compunctions about pleasing his partner with so cheap a concession as a set of racial laws restricting the Jews in all fields of endeavor.

Even before these laws were passed in 1938, many Italian Jewish leaders reacted with fear at the first sign of a fascist attack about a year earlier. They vehemently professed their loyalty to fascism and, for good measure, declared their violent opposition to Zionism, which Mussolini then saw as a British threat to his imperial ambitions.

In 1937, when a group of rabbis, including Zolli, issued a declaration defying a fascist order that the Italian Jews cut their ties with world Jewry, other Jews, some convinced fascists, were horrified by this defiance. The community found itself bitterly split.

Foa, Almansi, and most other Jews occupying high places had no intention of voluntarily rejecting their source of bread and butter; nor would they give up hope in a system they had so loyally served, one they had simply accepted as a way of life, whatever its merits or defects. When they were finally forced out, they felt like children who had been abandoned by their mother.

Yet, despite their disillusion, they blamed Hitler far more than Mussolini. The Duce, they were sure, would still come to their aid if the Germans proved too overbearing.

CHAPTER 9

A Prisoner of Sorts

Soon after Ambassador Weizsäcker learned of the order to round up the Jews, information about the kidnap plot, apparently thanks in large part to him, was in the hands of Sefton Delmer, head of Britain's "black radio" intelligence operation. It produced programs that supposedly originated from undercover stations within Germany called the Fascist Republican Radio but were in fact broadcast from London. This was a counterfeit network posing as the real one, operated, as a Delmer associate would put it, "by members of the 'good' *Wehrmacht*, loyal Germans all, dedicated to the Fatherland but disturbed by the fanatical authoritarianism and corruption of the Nazi Party."

Delmer, who had been a war correspondent for a British newspaper until the fall of Paris, knew a great story when he heard it, and now he would use it to confuse the enemy and, he hoped, kill the plot.

On October 7, 1943, the false network, purportedly broadcasting from Salo, the capital of Mussolini's rump state, hinted at Hitler's "secret" by declaring that "quarters [were] being prepared in Germany for the pope."

British and Italian newspapers carried the warning, thinking it was delivered over the real fascist radio. Delmer would wryly remark after the war that "one of the 'mistakes' which [our] Fascist Republican Radio perpetrated was to be inexcusably rude and hostile to His Holiness the pope."

The pope, after learning of the "threat," was more alarmed than ever. A Vatican official, Monsignor Mella Di Santella, would tell a reporter that to lend "credence" to the false radio broadcast, a colonel (apparently Eugen Dollmann) came to a papal audience a few days later and, taking the pontiff aside, "confirmed" the report. Pius replied:

> I will not move from Rome. Here I was placed by the will of God and therefore by my own will or with my consent I shall not leave my seat. They would have to tie me up and carry me out, because I intend to remain here!

Nor was the pope, it seemed, greatly relieved when the colonel informed the Vatican that Wolff, as SS chief in Italy, had promised to do his best to thwart an attack on the Vatican. The general was apparently trying to win the trust of Pius, but at the same time hoped to raise enough doubt and fear in his mind to keep him from speaking out against the coming roundup and triggering the kidnap plan.

On October 8, the day after the counterfeit broadcast, Monsignor Giovanni Battista Montini, one of Pius's two assistant secretaries of state and the future Pope Paul VI, summoned Weizsäcker to the papal quarters.

The pope would be glad to see him the following day about the report from Salo, he said—a report that the ambassador knew had not originated in Salo but was intended to warn the Vatican of the plot and discourage Hitler from carrying it out.

◆

As Weizsäcker entered Pius's study on October 9, he was impressed by the serene manner and august bearing of the man sitting behind the large, neat papal desk. The visitor bowed stiffly, but with grace, and sat down in the glare of the light to his rear that illuminated the pope's thin, ash-gray countenance—so furrowed, despite the tight, parchment-like skin—with the worries of the world. The ambassador was "fascinated by his intelligent eyes, his expressive mouth, and his beautiful hands."

The man looked the part of a representative from heaven, even though the ambassador knew that he was more the shrewd, skillful diplomat resembling himself than the almost apparitional holy man his meek yet lordly presence suggested.

And this was the indelible impression of saintliness that intrigued most Allied diplomats who visited him. Sir Francis D'Arcy Godolphin Osborne, the British minister to the Holy See, for one, called Pius "the most warmly humane, kindly, generous, sympathetic, and incidentally, saintly, character that it has been my privilege to meet in the course of a long life."

Others found him less than warm or approachable, and some thought him simply wrongheaded. Even Osborne, who so admired him, would one day remark about his public silence during the Holocaust: "Is there not a moral issue at stake which does not admit of neutrality?"

Another diplomat would say: "[Pius's] thought was subtle. But he clothed it in an envelope of old-fashioned if not obsolete rhetoric, which had the effect of making every point that he made sound weaker. He grew up in a nineteenth-century tradition of Vatican circumlocution, fitted it naturally, and carried it to the ultimate."

Still another would remember Pius as looking and sounding unworldly: "His face was ascetic and pallid; his eyes were set deep in his head; his movements were controlled, his hands clasped."

Whatever qualities Pius possessed, Weizsäcker, himself a master negotiator, did not doubt that the pope was one, too; and so he would prove to be at that meeting on October 9 when he sought to elicit some hint of what might be in store for him. The perfect calm that was mirrored in the pope's bright, bespectacled eyes seemed not the least disturbed as he brought up the kidnap plot.

He had heard of the "rumor," Pius said, from "serious Italians" who had been informed by a high-placed German, apparently

Colonel Dollmann. But he was determined to stay in Rome unless he was carried out.

How long should his cardinals and assistants keep their bags packed? Pius asked.

Without denying the "rumor," Weizsäcker replied that he didn't know. But he urged the pope not to provoke Hitler. Like Wolff, he apparently sought to feed Pius's fear that the Führer was plotting against him. Fear that, if sufficiently infused, could seal his lips when truckloads of human cargo rumbled past the Vatican walls— and perhaps foil the plan to haul away the pope as well.

Aware that his visitor was warning him of such a fate, Pius expressed the hope that the ambassador would use his influence in the matter.

Weizsäcker, as instructed by Berlin, then asked Pius, would he publicly praise Nazi behavior toward the Vatican?

Pius tapped into his skills as a negotiator. If Berlin promised not to take any action hostile to Vatican interests in the future, the Vatican would agree to the ambassador's request.

As Weizsäcker would later report to Ribbentrop: "The German declaration, which could also be interpreted as a promise, would point toward the future if linked to a Vatican statement [praising German behavior]."

In other words, promise to call off the abduction plan permanently and the pope would "confirm" that the Nazis were treating the Vatican well.

To further convince Berlin that the pope was reasonable and undeserving of violent treatment, Weizsäcker would say with carefully deceptive language: "The pope was fully cognizant of the slanders which our opponents, and now Roosevelt himself, are spreading about our troops in Rome."

The ambassador added, hoping to demonstrate how the pope could be useful to Germany, that the pope could support a German mission against Russia. "Hostility to Bolshevism," he reported, "is, in fact, the most stable component of Vatican foreign policy, and the Anglo-American link with the Soviet Union is detested."

He would seek instructions from Berlin, Weizsäcker had told Pius, about the proposed exchange of promises. But as the days passed, none came. And the ambassador didn't expect any until Hitler either ordered the abduction or waited until he knew whether the pope would speak out when the Jews were dragged out of their homes.

The pope, however, had escaped the trap that Berlin had set for him. He had refused to be intimidated into praising the Reich for its friendly attitude toward the Vatican while it held a gun to his head.

But would the gun ultimately terminate his reign?

◆

History has suggested that it could. In 1798, Napoleon Bonaparte's French troops removed Pope Pius VI from Rome, and he died in their hands.

In 1809, Napoleon had Pius VII taken prisoner and brought to Fontainbleau, near Paris.

And in 1848, anticlerical rebels forced Pope Pius IX to flee the then powerful Papal States and take refuge in the sea fortress of Gaeta—accompanied by his solicitor, Marcantonio Pacelli, the grandfather of the future Pope Pius XII. They returned two years later, with French bayonets clearing the way. Marcantonio then served as secretary of the interior for all the papal dominions—until rebels attacked again in 1870 and this time permanently deprived the Vatican of its political power.

Pope Pius IX locked himself inside the Vatican as a voluntary prisoner, and the "black aristocracy," the families of the popes, kept the front doors of their palaces in Rome partially shut as a sign of mourning. In this same defiant spirit, Marcantonio disdainfully rejected the post of state councilor, and instead founded the *Osservatore*

Romano, the influential Vatican newspaper that today still voices the papal views.

Pius XII could well understand the distress of his grandfather since he was himself a prisoner of sorts. Soon the remaining remnant of Vatican authority, recognized by the Lateran Treaty with Italy in 1929, which established the sovereignty of Vatican City, might crumble in the hands of the most criminal ruler in history— with the exception, in his view, of Josef Stalin.

CHAPTER 10

Out of Fear of Men

The kidnap plot would climax a relationship of expediency, opportunism, and distrust between two of the most important leaders in modern history—Pope Pius XII and Adolf Hitler—a relationship that began at least ten years before the Führer came to power in 1933, when Archbishop Eugenio Pacelli, the future pope, was the Holy See's ambassador to Bavaria. In a letter to the Vatican dated November 14, 1923, Pacelli denounced the Nazi movement as an anti-Catholic threat and noted that the cardinal of Munich had condemned Nazi acts against the Jews.

The two men had thus harbored a consuming mutual contempt for one another since Hitler's early years as a rabble-rouser, with each eventually feeling threatened by the potential global power of the other. Pacelli would, as pope, exercise authority over a worldwide Church that in many ways controlled the minds of millions. And Hitler intended to stretch his rule across Europe and Asia and become the spiritual as well as the political leader of all conquered peoples.

But in their fear and distrust of each other, the two—Pacelli as Pope Pius XI's secretary of state and Hitler as Germany's new Führer—found it at least temporarily advantageous to rein in the conflict with a Concordat in 1933. This agreement, which called for the separation of church and state, made all German Catholics subject to canon law under the greatly increased authority of the Vatican. In return, the Catholics had to end all social and political action related to the Church. This meant, most importantly, that the Catholic Center Party, the only democratic political party remaining in Germany, would disappear.

German leaders crowed that this was a breakthrough victory for the Third Reich, and it came the same year Hitler rose to power. "By her signature," the German newspaper *Völkischer Beobachter* editorialized, "the Catholic Church has recognized National Socialism in the most solemn manner. This fact constitutes an enormous moral strengthening of our government and its prestige."

The claim was not without merit. The Concordat, as an Italian expert would write, "was a move to disarm German Catholicism and 'synchronize' it with the National Socialist system. . . . By the prohibition against priests mixing in political matters, [Hitler] had made it impossible for the Church to oppose the preaching of the racist creed."

For Pacelli, who in six years would inherit a papal throne wielding enormous power throughout the Catholic world, the Concordat represented his first important compromise answer to a savagely challenging moral dilemma. Was it morally acceptable, his critics asked, to sign an agreement that, in effect, could be interpreted as approval of an immoral government?

His superior at the time, Pius XI, was reluctant to make the compromise, but with little stomach for the intricate bargaining and bluffing of diplomacy, left most such matters to Pacelli, the consummate diplomat. He would express his confidence in his secretary of state when several Church officials thanked the pope for writing the encyclical that had so infuriated the Nazis.

"Thank *him*," the pope replied, pointing to Pacelli. "He has done everything. From now on, he will deal with everything."

In agreeing to the Concordat, Pacelli would explain "apologetically" to a British diplomat after the signing "how it was that he had signed [it] with such people." He said that a pistol had been pointed at his head and he had no alternative. He was given just one week to make up his mind. If the German government violated the Concordat—and they were certain to do that—the Vatican, the pope said, "would have at least a treaty on which to base a protest."

Although he felt only "disgust and abhorrence" of the Nazi "reign of terror," he had to choose between "an agreement on their lines and the virtual elimination of the Catholic Church in the Reich." Was not the safeguarding of the Catholic Church his first and most sacred priority, at whatever cost?

Pacelli despised Hitler and his top assistants all the more. Harold Tittmann, a U.S. representative in the Vatican, reported in 1940 that "the last thing the Vatican would welcome would be a Hitler victory" in the war, though it feared such a triumph. But what policy, some of his supporters still ask, could be more morally justified than one protecting and consolidating the trappings of God's kingdom on earth, which symbolized the very heart of Christianity?

As Pacelli suspected, it would take more than diplomacy to confront a ruthless dictator who would violate the Concordat at will and might still seek to eradicate the German Catholic Church.

◆

Whatever Hitler or Pacelli thought he had achieved from this opportunistic, contrived agreement, each felt a threat to his hold on the German Catholics. A mutual threat that would ultimately spawn the abduction plot, an extension of a vow that Hitler made to his henchmen in July 1942: "Once the war is over we will put a swift end to the Concordat."

And, in fact, the Führer did not wait long to begin its destruction. Church schools were suppressed or subject to requirements of Nazi teaching inconsistent with the Christian faith. Church property was confiscated or vandalized. Many priests and bishops were harassed and sent to concentration camps. A German church analyst would write about a Fulda pastoral delivered in 1942:

After more than eight years of systematic deceit, pressure, ridicule, faked morality, trials, and indoctrination, the Nazis have now succeeded in enrolling about ten million countrymen in their "German religion of God-believers." They are now in their definite all-out move against the churches, spreading defeatist moods claiming that the churches are already in full dissolution, and that further resistance is useless.

At the same time, Cardinal Michael Faulhaber, the archbishop of Munich, voiced in his pastoral his concern about the increasing number of apostasies, and also about "a certain number of unworthy priests who have chosen the easier way of collaboration."

When World War II broke out, Hitler, who was himself a nominal Catholic, feared that the pope might speak out about the Jewish genocide and turn German Catholics against him, even though their intimidated bishops constantly lauded Hitler's military triumphs. Since German Catholics comprised some 40 percent of the population, and more importantly of the army, the papal voice could adversely affect battlefield morale. The Führer knew that almost a fourth of the SS Catholic membership would not leave the Church even though pressured by Himmler to do so.

Pius, on the other hand, feared that if he spoke out, his German flock would turn against *him*. For most Germans were anti-Semitic and strongly supported the Führer—especially because most church leaders backed him, an attitude partly inherited from history but reinforced by fear and imposition. Indeed, the loyalty of some clerics to Hitler did not abate until his death. As Gordon Zahn, a Catholic professor, wrote:

Even in the midst of total military collapse, with the Third Reich tottering to its death, [German] bishops were raising their voices to inspire men to offer their last drop of blood. . . . We may justly conclude that the [German] Church did become an agency of social control operating on behalf of the Nazi State, insofar as insuring wholehearted Catholic support of the war was concerned.

In some cases, intimidation was clearly the principal instrument of social control. Many bishops feared that Hitler would crush their institutions and throw them into concentration camps, or even kill them if they didn't support his policies.

But some didn't have to be intimidated. They backed the Führer's nationalistic aims voluntarily, especially his vow to wipe out the communists. And they were not too concerned, either, by Hitler's totalitarian aims, though almost all opposed his racial philosophy and other cruel components.

Didn't their forebears from the nineteenth century reject the secular democratic views of the Enlightenment and the French Revolution? Didn't the democracy of the Weimar era that followed the German defeat in World War I bring only economic disaster and spiritual vacuity to the country? In any event, under the terms of the Concordat, it was not the business of Catholics to concern themselves with politics.

A few clerics in the 1930s went beyond silence and voluntarily collaborated with the Nazis, even hijacking Nazi concepts. Vicar General Miltenberger of Würzburg wrote in a directive to the clergy of his diocese:

If a priest should heap scorn on or ridicule the concepts of blood, soil, race, he would thereby not only risk political attacks and legal prosecution, but also offend his Church theologically. . . . One must help the people to incorporate all these concepts which are presented to them with great enthusiasm into their religious world.

Such servile statements actually spurred the Gestapo to charge that the Church was trying to conquer Nazism from within. Formerly, it pointed out, the clerics had emphasized "liberty, equality and fraternity"; now they spoke of "nationality, authoritarian leadership, blood and soil." Ironically, some anti-Nazi voices offered the same criticism.

However tactically obsequious many German bishops were to their masters, they did not believe that the Germans were a master race and that the Jews were inherently inferior. To some, what was supremely important was the need to protect the Church from communism, which the Jews, many claimed, were trying to foist on Germany. Yes, the Nazis were also anti-Christian, the bishops realized, but *they* could be bought with political compliance and cheerleading.

Archbishop Konrad Gröber of Freiburg, for one, apparently thought so. He wrote that Marxism was "the materialistic socialism founded by the Jew Karl Marx," and that Bolshevism was "an Asiatic state despotism in the service of a group of terrorists led by Jews." Such statements, though deplorable, were moderate by Nazi standards.

In March 1933, shortly after Hitler came to power, the bishops expressed their basic public view of National Socialism: "Catholic Christians, to whom the voice of their Church is sacred, do not require at this time a special admonition to be loyal to the lawful authorities and to fulfill conscientiously their civic duties while rejecting on principle all illegal or subversive conduct."

In other words, churchgoers should obey Nazi laws, unless a law was unlawful. The Concordat would cement the fateful compromise.

Hitler was delighted with the Concordat. He had taken the first step toward consolidating his power as Führer and felt confident enough to throw his anti-Semitic designs in the face of the now captive clergy. Had not the Church always considered the Jews parasites and confined them to ghettos? He would simply follow in its footsteps.

And the German Church would follow in his, though more out of fear than conviction. Cardinal Faulhaber would thus tell the pope shortly after he came to power: "There are times when we doubt that the upper echelons of the [Nazi] party in general desire peace.

The [leaders] want to be combatants to such an extent that they would love nothing more than to be given a reason for fighting, especially when it concerns the Church. But I . . . believe that we, the bishops, should act as if we see nothing."

The British, however, saw a different role for the bishops. They could actually be the key to an Allied victory. On February 14, 1943, an official in the foreign office cabled Osborne:

It has been represented to me by one of our secret organizations that an important contribution to the overthrow of the present government in Germany would be made if the pope could be persuaded to instruct leading cardinals and bishops in Austria and Germany to denounce the German regime. Recent anti-Nazi declaration by [a] cardinal . . . suggests that Roman Catholic prelates might be willing to take such a step if they were given encouragement by the Vatican.

Reprisals would certainly be taken by the German government but it is suggested that the pope might not be unwilling to face these if he is becoming convinced of the essential justice of our cause and of the certainty of an Axis defeat.

Osborne replied with caustic shock that his superiors could be so unaware of the forces determining the political orientation in the Church:

I do not think that there is the remotest chance of inducing the pope to take this action. It would involve a not very creditable last minute abandonment of jealously preserved principle of Vatican neutrality as well as a violation of the pope's own congenital caution and passivity. It would compromise his cherished hopes of mediation. He has hitherto always declined to condemn Nazi crime on the ground, [believing] that to do so would bring greater hardship and sufferings on German Catholics and there is no reason to suppose that he would yield now.

Especially with Hitler waiting for an opportunity to show once and for all, at any cost, who was destined to become the world's most powerful leader.

If Pius feared such a showdown with the Führer, particularly in light of rumors afloat that Hitler wished to unseat him and destroy the Church at the appropriate time, he cannily tried to prepare for it. Yes, he hated Hitler and, in fact, would participate in an attempted coup against him in 1940. But how could he win over most of the German bishops who supported the man, or at least pretended to, thereby solidifying his hold over German Catholic laity? The pope chose a subtle, gradual way of turning them against Hitler. On July 20, 1939, he wrote to the Episcopal conference:

> The doubts and confusion surrounding the real intentions of the most influential forces concerning religion and the Church have as their consequence that among some people, whose fidelity to the Church can in no way be questioned, there are various ideas regarding what course of action is to be followed.

About a year later, on August 6, 1940, Pius wrote to an Episcopal conference, with no mention of "various ideas":

> A thousand influences opposed to the Church and to Christ, in speech, in writing, and in attitude, constantly flow from a more or less de-Christianized society upon the souls of believers. It subjects them to a moral pressure which, accompanied by coercion and harassment, often forces them to undergo trials that demand heroic fidelity to their faith.

And on June 5, 1942, he wrote to the bishop of Mainz:

> None of those who pretend to pass an objective judgment can still have doubts today; for in spite of the efforts of Our great predecessor, Pius XI, and Our own efforts to smooth relationships between

the Church and the state, the result that has been sincerely hoped for and seriously desired has remained null, and the responsibility for this failure should not be placed on the Church.

If the pope ultimately had to speak out publicly against the Nazis, would his grandiloquent condemnation reach the 40 percent Catholic share of the German population and persuade it to choose the keeper of their souls over the keeper of their minds? And would he lose 40 percent of the German army? Hardly encouraging was a pastoral letter issued by Bishop Maximillian Kaller of Ermland, Germany, in January 1941:

> We joyously profess our allegiance to the German [army] and feel ourselves linked to it in good as well as in bad times. . . . In this staunchly Christian spirit we also now participate wholeheartedly in the great struggle of our people for the protection of their life and importance in the world. . . . Especially as believing Christians, inspired by God's love, we faithfully stand behind our Führer who with firm hands guides the fortunes of our people.

True, the super-nationalist tone of the letter was at least in part a cover for a subtle plea for freedom to remain loyal to the faith without provoking Nazi retribution. But with the troops "brainwashed" by the bishops, might not patriotic sentiment turn them against the Vatican if the pope condemned Hitler? And even worse, the Führer could retaliate ruthlessly against the Church (though he could not invade the Vatican before occupying Rome later).

And even if he didn't, speaking out publicly would mean the pope was openly taking sides in the war and would kill his chances of mediating a peace treaty, his most cherished dream. Already the strain of "neutralism" was taking its toll on him. It was not easy urging soldiers on both sides to fight for their respective countries with valor in their efforts to kill each other, regardless of who was fighting for a just cause, and who not.

Even so, the pope, who deplored the Allied demand for "unconditional surrender," still had hopes of arranging a peace based on
compromise that would, as he wrote to Cardinal Faulhaber in 1944,
let Germany keep Austria and the Sudetenland—presumably without
Hitler at the helm. An accord must be powerful enough to keep the
Soviets out of Europe.

Meanwhile, Pius felt, he had to keep the German Catholics loyal
to the Church, wherever their war sentiments lay. It is unclear what
the pope thought of a statement courageously made by Cardinal
Faulhaber in 1936 that "the bishop no longer would be the servant
of God if he were to speak to please men or remain silent out of fear
of men." Nor can one know what the pontiff thought when the cardinal, like almost all his priestly German colleagues, followed the
papal example and remained publicly silent about the mass killing
of Jews "out of fear of men."

CHAPTER 11

Living with God
and the Devil

At least until he learned of the kidnap plot, Pius feared Stalin even more than Hitler. The Nazis, he believed, would probably lose the war and the Soviet Union would share in an Allied victory. And here merged the deepest interests of Pius XII and those of General Wolff, Ambassador Weizsäcker, and the other German officials who wanted to save the pope and the Vatican. A Soviet triumph would permanently threaten the Vatican while communizing Germany and other European countries.

Faced with a choice of evils, Pius was the pragmatic diplomat. He understood that Hitler, Bormann, Himmler, and other Nazi leaders had the same goal in mind as Stalin—to ban not only the Church but also Christianity as a religion. Pius felt, however, that eventually the Nazi chiefs would be overthrown by German military officers who, he hoped, would reach a negotiated peace with the Allies that would unite both sides in a joint crusade against the Soviets—exactly what the anti-Hitler German diplomats wanted. And the pope, with his diplomatic experience, they all agreed, would be just the person to mediate such a deal.

Yet, paradoxically, when Germany invaded the Soviet Union in 1941, the Vatican displayed no sign of glee, to Berlin's chagrin. According to Fritz Menshausen, the counselor at the German Embassy in Rome, the Vatican feared "that after a defeat of Bolshevism the Catholic Church, and indeed all Christianity, would, so to speak, go from the frying pan into the fire."

Menshausen added:

> If the pope should now speak against Bolshevism, against which the Holy See had after all spoken repeatedly in principle, he would also have to take a position against the anticlerical measures and tendencies hostile to Christianity in Germany; the reports "continually received" at the Vatican on this subject provided "overwhelming material" to justify such a step; the pope's silence was the best proof that he would like to avoid everything that would injure Germany.

Was it the "best proof"? The Vatican, after receiving a stream of reports on the horrors committed by Hitler, hoped that the Russians and Germans would destroy each other. The pope, however, found it morally impossible to make a statement calling for so bloody a struggle.

Monsignor Tardini, perhaps the most anti-Axis Vatican official, would tell colleagues he hoped that "in the providence of God" the war would end communism *and* Nazism. Communism might be the sworn enemy of the Church, but it was not the only enemy. "The swastika can hardly be presented as a crusader's cross," Tardini said, recognizing that the Allies were winning the war. He explained:

> It is true that in the hypothesis of a German victory only Nazism would be victorious, while the other nations would be enslaved to Nazism. On the other hand, on the hypothesis of an Allied victory, communism would not be the *only* victor but would have at its side two formidable powers, Britain and America.
>
> Nonetheless, . . . there is ground for fearing (a) that the war will end in a preponderantly Russian victory in Europe and (b) that the result will be a rapid diffusion of communism in a great part of

continental Europe and the destruction there of European civilization and Christian culture.

And the Vatican's concern about the communist threat grew
stronger even as the Allies urged the pope to stop demonizing Russia and thereby weaken the Allied side. Thus, on February 13, 1943,
several months before Hitler hatched his kidnap plot, Osborne
warned his London office that the Vatican had "shown some signs
recently of becoming more alarmed about Russian victories than
about German behavior. In fact the progress of the war, far from
making the Vatican more pro-Allied, may, on the contrary, make
them more inclined to make allowances for the Germans."

But if fear of both dictatorships kept the Vatican quietly on the
Allies' side, its enthusiasm was limited. For the Vatican did not happily look forward to having a single superpower—the United
States—as the only alternative power center in the world after the
war. Tardini felt some relief when he received a British promise that
there would be "no exclusively Russian victory," and that "strong
British and American armies [would remain] in Europe."

In a memorandum, however, reporting on a talk he had in September, 1942, with the American diplomat Myron Taylor, Harold
Tittman's usually absentee superior, the monsignor would write:
"All things considered, one must conclude that if National Socialism prepared and provoked the war, the U.S. is itself gravely infected with nationalism, which bodes all kinds of ills and excludes
every forecast of good."

Though this might be seen as true neutralism, the pope knew it
was in the Vatican's interest to maintain good relations with the
United States and did not ignore American pressure to stop attacks
on Russia in the interest of ending the war. He even informed American bishops that they should not let their hostility to communism
stop them from supporting President Roosevelt's Lend-Lease aid
program for Russia.

But more important, at least in late 1943, was that the pope, now aware of Hitler's kidnap plot, realized that the Nazis posed a far greater immediate threat to the Vatican than the more distant communist danger. Still, the route to this realization was a long and complicated one.

The fighting was not going well for Germany. It appeared, especially after the fall of Mussolini and the Nazi occupation of Rome, that, disastrously in the pope's eyes, the Allies would win unconditionally and without his mediation, without the possibility of a joint Allied-German force being formed to halt the Soviet plunge into Europe.

The pope had long been depressed about that prospect. As early as 1940, he had desperately pressed Roosevelt to make plea after plea to Mussolini to keep Italy out of the war, fearing that its entry in the conflict could result in a German-induced fascist attack on the Vatican, but to no avail.

He had then asked the British, Italian, and German governments to study the possibility of an agreement to end the war, and he failed again, with Hitler willing—if he could keep all the territory he had already won.

This negative reaction finally convinced him that there was almost no hope for a negotiated peace on any terms. Pius glumly told Myron Taylor, according to Tittmann, that he was "especially concerned over the future of Great Britain, which seemed very black indeed." If the British lost, who, he wondered, would be left in Europe to save the Church and its pope, especially with so little American aid arriving so late—too late to save him from either the Nazis or the communists?

Now, three years later, in 1943, Allied troops had landed in Salerno to the south and were likely to break out of Anzio to the southeast, while Rome had fallen into German hands, making the Vatican ripe for the picking. So why not face reality and submit to Allied pressure to refrain from verbally attacking the Soviet Union in order to spur an Allied victory, especially since Germany, with the fuse of the kidnap plan aglow, was now the greater immediate danger to the Vatican and the papacy? As the pope would tell an intimate, Father Paolo Dezza, in 1942, even before the Nazis marched into Rome and Hitler gave his order to General Wolff:

"The communist danger does exist, but at this time the Nazi danger is more serious."

The pope, however, still feared that if the Germans left Rome too soon before the Allies' arrival, the communists might fill the political and security vacuum. If this happened, would the Allies, after entering Rome, be reluctant to alienate Stalin by sweeping his proxies out of power?

After all, most Romans—bureaucrats, clerks, shopkeepers with little revolutionary bent—were passive toward the Resistance, an attitude that had permitted the Germans to occupy Rome so easily in the first place. The Romans were traditionally skeptics and trusted more to fate than themselves; and their skepticism had only grown when, after celebrating the ouster of Mussolini, they found themselves under the Nazi as well as the fascist boot—left in the lurch by their king and premier, who had fled to safety. To the Romans, their city was eternal, as the Church had taught. Armies could come and go; dictators could rule and perish; revolutionaries could revolt and retreat; but Rome would remain Rome, changeless in its grandeur and its ability to survive in a changing world.

With the coming of fascism, Romans had shrugged their shoulders and hoped for the best. In the golden days after Italy's conquest of Ethiopia in 1936, the Romans took pride in their new imperial status, acquired so cheaply. However, when the cost began rising during the Spanish Civil War, with long casualty lists, the gold began to tarnish. And as the Duce bowed ever lower before Hitler, finally flinging the nation into World War II, the Romans, mainly fascist-cultivated bureaucrats indifferent toward the leftist-dominated Resistance, shrugged again and waited for destiny to save them—just as it always had.

Communist leaders, on the other hand, were determined to shape destiny, not to be shaped by it, as the pope well understood. But, in

fact, divided and short of followers, they had little chance of succeeding. Some members of the Moscow-directed Communist Party
wanted to terrorize principally the Germans, believing that German
reprisals would presumably win the cooperation of the Romans
against the occupation. Other party members wanted to attack only
the Italian fascists, fearing that the reprisals sparked by an assault
on the Germans could seriously damage the party.

However, the farther left Communist Movement of Italy, or Red
Flag Party *(Bandiera Rossa),* argued that both strategies would
compromise the Resistance while yielding no compensatory advantage. Not indiscriminate terrorism, but sabotage and eventually military action, the Red Flags insisted, would hasten Nazi
withdrawal without weakening the forces of revolution. This party
had a larger but far less disciplined following in Rome than the Communist Party.

The two parties had little in common other than Marxist ideology. The Stalinist Communist Party simply looked to the Soviet
Union for guidance; the Red Flags not only leaned toward Trotsky-
ism but also embraced anarchists and various other leftist and intellectual ideologists. Its rank and file consisted mainly of poor,
uneducated workers, artisans, and small shopkeepers, in contrast to
the Communist Party, whose members came mainly from relatively
prosperous, well-educated middle-class families. The Red Flags deplored the Stalinists' absolute dependence on Soviet policy, while the
Stalinists viewed the Red Flags as unrealistic adventurers.

Red Flag members were effective saboteurs. Typically, by infil-
trating key ministries and services, they were able to "censor" spy
messages intended for the Nazis, create chaos in telephone communications, and falsify the census to thwart Mussolini's military draft.
An "official" report they prepared indicated that 90 percent of the
Romans were female and the rest mainly people younger than sixteen and older than eighty!

But though the left was so splintered that a successful revolution
seemed highly unlikely, the pope's fear of a communist takeover

never flagged. Nor did he distinguish between Stalinist communists and members of other leftist, or even some centrist, political parties, however well-meaning he felt some might be. For he feared that the communists of whatever stripe, better organized and more politically sophisticated than the other groups, would inevitably dominate them, especially during periods of chaos—to the detriment of the Church.

Still, the pope was strongly supported by at least one political entity, the Christian Democratic Party, a virtual Vatican agent, and the pope's main hope for preventing a communist takeover in a democratic era. Although it was a heterogeneous party embracing extreme conservatives as well as quasi collectivists, members were bound by a common desire to give a Catholic character to the Italian state.

Italian democracy had crushed Vatican temporal power in the revolution of 1870, victimizing Pius XII's grandfather in the process. Moreover, relations between the Vatican and the succeeding Italian governments remained strained—until Mussolini took power and set up an authoritarian hierarchy that the Church, with a similar power structure, could at least understand. Only in 1929, when the Vatican signed the Lateran Treaty with the Duce establishing the sovereignty of Vatican City, did the Church feel secure in Italy.

True, fascism eventually became despotic, and even menacing, when Mussolini began drawing too close to Hitler, who influenced him to view the Church as a dangerous competitor for men's souls. But if fascism had outworn its usefulness, it was wrong to think, in Pius's view, that complete political freedom should necessarily replace it, with the communists itching to grab power.

Anyway, the Italians were still too sluggish from the fascist narcotic to grasp *any* unfamiliar ideology, including Marxism. And the communists realized, as the pope apparently did not, that for this reason they would have an exceedingly hard time taking over the government.

But intense as his fear of communism was, Pius's primary concern in the weeks after the Nazis marched into Rome was the greater immediate danger—that the Allies might arrive too late to save him from abduction and the Vatican from despoilment. The Nazis could thus provide the communists with ideal conditions for a takeover of the area when the Germans, with the pope in hand, fled before the approaching Allies.

Actually, for all their fervor, the communists and other leftists were not the most powerful and certainly not the best-armed members of the Roman Resistance. The democratic political parties and the scattering of Italian soldiers, especially the monarchists, who, for a while, stood their ground against the Nazi occupiers, were just as active and were confident they could frustrate the communist designs that the pope so feared would turn Rome and the Vatican into Soviet territory.

Indeed, as all governmental and military authority gradually melted away and Italy sank into deadly chaos, an alliance of six parties, unable to contact the king, set up a revolutionary authority, the Committee of National Liberation (CLN). Politically, the CLN demanded that the king abdicate and that Badoglio resign to make way for a democratic party regime that, once in power, would decide whether to keep a monarchical system.

The political parties, though split ideologically, agreed that the king and Badoglio must go, but Italian military officers in the Resistance, the *Carabinieri,* disagreed. True, these officers, like the politicians, deplored the royal flight from Rome, which left them without orders and at German mercy, but they nevertheless remained unshakably loyal to the king. They had served fascism because the king had served it; now they would serve the Allies because the king did.

Whatever the initial reservations of these officers, their devotion to the Allied cause grew with every Nazi atrocity committed against the Romans. They were even willing to cooperate with the CLN leaders, who had been their enemies under fascist rule, though they feared, like the pope, that the CLN wanted to destroy Italian tradition, promote drastic social change, and perhaps set up a communist government. They had built up large arsenals, one of them—with the apparent collusion of priests—in the Basilica of San Paolo Fuori le Mura, which was, by treaty, Vatican territory.

Most of these officers, though the cynical products of fascism, were brave men; men who were suddenly to discover, often to their own amazement, that there were things of genuine value worth fighting and dying for. They vowed to thwart a possible communist takeover of Rome before the Allies arrived—and to prevent a Nazi takeover of the Vatican before the Germans departed.

But all this political uncertainty unnerved the pope, and, in his view, could spell disaster, with the Red Army closing in on Europe and the local communists and their gullible partners waiting to strike. Worse, what if the Nazis struck first—with him the target? And they almost surely would if he publicly condemned the roundup of Jews. They might not occupy the Vatican for long since Allied troops were approaching, but with the Vatican ravaged and its leaders in chains or dead, the communists would find it all the easier planting their red flag in the ruins before the Allies arrived.

◆

Pius's uneasiness was reflected in his failure to protest openly against Mussolini's torture of suspected leftist leaders in Rome before the Duce was overthrown. The Italian dictator was a proud man, but he had to admit that his regular fascist police force in Rome lacked the ideological militancy to handle torture with the necessary ardor. Ruthless men were needed, men who would not hesitate to use any means to obtain information, men who could show the Nazis a thing or two about dealing with the enemy.

When the Nazis occupied Rome, ruthless men had thus set up a "social police department" in Braschi Palace, Fascist Party headquarters on Via Tasso. They often arrested people on false charges so that they could steal their possessions and obtain ransoms for their release. Soon, the palace became not only a torture house but a storehouse—for stolen goods that included clothes, foodstuffs, cigarettes, and even a live cow.

Colonel Dollmann and Consul Möllhausen, among other moderate Germans, were scandalized. What right did the Italian fascists have to behave like the German Nazis—torturing people and stealing their wealth? Right or wrong, the Nazis at least acted in defense of an ideal. They tortured only legitimate suspects and stole only from the guilty—except, of course, when it came to Jews. The Italians, however, were simply gangsters.

When the Germans occupied Rome, Dollmann even moralized about the "scandal" to Colonel Kappler, who ran the torture chambers with great efficiency, and Kappler agreed that a "cleanup" was necessary. No opportunistic Italians were going to compete with him!

Kappler inspected the store of goods that the fascists had accumulated, and the sight only confirmed to him the crudity of the Italian people. While he collected art treasures from his victims, they collected cows.

From his Vatican home, Pius could almost hear the cries of the hideously tortured echoing from Via Tasso. But as with the Jewish problem, he found himself reeling with an inner torment of his own. Could he speak out without restraint on behalf of these victims and risk Nazi retaliation against the Church—especially when he felt compelled to show restraint in publicly condemning the mass murder of innocent Jews?

He would seek to help individual victims quietly behind the scenes through German and Italian contacts.

CHAPTER 12

A Blueprint for
Massacre

As reports of a Nazi plot against the Vatican mounted, the pope's anxiety kept pace, especially when he learned of the arrival in Rome in autumn 1943 of Ludwig Wemmer, an official of Bormann's National Socialist Party chancellery. As Bormann's religious affairs adviser, Wemmer would be the appropriate man to help carry out a papal kidnap plan. Though it could only be surmised at the time, Wemmer's main job was to spy on Weizsäcker to make sure he was not conspiring with the pope against Nazi interests.

The Vatican took the reports so seriously that the pope had his personal archives sealed up in a false floor and documents of the secretariat of state scattered in obscure corners. At one point, some papal assistants in the secretariat were given orders to pack their bags and be ready to accompany Pius in flight on short notice, even though the pope had vowed to remain in Rome. At the same time, Allied diplomats living in Vatican City decided to burn their official papers on the advice of Cardinal Maglione.

And at a meeting of the diplomatic corps on September 14, according to a report cabled to Washington by American diplomat Harold Tittmann, "it was unanimously decided that if the pope should be forcibly removed by Germans, not only would the diplomats protest against the violence perpetrated but would also ask that they be allowed to accompany His Holiness."

The threat to the Vatican had become critical, and the German diplomats in Rome were as edgy as the pope and the curia. Kessel, who, like his superior, Weizsäcker, despised the Führer, would later write:

> It must be reasserted that Hitler, kept at bay by the Allies, like a beast of prey pursued by a pack of hunters, was capable of absolutely any hysterical act of crime. The idea of taking the pope prisoner and transporting him [elsewhere] had entered into his calculations. . . . We had specific information that if the pope had resisted, there was the possibility that he would be shot—while attempting to escape.

Kessel was clearly referring to a plot called Operation Rabat, apparently the one Hitler had in mind when he ordered Wolff to prepare a kidnap operation. The fascist leader in Como, Italy, Paolo Porta, described the plot in a letter he wrote to his counterpart in Milan, Vincenzo Costa. The letter's heading, *Massacre of Pius XII With the Entire Vatican,* reflected the ferocity of the plan, which was concocted in September 1943, about the time Wolff was given his mission, and tentatively scheduled to burst into deadly reality in January 1944. According to the letter, which repeated what a high SS official had told Porta, the purpose of the plot was to avenge "the papal protest in favor of the Jews"—no doubt including an expected papal outcry when the Jews were rounded up.

The plan, presented in greater detail than Wolff revealed to me, called for soldiers of the 8th Division of the SS *Florian Geyer* Cavalry, disguised in Italian uniforms, to launch a night attack against the Vatican. They would kill all members of the curia and take the pope prisoner. Then troops of the Hermann Göring panzer division would surge into the Vatican to "rescue" the pontiff and kill the disguised SS men, thinking they were Italian assassins rather than SS compatriots. Thus, no witnesses. If the pope tried to escape (or apparently was "perceived" as trying to), he, too, would be shot. The world, like the panzer soldiers, would thus be led to believe that the "Italians" and not the Nazis were guilty of murdering the curia and probably Pius.

If the pope somehow survived, he would be deported to Germany or Liechtenstein, where, Germany would proclaim, he had been taken for his own safety, as Wolff indicated to me.

Was the general informed of the most gruesome details at the meeting with Hitler that he described to me? Was he the SS official who informed Porta of the plot? If so, that might further explain why he was determined to sabotage it. Having come to believe, without being passionately ideological, that the SS was a fine symbol of true Germanism, he would find it extremely difficult to support the murder of such dedicated men, even if they were dedicated mainly to murdering others. But if it came down to them or him—well, he didn't want to die.

Himmler, the SS chief, by contrast, would kill almost anyone, even at the cost of more painful head and stomach aches, if it was in his interest to do so. And it was in his interest to disabuse Hitler of suspicion that he might not be completely loyal, even as he dickered with the Resistance—and also a rare opportunity to drive a stake through the heart of the Church he hated. Bormann, who surely was involved in the plot, would, for his part, pursue any means of getting rid of Christianity itself and filling the spiritual void with worship of Adolf Hitler.

Faced with such a nightmare, Weizsäcker struggled ever harder to frustrate the plan, whatever its details. He "had to fight on two fronts," Kessel would write. "On the one hand he had to advise the pope not to undertake anything unpremeditated, that is, actions with possibly deadly consequences [meaning condemnation of Jewish deportations, he would tell me]." At the same time he had to convince Hitler with subtly worded reports that the Vatican was well-disposed which, as far as Hitler was concerned, meant weak.

Weizsäcker would write that he (and presumably his colleagues who knew of the plot, including General Wolff) had agreed to a plan to save Pius before German soldiers could whisk him away. The governments of both Spain and Portugal had invited the pope to "vacation" in their countries; despite the pope's protestations that he would remain in Rome, persons close to him had arranged for his escape, if necessary, according to a papal assistant.

The ambassador was apparently referring to this plan, which was drawn up by Count Enrico Galeazzi, architect of the Apostolic, Monsignor Eduardo Prettner Cippico, and Milo di Villagrazia, an attorney. They met secretly with Sister Pasqualina Lehnert, Galeazzi's sister-in-law, and plotted to have the pontiff driven to San Felice Circeo, north of Naples, where he would hide in a villa on a cliff overlooking the sea, accessible only over a steep, narrow, easily defended path.

After remaining there for about forty-eight hours, he would sail to Spain, where General Francisco Franco would place him under his protection. Sister Pasqualina, according to this account, went in advance to San Felice Circeo and arranged for the pope's planned brief stay there, injuring her foot when she slipped on the precarious rocky path.

About the same time, on September 20, a Madrid correspondent of the Swedish newspaper *Social Demokraten* filed a report: "Spanish Catholic circles are very worried about the situation in Rome and especially by the fact that large German forces 'protect' the Vatican and have taken up positions in St. Peter's Square. In Spain and Portugal the population looks up to Rome, and if any power outraged the head of the Catholic Church, it would be very difficult for the governments to remain inactive."

CHAPTER 13

An Agonizing Dilemma

Some critics have charged that Pope Pius did not strongly and specifically condemn the Nazis for their genocidal policies in part because he was essentially a coldly indifferent anti-Semite. But other observers strongly disagree, even though they might be critical of his judgment, pointing out that the evidence disputes this charge.

Pius was mainly driven, many believe, by an obsessive desire to preserve the power and earthly trappings of the Church at almost any cost; and he used neutralist policy to achieve this end.

In some critical eyes, Pius acted out of a sincere if mistaken view of the Church's role in implementing the moral priorities taught by Christ. A view perhaps nurtured by the pope's long training in the art of temporal-style compromise diplomacy, which often involved practical political matters or sacred but lifeless real estate.

Some concede that he was burdened by a bureaucracy that harbored pro-Axis priests who, often acting on their own, supported Berlin's policies and even helped Nazi officials flee Europe after the war. And many feel that Pius XII was a decent, well-meaning man whose noble aura softened the rough edges of a complex, pragmatic mind. A man who acted as best he could, or thought he could, within the rigidly defined moral perimeters set by personality, education, experience, cultural environment, and historical conditioning.

But, when Pius XI died in 1939 and Eugenio Pacelli wrapped himself in the white robes of Pius XII just in time to deal with World

War II, his first priority was, say his critics, to save his sacredly immortal Church, not necessarily those transient mortals who might
be endangered. And in pursuing this priority, even when persecution
of the Jews turned into genocide, they assert, he constitutionally
could not bring himself to put the very epitome of his life at risk by
switching priorities. But, they ask, shouldn't he have taken the risk?

Pius XII's supporters reply that the pope had served God by trans-
forming the Church into a holy spiritual mecca stronger, more united,
more disciplined than it had ever been in modern times. Would he be
serving God by virtually assuring the destruction of this blessed hand-
iwork with sermons of outrage that might actually escalate the
killings? Hitler, in retaliation, would simply raid more monasteries,
more convents, more churches, and maybe even the Vatican, and kill
many of the Jews, priests, and nuns found there. And the peril grew,
the pope knew, when he heard that Hitler was plotting to abduct him.

Moreover, it is pointed out, almost as soon as Pius became pope,
he created a special department for the Jews in the German section
of the Vatican information office to make it easier to protect them.
And when Goebbels silenced Vatican Radio, which often protested
against Nazi extremism, he said that its programs were "more dangerous for us than those of the communists themselves."

Anyway, supporters ask, what choice did Pius have but to re-
strain his public rhetoric if he wanted the Church to remain eternal?
Neutralism, it seemed, was the only way. So how could he openly
condemn Hitler's crimes, the sympathizers further ask, without condemning those of the Soviet Union and the Allies themselves? Would
that be in the Allies' interest?

Nor had Pius seen, the Vatican claimed, any absolute proof that
the Nazis were committing genocide. Though mounting eyewitness
accounts of genocide were pouring into the Holy See, the pope told
Harold Tittmann that he believed Allied information "contained a
small element of exaggeration for the sake of propaganda."

The underlying problem was, the critics argue, that the Vatican
treated the various individual mass murder stories, even those coming

from its own clerics, as individual atrocities of war, evil as they were, and did not, and didn't wish to, integrate them into a distinct pattern of genocide. Thus, few people recognized the crimes as such, a recognition that might have roused even some Germans to stand up to Hitler whatever the consequences, or at least seek to slow up the machinery of mass murder.

After the war began, a general papal condemnation of atrocities, the Vatican found, did not elicit an especially vitriolic Hitlerian response. But the Vatican and the anti-Hitler German diplomats based there feared that even the most indirect allusion to genocide would set off an explosion that would intensify the horrors, great as they already were, and engulf the Church itself.

Still, some high Church officials favored taking the risk. For example, Konrad Preysing, the bishop of Berlin, pleaded with his fellow bishops and the pope himself to publicly condemn Hitler for the killings and even urged the Vatican to break off diplomatic relations with Germany as the only moral thing to do.

While what would become known as the Holocaust raged throughout Europe, what seems to have bothered the pope most, understandably, was the threat posed to his own Roman Jews, his neighbors. How he reacted to it would be the ultimate litmus test. If the threat materialized, could he claim, in submitting to what amounted to blackmail, that the stories of genocide were exaggerated?

As Kessel, the secretary of the German Embassy, would say after the war, "I was convinced then and am still convinced today that he almost broke down under the conflicts of conscience."

Would blackmail tip the scales?

Whatever the answer, Pius's knowledge that Hitler was plotting against him and the Vatican did little to encourage him to submit to the growing pleas by the Allies that he speak out directly and unambiguously against the genocide. The British minister, Osborne, in an audience with the pope on January 5, 1943, for instance, "impressed upon him that Hitler's policy of extermination was a crime without precedent in history." And in his diary, Osborne, normally an admirer of the pope, would write: "But is there not a moral issue at stake which does not admit of neutrality?"

When Tittmann told the pope in the fall of 1942 that his broadcasts were too vague and that "we need something more explicit," he replied:

"Well, I am sorry. I cannot do it. . . . There are over forty million German-speaking Catholics. If I should denounce the Nazis by name as you desire and Germany should lose the war, Germans everywhere would feel that I had contributed to the defeat, not only of the Nazis, but of Germany herself; for the German population not to be able to make the distinction between the Nazis and the Fatherland would only be human in the confusion and distress of defeat.

"I cannot afford to risk alienating so many of the faithful. One of my predecessors, Pope Benedict XV in the First World War, through an unfortunate public statement of the type you now wish me to make, did just this and the interests of the Church in Germany suffered as a result."

In other words, the Church's welfare, as the pope perceived it, was his primary priority. This statement, the historian Michael Phayer would write, was "disconcerting because of the warped standard that is implied—German disappointment with the pope as opposed to millions of innocently murdered Jews."

The strongest justification offered for Pius's public silence was that any papal protest would provoke Hitler into drastic retaliation. The pope's supporters argue that because Dutch prelates protested vehemently against Hitler's deportations in Holland, several hundred additional victims, mostly Jewish converts, including Edith Stein, the philosopher, were dragged out of Church institutions to their death. And the supporters further note that about 80 percent of Holland's Jews were ultimately deported, a higher percentage than in any other Nazi-occupied country.

Critics respond that Hitler was far less likely to respond violently to condemnation by the powerful leader of a worldwide religion than to denunciation by prelates with little influence outside their own countries.

They point out, too, that the pope's protest against Hitler's euthanasia program had brought an end to it; so why not do the same with the genocide program? Also, when at one point the gentile wives of Jewish men protested as a group against the roundup of their husbands, the Nazis backed down and released them.

The kernel of the critics' argument: If the pope had publicly and explicitly spoken out, several hundred thousand more victims *might* have been deported, but millions *might* have been saved. If he remained silent publicly, several hundred thousand *might* have remained safe, but several million were *certain* to die.

Was it morally justifiable, these critics ask, to witness a crime, especially one so incomprehensibly vast, without crying out to the heavens in protest, whatever the risk or sacrifice, if only to reassure future generations that man has not lost his soul? Was this not a sacred duty of a pope, or any other spiritual leader?

The kernel of the supporters' answer was expressed by Kessel when he said with pragmatic logic, reflecting the view of the anti-Hitler German diplomats: "We were convinced that a fiery protest by Pius XII against the persecution of the Jews would have in all probability put both the pope himself and the curia into extreme danger but . . . would certainly not have saved the life of a single Jew."

Pius himself had warned the cardinals on June 2, 1943, to be cautious in their language, whatever action they took to save Jews: "Every word spoken by us to the competent authorities, with [saving Jews] the end in view, and every reference made in public by us have to be most seriously pondered and weighed in the interests of those who are suffering, in order not to render, unwittingly, their situation even graver and more unbearable."

The pope surely had in mind a report from Monsignor Cesare Orsenigo, the papal nuncio in Berlin, that described a meeting he had with Hitler in early 1943:

As soon as I touched upon the question of the Jews and Judaism, the serenity of the meeting ended at once. Hitler turned his back to me, went to the window and started drumming his fingers on the pane . . . Still, I went on, voicing our complaints. Hitler suddenly turned around, went to a small table from which he took a water glass and furiously smashed it to the floor. In the face of such diplomatic behavior, I had to consider my mission terminated.

(This statement was seen by some observers as an argument against pressing Hitler to moderate his "Jewish" policies, Orsenigo being reputed for his warmth toward the Nazi regime. He refused even to receive an SS officer with a bad conscience who in August 1942 had witnessed a gas execution and wanted to send an account to the Vatican. The officer finally did through other Church contacts.)

Even before Hitler had given his order to General Wolff, Pius regretted finding himself "sometimes before doors which no key can open." The hardest he would pound on the door, his critics argue, was to say in his 1942 Christmas message that he deplored the fact that "hundreds of thousands . . . through no fault of their own, only because of their nationality or descent, [were] condemned to death."

Supporters of the pope argue that the Nazis' fiercely wrathful response to this statement, including a charge that he was a "Jew-lover," the worst possible indictment in the Nazi justice system, proves that listeners understood only too well that the pontiff was referring to the Jewish killings.

Nevertheless, some critics wonder why the pope made no distinction between the conventional atrocities of war, including the killing of captured partisans, and calculated genocidal murder having nothing to do with the fighting. Wasn't this crime morally more demanding of fiery protest than the battlefield kind?

Yes, some argue, additional innocents might have died if the pope had spoken out, perhaps even the pope himself. But was it, they ask, morally acceptable, especially for a religious icon, to refrain from risking the lives of some in an effort to stop the murder of many—indeed an entire people, whatever temporary abuse an ageless Church might suffer in pursuing its most fundamental mission: fighting evil?

True, the critics say, some Church notables, as in Holland, had dared to speak out, and the Church and those protected by it had paid a heavy price in blood. But they were doing only what they were morally obliged to do as self-chosen servants of God.

Supporters of the pope contend that Pius ordered or encouraged churches "to save lives by all possible means," an effort that is estimated to have helped save anywhere from one hundred thousand to more than seven hundred thousand Jews throughout occupied Europe. There is little written evidence of such efforts, but the Vatican was not eager to risk having "incriminating" documents fall into the hands of the Nazis, especially with the very existence of the Vatican at stake.

◆

Pius feverishly sought to solve his dilemma, hoping the world would understand that his refusal to condemn more vigorously the specific crime perpetrated against the Jews was rooted in his desire to *save* lives, and that it should not be interpreted as an expression of anti-Semitism.

When in May 1940 atrocities, including killings and forced labor, were committed against the largely Catholic public in Poland, he used the same rationale as he did with the Jews for refusing to speak out strongly. Dino Alfieri, Mussolini's ambassador to the Holy See, said then:

"We ought to speak words of fire against the atrocities in Poland, and the only thing which restrains us is the knowledge that words would make the fate of those wretches even worse."

And after one priest coming from Poland informed Pius of the deplorable conditions there and pleaded the opposite, imploring him to excommunicate Hitler and his Catholic cronies, the pope fell to his knees and raised his arms as if beseeching God to rescue the victims. But for his own part, he said, though he wanted to follow the priest's suggestion, his protest would evoke "the fiercest reprisals."

Pius did privately protest the persecution of Poles and Jews to Foreign Minister Ribbentrop when he visited Rome in March 1940. And when Ribbentrop told him not to meddle in politics, Cardinal Maglione gave him a list of German atrocities. The foreign minister was unfazed; he handed the cardinal in turn a list of alleged atrocities committed by Poles against Germans—a show of arrogance that did nothing to signify to Pius that Hitler would take heed of any public papal condemnation of the Jewish mass killings.

Thus, Pius's failure to publicly attack the Nazis for their cruel treatment of the Poles, who were mainly Catholic, suggested that the pope's silence about the Jewish deportations was rooted not in bias but in a real fear of Nazi retaliation against the Church. He appeared to confirm this when he quoted in a speech a statement by his predecessor, Pius XI, who was far more outspoken in his anti-Nazi views: "It is impossible for a Catholic to be an anti-Semite: Spiritually all of us are Semites."

The Vatican radio would expand on this theme: "He who makes a distinction between Jews and other men is unfaithful to God and is in conflict with God's commandments. As long as men make differences in the treatment of members of the human family, the peace of the world, order and justice will be at stake."

And Pius would tell an Italian priest: "Perhaps my solemn protest would have gained me the praise of the civilized world, but I would have brought on to the poor Jews a still more implacable persecution than the one they now suffer. I love the Jews. Was it not from among them, the Chosen People, that the Savior was to be born? And did not the Virgin Mary, the Apostles, and the first sons of the Church belong to this people?"

Moreover, his experience as a child seemed to reflect this ecumenical sentiment. At his elementary school, he developed a close friendship with a Jewish schoolmate, Guido Mendes, and the two boys often visited each other's home, where they would discuss their religious differences in a friendly spirit. Mendes would describe his friend as the top student in his class and a careful dresser who was never seen without a coat and tie. Years after their graduation, when the fascists began to threaten Jews in Italy, Pacelli, as the Vatican secretary of state, helped the Mendes family flee to Jerusalem, and the two friends kept in touch with each other over the years.

Although the pope commented that "spiritually, all of us are Semites," "all of us" could not be accurate, the pope's critics say. And they point mainly to a situation that occurred when he served after World War I as papal nuncio in Munich and the Bolsheviks attempted to take over Germany. He sent a letter to a Vatican official describing the revolutionary events as reported by a subordinate, who wrote: "Absolute hell. An army of employees [in the captured royal palace] were dashing to and fro, giving out orders, waving bits of paper, and in the midst of all this, a gang of young women, of dubious appearance, Jews like all the rest of them, hanging around in all the offices with lecherous demeanor and suggestive smiles."

Why hadn't Pacelli deleted the anti-Semitic aspects of the letter before sending it to *his* superior? Critics have wondered if he had ever placed in proper focus his early allegedly confused image of Jews and communists that projected little distinction between them. His supporters say he simply dispatched the letter without carefully reading it and claim that it was mistranslated.

Furthermore, they also point out that some notables known for their friendly relations with Jews, such as former President Richard Nixon and the Reverend Billy Graham, have made real anti-Semitic remarks in private and have never been seriously censured for them.

True, in Italy, the Vatican pressed the government to change regulations decreed by the 1938 anti-Semitic laws only for Jewish converts to Catholicism insofar as they violated Church traditions involved, for example in, marriage.

But in the context of Pius's fear-ridden reign, it would seem that once more he was motivated not by anti-Semitism but by the psychological compulsion to avoid "unnecessary" friction with a Nazi government that could threaten, at the least provocation, the Vatican with its sacred symbols and its papacy. He felt he had to maintain at any cost a façade of neutralism even in the biblically based realm of morality.

But, ask the critics once again, shouldn't he have let the world know in a lesson for posterity that the Vicar of Christ must never compromise with evil or fail to renounce it, whatever the cost? British diplomat Osborne would make this entry in his diary:

> A policy of silence in regard to such offenses against the conscience of the world must necessarily involve a renunciation of moral leadership and a consequent atrophy of the influence and authority of the Vatican; and it is upon the maintenance and assertion of such authority that must depend any prospect of a papal contribution to the reestablishment of world peace.

But Pacelli as cardinal secretary of state and later as pope did publicly protest on some occasions against Hitler's criminally anti-Semitic policies, though, in public, he usually referred to the Jews only in the more ambiguous and less inflammable context of "race." For example, on July 13, 1937, he defined Germany to an audience of Catholic pilgrims as "that noble and powerful nation whom bad shepherds would lead astray into an idolatry of race."

Pius also reserved his cautious means of expression for Jewish converts, whom he is accused of favoring. On one occasion, after their roundup in the Netherlands in 1940, according to the pope's assistant and confidante, Sister Pasqualina Lehnert, he scribbled a strong protest in their support. But then he suddenly decided to burn the protest in his kitchen and remained there until the document was completely consumed.

"I thought about filing it," he told the sister, "but if the Nazis come and find it, what will happen to the Catholics and Jews in Germany? No, it is better to destroy this strong protest."

Pacelli wrote his most biting condemnatory statement for Pius XI, an encyclical known as *Mit brennender Sorge (With Burning Concern)*. Distributed to the German bishops, it referred to the Nazi Party and its "arrogant apostasy from Jesus Christ, the denial of Christ's teaching and redemptive work, the worship of force, the idolatry of race and blood, and the oppression of liberty and human dignity."

The encyclical further stated: "True Christianity proves itself in the love of God and the active love of one's neighbor. . . . Only ignorance and arrogance can blind one to the treasures of the Old Testament. He who wants to banish biblical history and the wisdom of the Old Testament from school, and church, commits blasphemy against the Word of God."

This was a strong and forthright protest, though some Jews were disturbed by a sentence ironically made in an intended context of tolerance: "He negates the faith in the incarnate Christ, who took on human nature out of that people which was to crucify him."

These few words mentioning Jewish responsibility for the crucifixion of Christ, even if referring to individual Jews of the biblical period and not to their descendants, were words sprouting from the seed of anti-Semitism planted two thousand years ago and codified by the New Testament references, for example, to "pernicious" Jews. The seed that would infect much of Christendom over the centuries and finally yield the Holocaust before being rooted out by the scriptural scalpel of Pope John XXIII, Pius XII's great reformist successor.

The encyclical was, in any event, strong enough to elicit the most venomous fury the Nazis had ever directed at the Vatican. The SS publication *Das Schwarze Korps* called it "the most incredible of Pius XI's pastoral letters; every sentence in it was an insult to the new Germany." And Pacelli's language drew a comment in *Völkischer Beobachter* referring to the "Jew-god and his deputy in Rome."

Hitler even threatened ominously to cancel the Concordat, raving that his government "had to consider the pope's encyclical as a call to battle . . . since it calls upon Catholic citizens to rebel against the authority of the Reich."

A call to battle? This violent reaction no doubt had a powerful psychological effect on Eugenio Pacelli. Even an ambiguous reference to Nazi "ignorance and arrogance," it seemed, had threatened to set off an explosion in Hitler's mind that could destroy the Vatican. How much greater would the explosion be, he surely asked himself, if he used similar language to condemn the murder of millions?

Two years later, in 1939, after inheriting the papal throne, Pacelli shelved another encyclical condemning racism and anti-Semitism that his predecessor had prepared. It seemed to him hardly the time to light another fuse. But if the future pope had been intimidated into public silence, he was a moderate in the breadth of papal history.

Unlike the ghettos and "pales" of northern and eastern Europe, the ghetto of Rome was neither a symbol of popular hatred nor a means of protecting the Jews against violence, for the Italian Christians never rejected the Jews. On the contrary, under papal rule the Italian Christians were to be protected *from* the Jews, or at least from their unholy influence.

At the same time, little effort was made to convert more than a handful. The Jews of Rome had come from Jerusalem, many as slaves of their Roman conquerors, more than two thousand years ago, and they formed the oldest Jewish community in the Diaspora. They were to serve as eternal witnesses to the truth of the Christian revelation. Indeed, they were a part of Christian ritual.

Some students of the Church never reached this relatively moderate level. In 1934, *Civilta Cattolica*, the Jesuit magazine published in Rome, observed regretfully that Nazi anti-Semitism "did not stem from the religious convictions nor the Christian conscience . . . but from [the Nazis's] desire to upset the order of religion and society." It added: "We could understand them, or even praise them, if their policy were restricted within acceptable bounds of defense against the Jewish organizations and institutions."

In 1936, the same publication clarified its viewpoint:

Opposition to Nazi racialism should not be interpreted as a rejection of anti-Semitism based on religious grounds. The Christian world, without un-Christian hatred, must defend itself against the Jews by suspending their civic rights and returning them to the ghettos.

Certainly not by killing them.

◆

No one will ever know how many Jews, if any, might have been saved had the pope spoken out publicly and powerfully. But, say critics, this uncertainty should not have nullified the sacred duty of the leader of a religious faith to protest to the world in the strongest possible terms, whatever the consequences, against an unprecedented evil that was defiling every human value God has instilled in man.

Many Jews agree, including the Jewish leaders in Rome, among them the descendants of the dead.

But in judging Pius's World War II record, others argue, one should take into account the fact that many who did survive might have died if not for his direct or indirect involvement. Among those who have harbored this view are some Jewish notables, from the late Prime Minister Golda Meir of Israel to the historian Martin Gilbert. Rabbi David G. Dalin would even quote the Talmud in lavishing praise on the pope:

The Talmud teaches that "whosoever preserves one life, it is accounted to him by Scripture as if he had preserved a whole world." More than any other twentieth century leader, Pius XII fulfilled this Talmudic dictum, when the fate of European Jewry was at stake. No other pope had been so widely praised by Jews—and they were not mistaken. Their gratitude, as well as that of the entire generation of Holocaust survivors, testified that Pope Pius XII was genuinely and profoundly, a righteous gentile.

The pope helped to arrange for several thousand to escape to countries that would accept them, notably the Dominican Republic and Brazil. He vigorously protested against the deportations ordered by the Slovakian government, and after six appeals managed to have them stopped, with Cardinal Angelo Roncalli, the future Pope John XXIII, supplying survivors with thousands of transit visas to Palestine. And in conjunction with the cardinal, Pius urged the governments of Bulgaria and Romania to spare Jews and dispatched money to help them survive.

At the same time, convents, monasteries, and other Vatican institutions, not all of which would have volunteered to risk their own survival by sheltering Jews, took the risk either on receiving direct orders from the pope or simply knowing his desire. Actually, canon law forbids sheltering in cloistered places anyone outside the Church establishment without the pope's express approval. Therefore, according to Church legal authorities, all those clerics who hid Jews must have received papal approval through some means. They conceived, however, that such approval is not essential in an emergency, and the Holocaust would certainly qualify as one. Even so, the pope, to make sure that the clergy understood his wish, spread the word in his oral communications with the clergy.

When refugees requested asylum in convents, which normally welcomed only females, confusion sometimes arose. In one case, after a Jewish couple sought refuge in one convent in Rome, only the wife was initially accepted—until the pope personally ordered the convent to accept the husband as well. Thus, doors, in effect, were opened at convents to Jewish men and other threatened males in all occupied countries.

Altogether in the Eternal City, a little over half the city's eight thousand Jewish residents ultimately found refuge in more than 150 convents and monasteries, mostly situated on Vatican property, and some three thousand in Castel Gandolfo, the pope's summer residence. Another sixty lived at the Jesuit Gregorian University, a few slept in the cellar of the Bible Institute, and around four hundred were fictitious "members" of the Vatican's four-thousand-man Palatine Guard.

And some, whether influenced or not by the Church's teachings, hid in the homes of lay Catholics—among them Israel Zolli, the chief rabbi of Rome.

CHAPTER 14

The Art of
Examining Walls

Though Chief Rabbi Zolli was terrified as he set out on his desperate mission early on September 28, a strange prosaic self-consciousness seized him. He was on his way to the Vatican wearing a shabby suit!

"I am dressed like a beggar," he lamented to his friend, Giorgio Fiorentini, the lawyer who was driving him.

But Zolli had no other suit. In his rush to escape the Germans when they occupied Rome eighteen days earlier, he had left almost all his belongings in his apartment. After staying the first fear-filled night there, he had spent the next three scrambling from one friend's home to another until finally Amedeo Pierantoni, a Catholic whose son, Luigi, worked for the Resistance, gave him refuge.

But now he had to come out of hiding and risk capture. He would try to save his people—many of whom held him in little esteem—whether they appreciated it or not. He would seek help from Pope Pius XII.

This was a mission not only of mercy for his people, including himself, but of love for the pope. He would later say that "the influence of the Vatican was great, and open persecution was certain to produce a great outcry from the pope." And his faith in Pius was fed by his secret feeling that the sign of the cross would ultimately save his people, or at least their souls.

Zolli, a native of Austria, did not view belief in both Judaism and Christianity as contradictory. His mother belonged to a family of learned rabbis and had urged her son to become one, too, though the pay would be little and the family, after losing its business, had been thrust into poverty.

He had first sensed the meaning of Christianity when he spent afternoons at the home of his friend, Stanislaus, where they worked on their homework together in a large white-walled room. On one of those walls hung a crucifix of plain wood, with the branch of an olive tree suspended over it.

The young Zolli wondered why he kept raising his eyes to stare at the crucifix, why he felt so strange in its presence. As strange as he had felt when, as a very young child, he would take his father's Bible and read it line by line, page by page, fearful of missing the thread of the story, while other children frolicked in the sun. In the white-walled room, as in his father's library, he had yearned, he would write, for "something infinite and indefinable."

After studying for the rabbinate, Zolli rose in the ranks to become chief rabbi of Trieste, which had become part of Italy when World War I ended in 1918. One afternoon he was alone at home writing an article when suddenly he began, as if in a trance, to invoke the name of Jesus:

"I found no peace until I saw him, as if in a large picture without a frame, in the dark corner of the room. I gazed on him for a long time without feeling any excitement, rather in a perfect serenity of spirit. . . . Was this experience objectively real or only subjective? I do not know."

Zolli would explain: "The Israelite community and the Church represented religious life for me, each in itself. I felt myself to be a Hebrew because I was naturally Hebrew, and I loved Jesus Christ." But many Jews, though not suspecting his spiritual conversion, were, Zolli admitted, "dissatisfied" with his appointment as chief rabbi.

"I know how to love better than how to make myself loved."

And this was especially true when he took over the same post in Rome. The Jewish community, especially its temporal leaders, viewed him as an eastern European "foreigner" who lacked the credentials to serve as a spiritual inspiration for people whose Roman roots reached back to ancient times. And he seemed to many a haughty intellect whose professed love for the community was condescendingly—and insincerely—modeled after God's blanket love of humanity.

Thus, rejected by many of his people, he would, on his own, visit the Vatican on a mission to save them even as he contemplated abandoning them when God decided he should. He wrote in his memoirs:

> Conversion consists in responding to a call from God. A man is not converted at the time he chooses, but in the hour when he receives God's call. When the call is heard, he who receives it has only one thing to do: *obey*. . . . Conversion is light renewed, love of God renewed. The convert is a man who has died and has risen again.

While thus awaiting the call to die, Zolli would seek the help of the man who would eventually show him the road to resurrection. Though he was saddened by the antagonism that he aroused in his fellow Jews, there seemed something symbolic in his mission to the Vatican, something that made him rejoice in what he felt was his boundless love for his people and all mankind.

His people were somehow immune to his protestations of love. They refused his embrace and his advice, sensing, it seemed, that his words had only a cold, mystical meaning to him, abstract words that Zolli fitted neatly into his brilliant theological sermons and treatises but could not transform into feelings of the heart.

Zolli appears to have been at once too mystical and too rational for his flock—tendencies that were in constant conflict within himself. His mysticism led to a fatalistic dependence on prayer, which the rabbi claimed gave rise in him to emotional ecstasy with infusions of reality—the reality, in particular, of a likely Nazi crackdown.

When Zolli was chief rabbi in Trieste, he read countless documents and spoke with many Jewish refugees from Germany and eastern Europe about Nazi atrocities. He knew that when the Germans occupied Rome they would attempt to destroy the Jews there, too. But his flock would not believe him, preferring the more comforting advice of their secular leaders—that there was no need to leave their homes and hide, that this was, after all, Italy, where little anti-Semitism existed.

The trouble was, Zolli thought, the community leaders had fooled themselves into thinking that their fascist friends would come to their aid. He himself had always opposed fascism and had even argued against it with one of his two daughters, Miriam, who as a student had been an ardent fascist herself. But now fascism was more dangerous than ever, at least for the Jews, for it offered false hope to those who, after having served the system for so long, still could not believe that it would betray them so ruthlessly. As ruthlessly as *they* had betrayed *him*.

Perhaps with his visit to the Vatican to seek gold, God was signaling that it was time for the rebirth of Chief Rabbi Zolli.

At the same time, it could remind his congregation of the involuntary visits by chief rabbis in past centuries . A newly elected pope, after crowning in St. Peter's Square, would mount a white horse and, on the way to the Basilica of San Giovanni in Laterano, pause to receive the Pentateuch from the chief rabbi of Rome. The pope would hold the book for a few moments and then turn it upside down, and the rabbi would bow his head and extend his hand. The *camerlengo,* or papal chamberlain, would then place twenty pieces of gold in the hand, supposedly making the rebuke tolerable, though actually adding to the humiliation.

The pope's flock was to observe in unmistakable terms the degradation of those who blinded themselves to the biblical revelation they had themselves witnessed. No, the Jews were not to be physically attacked, driven out, or even converted. They were needed—as Jews. But the gold was to remind everyone why they should be shunned.

These were modern times, however, and Zolli sensed that the Jewish community and synagogue leaders would not grant him the honor of going to the Vatican to seek new pieces of gold. He thus decided to do so without consulting them. Why didn't he ask some influential priest to request aid from the pope, someone who would not have to sneak into the Vatican at great risk?

Zolli clearly hoped to meet the pope personally and, without bowing and groveling, perhaps even be invited to stay in the Vatican with his family. After all, it would seem only proper for the spiritual leader of the worldwide Catholic community to welcome the chief rabbi of Romans, who traditionally looked to the pope, good or bad, for protection.

"We shall go in by one of the back doors," Fiorentini told Zolli as he drove toward the Vatican gate. "The Vatican is always guarded by the Gestapo. A friendly person will be waiting for you, and so that you can avoid showing personal documents stamped 'Hebrew Race,' you will be presented as an engineer, called to examine some walls that are being constructed."

"The art of examining walls has always interested me," Zolli wryly replied.

At the Vatican, the builders greeted the plump, bespectacled "engineer," who, after carefully inspecting their construction plans, nodded his approval. The two visitors then nonchalantly walked to the office of the Vatican treasurer, who welcomed them warmly. As the treasurer left to see the pope about obtaining the needed gold, the chief rabbi pleaded:

"The New Testament does not abandon the Old. Please help me. As for repayment, I myself shall stand as surety, and since I am poor, the Hebrews of the whole world will contribute to pay the debt."

As surety, he seemed to suggest, he would agree to be confined to the Vatican.

◆

The debt would be for Vatican gold to buy Jewish lives, and this time far more than the traditional twenty pieces given to a chief rabbi to ease his humiliation. Two days before, on September 26, the two top Jewish lay leaders, Dante Almansi and Ugo Foa, had been summoned to the headquarters of Colonel Kappler, the young, blond Gestapo chief in Rome.

The colonel greeted them courteously, even expressing regret for any inconvenience he may have caused. The two Jewish leaders cringed. They knew that the mildly sounding, even kindly opening words uttered by this feared torturer were a mocking prelude to some terrible edict of doom.

Kappler was a slavishly loyal instrument of the Nazi Party, yet, more than with most top Nazi bureaucrats, pragmatism and common sense often triumphed over ideological zeal. For example, he had considered the rescue of Mussolini from his captors as unwise, believing that fascism was dead and that if the Duce returned to power he would have to rule "by the strength of German bayonets," as Kappler testified to a court after the war.

Yet the Gestapo chief obediently played a key role in the dictator's rescue after discovering where he was being held. If he had a soft spot, it was his love of Rome, his "second home," with its rainbow array of flowers, its splendid antiques. But little of that affection was transferred to the Italians, some of whom he ordered mercilessly tortured after the occupation of Rome if suspected of the least resistance to Nazi rule.

Even so, Kappler, like his SS superior, General Wolff, opposed large-scale roundups of real or suspected enemies, including Jews, not for humanitarian reasons, but for fear that such raids would energize the communists and other political agitators to bloody the streets of Rome in challenging Nazi power. Both men especially feared that Hitler would soon demand the roundup of the Roman Jews, a prospect that could yield a papal outcry and the chaos they wanted to avoid.

Moreover, if Wolff had not yet told Kappler of the kidnap plot, the colonel must have heard rumors of it—and would surely be involved. If it succeeded, he could expect an even greater explosion. So why light the fuse with a roundup? Anyway, the Jews numbered only about eight thousand and were mostly middle class and poor residents who posed no threat to the "real" Italians.

Indeed, Wolff and Kappler knew that most Italians, including King Victor Emmanuel III, vigorously opposed Hitler's anti-Semitic policies. Reflecting this attitude was an account in the diary of Count Galeazzo Ciano, Mussolini's foreign minister and son-in-law, of a meeting between the Duce and the king on November 28, 1938, shortly after the Italian dictator decreed the anti-Jewish laws:

> I found the Duce in a state of indignation against the king. Three times in the course of their conversation this morning the king said to him that he feels an 'infinite pity for the Jews.' He cited cases of persecution. . . . The Duce said that there are twenty thousand spineless people in Italy who are moved by the fate of the Jews. The king replied that he is one of them.

The king, in fact, was being true to an ancient Roman tradition. Particularly before the destruction of Jerusalem two thousand years ago, Roman leaders had often been good to the Jews by ancient standards. Julius Caesar had treated them so well that when he was assassinated they wept for him and chanted dirges. And they bewailed for a whole week the death of Augustus, who had enriched the Temple of Jerusalem with costly gifts and had encouraged the Jews to strictly observe their Sabbath. They did—refusing to lose their identity whoever sat on the conqueror's throne in Rome.

Kappler thought he had found a way to save the Jews, and, at the same time, enrich the Gestapo. And Wolff apparently approved of it. The colonel's tone thus suddenly changed in his confrontation with Almansi and Foa and his angular face hardened, accentuating the long, thin scar that crossed his left cheek.

"You and your co-religionists," he said quietly, "are Italian nationals, but that is of minor importance to me. We Germans consider you only as Jews and therefore our enemy. Rather, to be more precise, we consider you a distinct group, but not completely apart from the worst enemies we are fighting. And we will treat you accordingly."

Almansi and Foa listened with dread, finally realizing that their community was in grave danger.

"It is not your lives or the lives of your children that we will take—if you agree to our demands," Kappler went on. "It is your gold we want, in order to buy new arms for our country. Within thirty-six hours you must pay fifty kilograms of gold. If you pay, you will not be harmed. If you do not, two hundred of your Jews will be arrested and deported to Germany, where they will be sent to the Russian frontier or otherwise rendered harmless."

The shocked Jewish leaders persuaded Kappler to extend the deadline by more than four hours and pridefully turned down an offer of men and vehicles to help them collect the gold. As they were leaving, Kappler warned: "Keep in mind that I have conducted a number of operations like this in the past, and all ended well. I failed only once, and a few hundred of your brothers paid with their lives."

As Kappler departed, he felt rather proud of himself; the Jewish lives for gold idea was his own. He could only hope that Hitler and Himmler would realize it made sense and that, with the Jews safe, there was no need to take action against the Vatican.

❖

Almansi and Foa, who had both held high posts in the fascist hierarchy before Mussolini heeded Hitler's demand in 1938 to crack

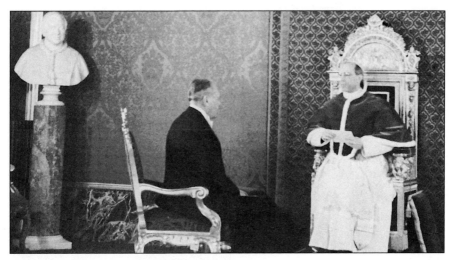

Pope Pius XII speaks with Myron Taylor, the chief American representative to the Vatican in February 1940. The pope, fearing the destruction of Rome's historic treasures, urged that the Americans stop bombing the Nazi-held city. And Taylor urged Pius to publicly condemn more forcefully the Jewish genocide, countering arguments that such a condemnation would push Hitler to kill even more people. The pope also feared that Hitler would retaliate by kidnapping him and the curia and looting the Vatican. (L'Osservatore Romano)

Cardinal Luigi Maglioni, the Vatican secretary of state, who warned German Ambassador Ernst von Weizsäcker that if the Nazis rounded up the Jews of Rome, the pope might feel obligated to speak out publicly against Hitler even though both men knew this could trigger a papal kidnap plot in progress. (U.S. Army)

German Ambassador Weizsäcker warned Pope Pius XII that if he spoke out publicly against the Jewish genocide, Hitler would implement the kidnap plot. In case Hitler did try this, the anti-Nazi diplomat involved himself in a plot to save the pope. *(Marianne von Weizsäcker)*

SS General Karl Wolff, who was ordered by Hitler to kidnap Pope Pius XII and loot the Vatican. But afraid that if the Allies won the war they might hang him for his role as chief of staff for Heinrich Himmler, orchestrator of the Holocaust, he betrayed Hitler and sabotaged the plot in the hope of winning the pope's support. *(Karl Wolff)*

SS General Karl Wolff as he appeared at his postwar German trial for his involvement in the murder of hundreds of thousands of Jews. He also helped to save several thousand in Rome, hoping to keep the pope from publicly speaking out against the genocide and inciting Hitler to implement his kidnap plan. He escaped indictment at Nuremberg because he surrendered the whole Nazi army in Italy to the Americans. *(Italian Communist Party Archives, Rome)*

SS General Karl Wolff with Italian dictator Benito Mussolini. Wolff, as SS chief in Italy, made sure the Duce would remain loyal to Hitler after being ousted from office and escaping with Nazi help to northern Italy, where he set up a rump fascist republic. *(Karl Wolff)*

Heinrich Himmler, the SS leader who directed the Jewish genocide and helped design the plot to kidnap the pope. At the same time, he flirted with the idea of ousting Hitler from power and leading Germany to the conquest of all Asia, fulfilling an ancient German dream. *(U.S. National Archives)*

A weak and scrawny man himself, Himmler sought desperately to meet the physical standards he had set for his SS members, who had to be perfect Aryans to have any hope of acceptance into the elite, murderous SS. They little imagined that some of them might be "eliminated," so they couldn't bear witness to their role in the kidnap plan—which could mean the killing of all members of the curia and perhaps the pope. *(Bundesarchiv, Koblenz)*

Martin Bormann, whose name was unknown even to most Germans, became Hitler's most powerful adviser and for years had been planning to kidnap the pope as the first step toward demolishing Christianity and replacing it with a new Nazi religion; this would have made the Führer the world's most influential spiritual leader. *(U.S. National Archives)*

Israel Zolli, the chief rabbi of Rome, sneaked through Nazi-infested Rome to the Vatican posing as a construction worker in order to ask the pope for gold to meet German ransom demands to save the city's Jews from deportation. Most of them were saved, in part because of counter-plotting by General Wolff and Ambassador Weizsäcker. After the war, Zolli, his first name changed to Eugenio in honor of the pope, returned to the Vatican—this time to work after converting to Christianity. *(Sophia Cavaletti)*

Field Marshall Albert Kesselring (center) converses with Benito Mussolini and Adolf Hitler. Strictly a military man, Kesselring opposed both the papal kidnap plot and the roundup of Roman Jews, but he remained loyal to Hitler until the Führer's death. *(U.S. National Archives)*

SS Colonel Eugen Dollmann, Karl Wolff's aristocratic assistant, impresses Adolf Hitler. Dollmann helped to arrange for the general a secret audience with the pope. Wolff managed what seemed the impossible: He won the complete confidence, simultaneously, of both the Vicar of Christ and the Antichrist. *(U.S. National Archives)*

A painting of Donna Virginia Agnelli, who, by devious means, helped Eugen Dollmann arrange for the secret meeting between Pope Pius XII and General Karl Wolff. *(Eugen Dollmann)*

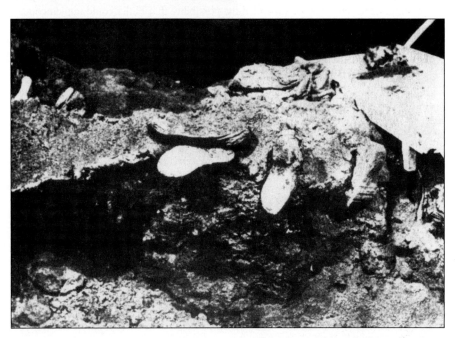

A corpse unearthed in Rome's Ardeatine Caves, one of several hundred people who were massacred by the Nazis in retaliation for a lethal communist attack on German troops. Pope Pius XII condemned both deadly incidents in keeping with his neutralist policy, hoping such neutralism would save the Church from Hitler's wrath. *(Communist Party Archives, Rome)*

General Mark Clark, lost on entering Rome, asks an American priest how to get to the center of the city. His arrival ended the possibility that Hitler could implement his papal kidnap plot. Pope Pius XII now felt safe, but he was disappointed that his dream of mediating a negotiated peace was dead and that the Soviet Union would share in the fruits of an inevitable German unconditional surrender. *(U.S. Army)*

A child salutes as crowds cheer American soldiers liberating Rome. *(U.S. Army)*

down on the Jews, visited their former fascist colleagues and argued that fascist sovereignty would suffer if Kappler's blackmail threat against the Jews was permitted. But failing in this effort, they called a meeting of members of the Jewish Community Council, the most influential Jews in Rome, to decide how to meet the Nazis' forty-eight hour deadline for the delivery of gold.

The atmosphere churned with tension, despair, and disbelief mixed with guarded hope as they sat together asking each other whether Colonel Kappler would keep his promise. Were the Jews of Rome to lose their homes, their lives? This isn't how their ancestors had described their destiny. According to Jewish legend, King Solomon and the pharaoh's daughter married and an angel then fixed a long reed in the sea, marking the place where the Eternal City would one day rise. An island gradually formed at this spot, and a forest grew on the island.

The first inhabitants built two huts of rushes, but the sage Abba Kolon then appeared and, seeing the huts collapsing, proclaimed that no hut could endure unless the earth had been moistened with the water of the Euphrates River. He thereupon undertook the long, hazardous journey to the Euphrates and returned with the water, and, on the dampened earth, he erected new huts, which now stood firm. Rome was born, to await the coming of the Messiah.

Had the Messiah now come to save them and their "huts" with this business of gold?

The Jewish leaders called on their people by word of mouth to come with their gold jewelry and trinkets to the great temple on the right bank of the Tiber River at 10:30 the next morning, September 27. They trickled in, and a half hour later the gold collection campaign began, with a jeweler and two goldsmiths, equipped with a scale, sitting behind a table in a hall of the temple.

The desperation permeating the temple grew as the leaders waited for their brethren to respond. Since most of the rich Jews had already fled the city, the task of saving the community would be left to the poor ones. Most of them lived in the slums of Trastevere, just across the river from the traditional ghetto—the rag-peddlers and laborers disdained by the wealthier Jews.

Little did they realize that Kappler, Wolff, Weizsäcker, and at least some of their fellow German officials were hoping the gold would buy not only Jewish lives but possibly the life of Pius XII. For if the Jews were saved, he would not be compelled to solve his dilemma with an outcry when he heard the sound of trucks crammed with Jews thundering through the night—a choice that could spell his own doom.

CHAPTER 15

A Question
of Priority

The pope's dilemma—whether to publicly condemn the genocide or not—was all the more painful because he had grown to love the Germans while serving the Church in Germany after World War I. It was hard to wish ill to his friends and their children now fighting under a tyrant determined to destroy the Church and murder millions of innocent people. At the same time, he did his best to disbelieve reports that the atrocities being committed against the Jews amounted to genocide, an admission that would add enormously to an already almost unbearable pressure on him to speak out publicly.

Though the pope was wrong in this wishful appraisal, which essentially stemmed from an iron resolve to save the Church, he wasn't the only world leader who can be accused of failing to exert a maximum effort to stop the genocide because a "greater cause" was at stake. Other leaders during that period of heinous inhumanity were blinded by long-term objectives they felt had to be pursued with greater priority. However inadvertently, they greased the machinery of genocide that swallowed up millions of innocent victims who had nothing to do with the waging of war.

President Roosevelt and Prime Minister Churchill refused to bomb the gas chambers or the railroad tracks leading to them, arguing that they needed all their planes to fight the war—and that only victory would save the Jews.

To ward off popular pressure to stop the genocide, they seldom mentioned it publicly, even after they received credible reports of it in 1942. Some victims who were gassed would have been saved if three years earlier Roosevelt had not turned back the ship *St. Louis* with its load of Jewish refugees fleeing from Nazi Europe, after it had arrived in American waters.

And on February 25, 1943, Secretary of State Cordell Hull wrote to the British Ambassador in Washington: "The refugee problem should not be considered as being confined to persons of any particular race or faith. Nazi measures against minorities have caused the flight of persons of various races and faiths, as well as of other persons because of their political beliefs."

In other words, genocide was just another word for oppression.

Then, on April 20, 1943, Breckinridge Long, Roosevelt's assistant secretary of state in charge of refugee affairs, wrote in his diary, referring to American Jewish leaders who were trying to pressure their government to take some action:

> One danger in it all is that their activities may lend color to the charges of Hitler that we are fighting this war on account of and at the instigation and direction of our Jewish citizens.

The British, like the Americans, made little distinction between the persecution and random political killing of non-Jewish refugees and the calculated genocidal murder of millions of Jews. When the British government first received reports of mass gassings in death camps shortly after the first deportations from the Warsaw ghetto on July 22, 1942, it regarded them as exaggerated and would not broadcast them. And on August 27, the foreign office cabled Washington about a planned joint public declaration concerning German atrocities in Poland:

"On further reflection we are not convinced that evidence regarding use of gas chambers is substantial enough to justify inclusion in a public declaration."

Two months later, in October, Jan Karski, a Polish Home Army lieutenant, met with two leaders of the Jewish underground in Warsaw and confirmed that the reports of genocide were not exaggerated.

"What's the good of talking?" one of the leaders said. "What reason do I have to go on living? . . . If all the Jews are killed they won't need any leaders. . . . But it's no use telling you all this. No one in the outside world can possibly understand. You don't understand. Even I don't understand, for my people are dying and I am alive."

Karski, overwhelmed by what he learned, headed for London and Washington and told the story to Churchill and Roosevelt. Now they knew. There really were gas chambers. But the Jews would just have to wait until the war ended. As a press release issued by the Department of State read in part: "Nothing could be recommended that would interfere with or delay the war effort of the [Allies]."

The British Embassy in Washington, D.C., on the other hand, sent a memorandum to the Department of State on January 20, 1943:

> The refugee problem cannot be treated as though it were a wholly Jewish problem which could be handled by Jewish agencies or by machinery only adapted for assisting Jews. . . . There is a possibility that the Germans or their satellites may change over from the policy of extermination to one of extrusion, and aim as they did before the war at embarrassing other countries by flooding them with alien immigrants.

Extermination at least eased the refugee problems of "other countries"!

Nor would the British, who controlled Palestine, permit Jews trapped in Europe to seek refuge there for fear of upsetting the

Arabs. In fact, Haj Amin al-Husseini, the Palestinian leader, was in Germany busily helping Hitler round up Jews for disposal in the gas chambers. "The Jews of Europe," he told me after the war, "had no right to go to Palestine."

Even David Ben-Gurion, who headed the Jewish Agency and in 1948 would become Israel's founder and first prime minister, fell into line. Although some colleagues pressured him to urge the Allies to bomb the killing facilities, he argued that he must reserve his limited influence for the struggle to win support for a Jewish state in British-controlled Palestine after the war—the only long-term answer, he felt, to anti-Semitic atrocities. At one point in the war, Ben-Gurion felt he had to choose between saving the Jews already in the Holy Land and the millions in Europe.

Yitzhak Gruenbaum, who served under Ben-Gurion, would say that "we knew about the massacres in August [1942] but didn't reveal the information in public because [Field Marshal Erwin] Rommel was then threatening Palestine, and the *Yishuv* [the Jewish community] had to devote all its attention to making a last stand. We had to instill in the people's hearts the recognition that it was necessary to fight and not to be like sheep led to the slaughter. How could we then talk about what was taking place in Poland?"

Ben-Gurion himself showed no public sign of even knowing about the Final Solution. He spoke of a Jewish army and other subjects, but not a word about the mass slaughter, except for one passing reference to the "disaster that has happened to Polish Jewry." His job was to preach the need for a Jewish state, to spur Britain to forge a Jewish army, and to propel Chaim Weizmann, his principal rival, into political oblivion—essential steps, he felt, toward a state. And Ben-Gurion, one of the greatest Jewish leaders in history, would not let any storm obscure his path. In 1948, the path would finally lead to a Jewish state—but without the millions of Jews who would not live to inhabit it.

The tactical follies of these political giants, however, cannot excuse Pius's restrained public condemnation of the genocide, his critics say, especially since he was a holy man who had chosen to devote himself to the salvation of human life.

As for the destruction of sacred land and treasures, it is asked, did not the very essence of faith require religious leaders to make any material sacrifice necessary to save lives, or to create conditions that would ultimately save lives, if only to affirm that the human spirit, unlike the flesh, can never perish?

Before the Nazis stormed into Rome, this question had crystallized into a moral quandary when the Americans started to bomb what they viewed as military objectives scattered among the ancient churches, monasteries, and monuments.

❖

Pope Pius XII had been chatting with foreign diplomats on the morning of July 19, 1943, when suddenly the sharp crack of antiaircraft guns interrupted the conversation. After a short, startled silence, explosions shook the earth. The pope rose from his desk and hurried to a rattling window of his study. The diplomats saw him grow pale as he observed columns of black smoke rise like huge, grasping fingers and converge into a fist thrust into the blue summer sky.

Despite the pope's desperate pleas to both the Allies and the Axis to declare Rome an open city, Allied planes were already streaking across the city, unloading their bombs on the marshaling yards in the district of San Lorenzo, a poor workers' area on the eastern edge of the metropolis.

For two hours Pius stood at the window watching the tarnished heavens, whispering prayers, removing his spectacles occasionally to wipe the moisture from his eyes. Finally, he went to his desk and called Monsignor Montini.

"How much cash is there in the Vatican bank?" he asked.

"About two million lire, Your Holiness."

"Draw it immediately and take the first car you find in San Damaso courtyard. We will join you."

The pope and Montini climbed into a small car and set off swiftly through the streets of Rome until they reached barricades blocking the way to the flaming railroad station. The two passengers descended, and an official, astonished to see the pope, informed him that bombs had partly destroyed the ancient Basilica of San Lorenzo and had struck the cemetery where Pacelli's ancestors were buried, scattering the remains of his own father and mother.

As the pope plodded through the smoking rubble of charred houses where more than five hundred dead victims were strewn, survivors struggled to touch his white cassock. Then a laborer spread his jacket on the cobblestones and the pope knelt upon it to pray. Before departing, he cradled a dead infant in his arms and ordered Montini to distribute alms from his bag.

To Pius, Rome lay in the Vatican's embrace spiritually and traditionally. He was the bishop of Rome and his papal predecessors had once ruled the city. Its people were his flock, and its churches and other Catholic institutions an integral part of the Vatican. His devotion was all the stronger because he was himself a native Roman, full of the exquisite memories of growing up in this sacred city. At his ordination in 1899, Father Pacelli had chosen to read his first Mass in the Borghese Chapel of the Basilica of Santa Maria Maggiore, because over its altar hung the painting of the Virgin Mary, "Salvation of the Romans."

And now his beloved Rome, so spiritually interwoven with God's home on Earth, had been bombed—by the Allies.

On his return to the Vatican that day, the pope immediately penned an emotional protest to President Roosevelt, writing in part:

> We have had to witness the harrowing scene of death leaping from the skies and stalking pitilessly through unsuspecting homes striking down women and children; and in person We have visited and with sorrow contemplated the gaping ruins of that ancient and priceless Papal basilica of St. Lawrence, one of the most treasured and loved sanctuaries of Romans. . . .

God knows how much we have suffered from the first days of the war for the lot of all those cities that have been exposed to aerial bombardments, especially for those that have been bombed not for a day, but for weeks and months without respite. But since divine Providence has placed Us head over the Catholic Church and Bishop of this city so rich in sacred shrines and hallowed, immortal memories, We feel it Our duty to voice a particular prayer and hope that all may recognize that a city, whose every district, in some districts every street, has its irreplaceable monuments of faith or art and Christian culture, cannot be attacked without inflicting an incomparable loss on the patrimony of Religion and Civilization.

◆

One can understand the extreme pain the pope felt as he witnessed the destruction of such sacred patrimony. But critics note that in this passionate plea for the salvation of some of the world's holiest and most artistically magnificent structures, this divinely composed collection of bricks, stone, and plaster, he did not refer to the murder of millions of civilians in a calculated genocidal program—an ideological one not even related to the normal horrors of war committed to win military advantage. But then, critics point out, the Germans had not yet occupied Rome and the pope could still assure himself and others that reports of genocide elsewhere in Europe were exaggerated.

Still, these detractors ask, shouldn't even exaggerated reports of the deliberate destruction of a whole people have aroused at least as much passion in him as the inadvertent destruction of soulless monuments, however sacred? The greatest masterpieces, it is argued, were created by man, but it was God, after all, who created man. Should not man have had priority over his creations?

British Minister Osborne, who normally praised the pope for his wisdom and modest nature, would write in his diary:

The more I think of it, the more I am revolted by Hitler's massacre of the Jewish race on the one hand, and, on the other, the Vatican's apparently exclusive preoccupation with the effects of the war on Italy and the possibilities of the bombardment of Rome.

Osborne's revulsion might have stemmed in part from a conversation his close friend, Harold Tittmann, had had with Pius: "[The pope] immediately brought up the subject of the bombing of Rome. . . . He made it clear [before the San Lorenzo bombing] that he would be obliged to make a solemn and public protest and added that he was certain that the combined effect of the bombing and protest on Catholics throughout the world could only be hurtful to the cause of the Allies."

A public protest against an Allied military initiative but public silence when the Nazis were deliberately murdering millions of civilians?

The pope realized that he had little to lose by threatening to speak out against the Allies; even if the threat couldn't stop them from bombing, it was not likely to provoke retaliation against the Vatican itself. But speaking out against the mass murders could, he no doubt felt, result in terrible retaliation by the Germans, not to mention an end to papal hopes of mediating a negotiated peace.

With a touch of sarcasm, Tittmann's superior, Myron Taylor, wryly remarked to Cardinal Montini in starkly geographic terms: "I am not clear whether the Holy See has condemned the bombing of London, Warsaw, Rotterdam, Belgrade, Coventry, Manila, Pearl Harbor, and places in the South Pacific."

A few weeks later, in August 1943, the pope's "misplaced priorities" are highlighted in the draft of a letter written by a leader of the small Catholic Resistance at the urging of Cardinal Preysing. It was to be signed by all the German bishops, who could no longer deny that the Jews were being massacred, though they knew less about the killings than the Vatican did. The letter, called a "Draft for a Petition Favoring the Jews," read:

With deepest sorrow—yes, even with holy indignation—have we German bishops learned of the deportation of non-Aryans in a manner that is scornful of all human rights. It is our holy duty to defend the unalienable rights of all men, guaranteed by natural law. . . . The world would not understand if we failed to raise our voice loudly against the deprivation of rights of these innocent people. We would stand guilty before God and man because of our silence. The burden of our responsibility grows correspondingly more pressing as . . . shocking reports reach us regarding the awful, gruesome fate of the departed who have already been subjected in frightfully high numbers to really inhumane conditions of existence.

Notably, the writer, knowing that a reference to "genocide" might invite a terrible vengeance, did not mention that horror—though it distinguished the fate of Jews from that of all other Nazi victims except that of the Gypsies. Yet all but a few bishops rejected the draft. How could they agree to it? Weren't they bound by the Concordat to keep out of the government's business? That was a Church teaching. Besides, why die unnecessarily? Still, the draft, which was seen by many eyes, might well have shaken the pope with its passionate, undiplomatic language that, especially with the fate of the Church uncertain, was anathema to him.

In any event, Roosevelt could hardly have regretted bombing Rome when on July 26, six days after the attack, Mussolini was booted from office partly because it dramatically underscored the failure of his policy. The pope asked the Duce's successor, Marshal Badoglio, to demobilize the city as the Allies demanded, but before the new premier could act, planes struck once more on August 13, barely missing the Basilica of San Giovanni in Laterano.

Pius again rushed to the scene to comfort the injured, pray for the dead, and distribute alms to the homeless, and returned to the Vatican this time with his cassock blood-stained. Nor did the raids stop when the Germans occupied Rome on September 10. They, too, ignored the pope's pleas to make Rome an open city, for they had to send troops and supplies from the north through its streets, thereby provoking still more Allied air attacks there.

The pain these attacks inflicted on the pope suggested to some Allied diplomats that in his fury he might refrain from making any moves harmful to German interests, especially denouncing the genocide. But with Mussolini's overthrow and the subsequent German occupation of Rome, the Führer, convinced that the pope supported the Allies and the coup despite the bombings, ordered in *his* anger a coup of his own—against the pope.

But more than anger drove the Führer. He and his cohorts feared the pontiff might feel compelled to end his silence once the Jews of Rome, the pope's own Jews, were rounded up for deportation. Allied leaders, on the other hand, hoped this threat would in fact induce the pope to speak out, apparently seeing such a decision as a conscience-soothing alternative to taking action of their own to save the doomed.

On Washington's instructions, Harold Tittmann, in August, met again with the pope to press the case. But he ran into the same arguments that all other diplomats at the Vatican encountered: If he spoke out about the Jewish killings specifically, the situation would only grow worse.

Pius spoke with such artful rationale that Tittmann departed feeling that the pope's argument made sense to him even though he was bound by Washington to press the opposite view.

"Personally," he would say years later in his memoirs, "I cannot help but feel that the Holy Father chose the better path by not speaking out and thereby saved many lives. Who can say what the Nazis would have done in their ruthless furor had they been further inflamed by public denunciations coming from the Holy See?"

Spoken, others would comment, like the master diplomat—Pope Pius XII himself.

In any case, Washington did not ask Tittmann to resume the effort to change the pontiff's mind. Perhaps, it was now felt, the best way to "Save the Pope," the slogan adopted by Roosevelt, was to let him remain silent. The Jews—those who survived—would just have to wait until Germany surrendered. Yet, no one was sure whether the pope, seeing his own Roman children dragged to their deaths, would, or could, ignore their cries for help.

If Pius's dilemma consumed him mentally and spiritually, he would not let fear for his own safety determine his decision. He had proved his physical courage in the past, much as his grandfather Marcantonio had. When Eugenio Pacelli served as Vatican representative in Munich in 1919, the communists, who had temporarily seized the city in the chaotic wake of World War I, raided his nunciature armed with guns, butcher knives, and other weapons and demanded he give them his limousine. But Archbishop Pacelli, a slim figure in black robes, confronted them as if backed by an army, even as a pistol was pointed at him.

"You must leave here," he said calmly. "This house does not belong to the Bavarian government but to the Holy See. It is inviolable under international law."

And eventually the intruders gave up and left.

But if Pacelli did not lack physical courage, he wasn't looking for a confrontation, any more than he was now when he faced the Nazi threat. When, as a child, he had been told by his uncle the story of a missionary priest who was crucified by pagans, he commented: "I think that I, too, would like to be a martyr."

He added, however, a reservation: "Yes, I would like to be a martyr—but without nails!"

◆

Chief Rabbi Zolli also had a conditional wish for martyrdom.

He was the one important Jewish leader who had not attended the meeting in the temple on September 27. He writes in his memoirs that he remained in the home of Amedeo Pierantoni and sent word through his friend Giorgio Fiorentini that his presence would "not be in the least helpful, since the discussion would be of financial matters." If he could be useful, however, the community could count on him.

Zolli contributed his gold chain and five thousand lire, and instructed his younger daughter, Miriam, to collect gold rings. (His elder daughter, Dora, was living elsewhere in Rome with her husband and child.)

At seven the next morning, after learning that the community had managed to gather only about thirty-five kilograms of gold, fifteen short of the requirement, he agreed to Fiorentini's suggestion that he ask the Vatican for the balance. After all, he was the chief rabbi of Rome. It might have occurred to Zolli that the pope would even invite him and his family to stay in the Vatican, where a number of endangered guests were hiding out.

Zolli immediately agreed to his friend's suggestion. And now he waited prayerfully while the Vatican treasurer spoke with the pope. The New Testament, as Zolli had remarked, did not abandon the Old. And no one, he felt, knew this better than he, for his knowledge of the New was almost as profound as that of the Old.

The Vatican treasurer finally returned from his talk with the pope about the request for gold and told Zolli: "Come back shortly before one o'clock. The offices will be deserted, but two or three employees will be here waiting for you and will give you the package. You may leave a receipt in the form of a simple note. There will be no difficulty."

"Please give my thanks to His Holiness," Zolli said.

But he surely must have been disappointed that a mere "employee" would be waiting for him.

Zolli apparently did not know that the Jewish Community Council had, on the previous afternoon, sent two other representatives on the same mission. Renzo Levi and a fellow Jew had visited Father Borsarelli, the vice abbot of the Sacred Heart Monastery, to request that he obtain the gold from the Vatican. The priest said he would ask the Vatican and advised them to return two hours later, at 4:00 P.M., for a reply.

But by the time the two Jews got back to the temple, many people had gathered at the entrance waiting to contribute to the collection.

Most were poor Jews dressed in tattered, patched clothing who had pathetically come with wedding rings, lockets, bracelets, and whatever other gold trinkets they had treasured. But some were wealthier Jews, and a few, rather self-conscious non-Jews who seemed, strangely enough, unsure whether their contributions would be accepted. Some of these "contributors" agreed only to *sell* their gold—and received four hundred lire per gram, paid with cash donations from others.

More and more people joined the crowd, ready to add their bit to Hitler's store of loot. And as each item was placed on the scale and its weight duly recorded, it appeared that the total might reach the required fifty kilograms after all.

Renzo Levi was thus elated when he returned to Sacred Heart Monastery, where additional good news awaited him. Father Borsarelli reported that the Vatican had agreed to the request for gold.

"Yes," the priest said, "we are ready to lend you any quantity of gold you may need. But it is obvious we want it back."

The loan, which the pope himself had approved, could be repaid in installments, with no time limit for the final payment.

Levi was slightly surprised by the priest's emphasis that the gold was to be a loan rather than a gift, though the Jewish community would have repaid the Vatican regardless. Still, he was appreciative and thanked the priest for the offer, though he added:

"Now we are more confident that we will reach our goal. If I don't return here by 6:00 P.M., that will mean that we will not need the loan."

He never returned, for the Jews had collected enough gold without the loan. Thus, when Zolli went to the Vatican the next morning, also to ask for gold, the Vatican thought his visit was connected with Levi's request and, apparently not yet informed that the gold wasn't needed, told him the gold was still not ready.

Zolli later learned his mission to the Vatican had been unnecessary when he sent Miriam to Foa with a note about the Vatican offer and with an oral message saying that he would volunteer to be first on the list if hostages were demanded.

Foa was not impressed by Zolli's fruitless Vatican mission and hostage offer. It was shameful, he told colleagues, that the community should have as its chief rabbi a "cowardly" man who, instead of nourishing the spirit of his people, worried only about saving his own skin. But Zolli was not discouraged. It was God's will that he must wait a little longer for the light emanating from heaven to shine down upon him. And then he would be with people who loved him. And to see the pope, he would not have to pose as a constructor of walls. Meanwhile, just in case the life-for-gold bargain was simply a Nazi trick, he would concentrate on trying to save his people—with the pope's help.

It took only one day to learn that the bargain was indeed a trick. On September 29, Kappler's men burst into the temple to search for "evidence" that the Jews had been helping the antifascists. The intruders wrecked everything and even threw the sacred Torahs to the floor before leaving with truckloads of files. A few days later, German experts came and removed the temple's priceless collection of rare books after they had, with delicate, caressing fingers, leafed through the yellowed pages with the care, skill, and passion of true art lovers.

But the ghetto Jews were not unduly alarmed. Had not their leaders assured them that the looting of books by no means presaged the roundup of people? To some ghetto residents the books were not really that important, for they could not read. If President Foa was not afraid and refused to hide, what was there to fear?

They were not aware that Almansi and some other Jewish leaders had switched apartments in the past week. Nor did many know that the only complete and up-to-date address files of the community had fallen into German hands. Why, Zolli wondered, hadn't Foa destroyed the files before the Germans could find them? Their confiscation did not greatly alarm temple members, though, for hadn't the ransom of gold been paid?

But Zolli's skepticism grew. Would he have to knock on the pope's door once more? Though he revered the pope, he could not have been happy being an uninvited courier again. But he probably realized that the pope would be placing the Vatican at greater risk if the Nazis invaded it and found the chief rabbi there.

Actually, was the Vatican selective in choosing who could take refuge in the Vatican itself? "Several times we asked the Vatican to grant asylum to refugees who came to us for help," Donald Pryce-Jones, assistant for Italy to OSS director Allen Dulles, told me, "but they refused." They did, however, "take in some people for money," he said, because "the Vatican hierarchy was filled with German priests" (not because of a papal decision). He did not criticize the outside Vatican institutions, which were packed with refugees. Vatican officials, however, vehemently deny there was discrimination of any kind in any of its places of refuge.

◆

Albrecht von Kessel was thunderstruck, he told me, when he learned of the gold ransom deal. Instead of fleeing like his friend, Alfred Fahrener, had warned them to do, the Jews, who he felt must be harboring a "death wish," were bargaining with those who would murder them.

Kessel returned to Fahrener, who had apparently contacted some Jews, but not the heads of the community. There was nothing to worry about now, Fahrener told him. After all, calm and order had been restored, and the Germans had been behaving correctly. In fact, Jewish refugees from Vichy France were pouring into the city they felt was a safer haven.

Kessel said that he was aghast and warned Fahrener that if the Jews didn't "vanish" at once, every last one of them would be deported. "If they are killed," he added, "their blood will be on my head and on the heads of my friends—and we don't deserve that. I implore you to take my advice seriously and use all your influence with the Jews in Rome!"

CHAPTER 16

Eve of Desperation

Kessel may have been especially aggrieved because he was involved in new military plans to overthrow Hitler, and the next effort had been scheduled for October, about the time the Jews would be rounded up. If the coup succeeded, all the Jews would be saved. But it seemed the plot had been cancelled. Father Robert Leiber, a personal secretary and adviser to the pope, would tell American intelligence that a confidant had revealed to him the plot:

> [The attempt was] organized by a high army group, which had widespread support, but [was] called off because it was believed that the time for the removal of Hitler was not yet ripe. Even the strongest anti-Hitler elements feared that the Hitler legend would persist unless at the time of Hitler's downfall the German people believed that the defeat of Germany was inevitable.
>
> While, on the one hand, in order to counteract energetically the Russian menace, it would be desirable to come to an agreement with the western powers before Germany is completely beaten in a military sense. On the other hand, the following fear exists—a revolution at a time when the hopelessness of the war situation is not yet being acknowledged by broad masses of the German population could lead to a further maintenance of Nazi fanaticism. The legend would assert: Hitler could have still won the war if he had not been betrayed.

With the October plan aborted, Kessel now devoted his energy to saving the Jews. On September 25, General Ernst Kaltenbrunner, head of the security services, which included the Gestapo, circulated a list of countries from which Jews could now be deported, with Italy first on the list. On that same day, Himmler sent Colonel Kappler the message telling him of the Jewish roundup plan.

Even as Himmler ordered the roundup, he continued to worry, as Wolff did, that it might force the pope to speak out, trigger his abduction, stir up revolutionary fervor—and further diminish his chances of winning Allied cooperation later. But he was not yet ready to join the Resistance, still feeling morally obligated to obey the Führer's order to kill as many Jews as possible, and still fearful that Hitler might prematurely learn that he had been in contact with some Resistance leaders.

Nor could Himmler's fear have abated when a radio propaganda campaign by Sefton Delmer's "black intelligence" unit in London tried to show that he hoped to soon replace Hitler as Führer. On learning from a dissident Nazi source that Himmler had attended clandestine meetings, Delmer had set up a "Himmler for President" campaign. His "enemy" station reported that the SS was preparing to seize army munitions stores and other strategic points in the Reich.

It quoted speeches and articles about Himmler meant to popularize and glamorize him as the "people's friend," with photographers instructed how to do this. They must see that "the left side of [Himmler's] face has a kindlier expression while his right profile gives a more masculine and martial impression. . . . The SS pictures are to be issued showing predominantly the right side of [Himmler's] face while the left side is to be preferred for shots showing [him] in friendly conversation with folk-comrades or with children."

The station also "revealed" that Himmler was concerned about Hitler's failing physical and mental health and told of his preparations to replace the Führer if necessary. In addition, Delmer had distributed in Germany exact replicas of the "Oath of Loyalty to the

Führer" sworn to by German soldiers on joining the *Wehrmacht*. But he substituted the name "Heinrich Himmler" for the name "Adolf Hitler."

He also substituted Himmler's head for the Führer's on a postage stamp that he had distributed in Germany, seeking to convince Germans that Himmler, in his impatience to assume power, had ordered the stamp made and that it had been prematurely issued to the post office and the public.

Himmler desperately sent Gestapo agents to hunt for these stamps, but not all could be found. He could only hope that Hitler, who wasn't a philatelist himself, would not see a copy. At any rate, he was in no position yet to show the least resistance to his boss's demands, especially those dealing with Jews.

◆

Though Kappler believed that Himmler's order for a roundup was impractical and hoped that the gold deal would satisfy Berlin's demand for "blood," it didn't. And Kappler was not a man to disobey orders, whether he approved of them or not. Hardly had he read the order, however, when he was advised of a discreet way to evade it—by Eitel Möllhausen, the German consul.

Möllhausen had just taken over direction of the embassy in Mussolini's republic, temporarily replacing Ambassador Rahn, who had been hurt in an automobile accident. He had learned of Himmler's message earlier that day from General Rainer Stahel, the moderate-minded German commandant of Rome, who had surreptitiously read it, though it was intended for Kappler's eyes only. The message read:

It is known that this nucleus of Jews has actively collaborated with the Badoglio movement and therefore its swift removal will represent, among other things, a necessary security measure guaranteeing the indispensable tranquillity of the immediate rear of the southern front. The success of this effort will be assured by means of a surprise action, and for this reason it is absolutely essential to suspend the application of any anti-Jewish measures in the way of individual acts in order not to arouse any suspicion among the population of an imminent *Judenaktion*.

"I don't want to have anything to do with such *Schweinerei*," said Stahel, a *Wehrmacht* soldier without strong ideological convictions who knew of Hitler's kidnap order and feared that he might have to crush a popular rebellion if it materialized.

"All right," Möllhausen told me he answered, "then you should have no difficulty sabotaging the plan."

"I came to you precisely because there is nothing I can do," Stahel responded. "The order was sent directly to Kappler, and unless he informs us, we will have to pretend that we are ignorant of it. But I thought you could perhaps do something through the foreign ministry."

"How?" Möllhausen asked. "I'm only a second-grade diplomat. And the Jewish question concerns only the SS."

Möllhausen reflected for a moment and added: "Let me think about it overnight. I don't know what I can do, but let me think about it."

"I know you well enough. I know you will do something," concluded Stahel.

After all, Möllhausen, when based in Tunisia, had saved the Jews there from deportation with the help of a Nazi officer and, with the support of Kesselring, put them to work locally as laborers.

Möllhausen, who was half French, had a swarthy Mediterranean complexion that seemed entirely in harmony with his excitable, nonconformist nature. He had lived in Marseilles until shortly before the war, then returned to Germany, where the foreign ministry hired him because of his command of languages. While on assignment in Paris, he developed a friendship with Rahn, who was also based there, and, as Rahn's protégé, followed him to North Africa and then to Rome.

Through this combination of luck and connections, Möllhausen now found himself wielding considerable power—an extraordinary rise for a man so young and so adamantly opposed to joining the Nazi Party. Influenced by such people as Rahn, he had become an intense nationalist, but he could not swallow the Nazi ideology.

He decided simply to compromise by goose-stepping with nationalist fervor while ignoring, evading, or frustrating any Nazi policy repugnant to him. But though he would try to bend the system with enough zeal to ease his conscience, he would not risk his career—or his life—trying to eliminate the source of evil.

Now Möllhausen would try to work on another "Tunisian" solution. But would Kappler cooperate? He was already busily deporting more than fifteen hundred distrusted *carabinieri,* royal underground policemen.

"How did you know about this order?" Kappler demanded when Möllhausen had mentioned the secret cable to him.

"What is the difference? The order exists and I would like to know what you are going to do."

"I have been given an order and there is nothing I can do about it."

"You can pretend you never received it."

Möllhausen paused, adding cautiously: "You received the order from Berlin. But you also accept orders from Field Marshal Kesselring, don't you?"

The consul knew that Kesselring, the top military authority in Italy, was a rigidly disciplined soldier who would have nothing to do with the "Jewish problem," not only because he dreaded the thought of participating in genocidal actions and feared how his troops would react, but also because such actions could spark a papal protest. That, in turn, might induce Hitler to move against the Vatican and set off street riots that would disrupt his military operations.

Anyway, Hitler assigned the SS troops to deal exclusively with the "Jewish problem" since they had been psychologically trained to handle the matter.

Most of Hitler's intimates seldom dared challenge his powerful will, and, as Walter Warlimont, a Nazi general, told me, lost "their sense of logic" and "had their brains taken out of them." But the Führer seldom admonished Kesselring for modifying orders the field marshal questioned since he regarded the man as indispensable, especially with the Allies pressing dangerously toward Rome. And though a strike against the Jews would be carried out by Wolff's SS troops, not the *Wehrmacht,* Hitler might listen to Kesselring's advice this time, too.

Möllhausen would now need an excuse to exact advice from the field marshal that might save the Jews.

Möllhausen and Kappler immediately drove to Kesselring's headquarters outside Rome and informed the field marshal of the roundup order from Berlin. Did he remember, Möllhausen told me he asked the field marshal, how he had approved the "Jewish solution" adopted in Tunisia after convincing Hitler that the deportation of the Tunisian Jews would have "damaging consequences" for Germany? Well, why not the same solution for the Jews of Rome? Let the Jews work.

The two men exchanged long stares, and Kesselring, who knew that his regular troops would not be used for the roundup, asked Kappler a question apparently meant to elicit an answer that would give him an excuse for backing this solution.

"How many men," Kesselring asked, "will you need to carry out the operation?"

A motorized battalion in addition to his own SS men was the answer.

Kesselring replied: "Under those circumstances, I regret to say that I cannot give my approval . . . I need all available forces for the defense of the city."

But the Jews, he added, could be used to build fortifications around Rome.

Möllhausen and Kappler then departed. That was all they wanted to hear, if for different reasons. Now they could at least quote Kesselring in questioning the wisdom of a roundup. It was at this point that Kappler conjured up the idea of extorting gold from the Jews as an alternative to deportation—and presumably disaster in the Vatican.

◆

One Nazi leader who was unimpressed by Kappler's "pragmatism" was Adolf Eichmann, chief of the Gestapo's Jewish affairs bureau. He decided to send to Rome his most experienced "Jewish expert," Theodore Dannecker, who had made a name for himself rounding up the Jews of Paris. A facial tic revealed his tension, which, it seemed, was eased only when praise poured forth from his bosses for his expertise in rooting out Jews from their hiding places.

On hearing of Dannecker's arrival in early October, Weizsäcker, Kessel, and Möllhausen, apparently with the knowledge of Wolff and Rahn, met to draw up a counterplan. Kessel would set the tone of the meeting when he passionately declared: "Those gentlemen in Berlin [are] losing the last bit of sympathy Germany enjoyed in the Vatican. . . . And now, they must win the war totally and swiftly if they don't wish many other disappointments, because no one will ever be able to forgive them for the persecution of the Jews and for the fate of all those unhappy people who suffer and die in the concentration camps."

After helping with the counterplan and conferring with General Stahel, who approved it, Möllhausen sent a cable to Foreign Minister Ribbentrop on October 6 referring to the message about deportation that Kappler had received before the gold collection. His aim was to make Berlin think that word of the deportation had leaked out and that it could not, therefore, be implemented. Marked "very very urgent," though no official classification existed with more than one "very," the cable read:

For *Herr Reichsminister* personally. *Obersturmbannführer* Kappler has received orders from Berlin to seize the eight thousand Jews res-

ident in Rome and transport them to northern Italy, where they are
to be *liquidated* [author's italics]. Commandant of Rome General
Stahel informs me he will permit this action only on approval of the
Herr Reichsminister for Foreign Affairs. In my personal opinion it
would be better business to employ the Jews on fortification work,
as was done in Tunis, and together with Kappler, I will propose this
to Field Marshal Kesselring. Please advise. Möllhausen.

Kesselring, of course, had already supported this view, but Möllhausen did not wish to indicate that he had conferred with him
without notifying Berlin.

On the following day, October 7, Möllhausen sent another "very
very urgent" cable to Ribbentrop: "In connection with telegram of
the 6th, no. 192. Field Marshal Kesselring has asked *Obersturmbannführer* Kappler to postpone planned *Judenaktion* for the present time. If however it is necessary that something be done, he
would prefer to utilize the able-bodied Roman Jews in fortification
work near here."

These cables enraged Ribbentrop, partly because Himmler found
out about them and asked what the foreign office was doing inter-
fering in Gestapo affairs, but mostly because Möllhausen had used
the word "liquidated" in an official document for the first time. And
no one, other than top Nazi officials, was supposed to know what
ultimately happened to the Jews—the reason why Himmler's cable
of September 25, addressed to Kappler, indicated only that the Jews
were to be deported to "the north."

Ribbentrop furiously complained to Ambassador Rahn about
Möllhausen's cables. Didn't the consul know that he had used a forbidden word? Rahn, who had recovered from his injuries and had
by now established his embassy in Fasano, leaving Möllhausen as
his representative in Rome, was also furious, but for a different reason. How, he wondered, could Möllhausen have jeopardized the
conspiracy to save the pope with so stupid a violation of the rules?
He called Möllhausen and curtly demanded:

"Come immediately to Fasano and explain!"

Möllhausen left immediately and explained to Rahn that he had deliberately used the forbidden word in the hope of frightening his superiors into calling off the roundup. But Rahn severely reprimanded him, fearing disaster. And his fear grew when he learned that another cable from Berlin to Kappler had arrived with the admonition:

The *Herr RAM* [Reich Foreign Minister] requests that you inform Ambassador Rahn and Consul Möllhausen that on the grounds of an order from the Führer, the eight thousand Jews living in Rome are to be taken as hostages to Mauthausen. The *Herr RAM* requests that you instruct Rahn and Möllhausen that they are in no way to interfere in this matter, but are to leave it up to the SS.

But those Germans struggling to save the Jews knew that Berlin had lied in stating that the Jews would be taken to Mauthausen, a concentration camp but not an extermination camp—and that the transports from Rome were bound for Auschwitz.

◆

On October 10, Weizsäcker glimpsed a ray of hope when a BBC commentator quoted the counterfeit Salo broadcast suggesting that Pius might be kidnapped and linked the broadcast to the ambassador's meeting with the pope the day before. Though Weizsäcker knew the broadcast was fake, he had an excuse to cable Foreign Minister Ribbentrop that it might be advisable for the ministry to deny the report and thus to commit the Reich not to execute the plot. But the ambassador was alarmed when, two days later, Ribbentrop replied:

"No public denial of the rumors is envisaged."

Did this mean that Hitler was about to turn the "rumors" into fact—even before the Jews were rounded up? In near desperation,

Weizsäcker sent a second cable indirectly ridiculing the idea of removing the pope by recalling the anecdote from Napoleonic days: If the Emperor wished to seize the pope he would have in hand "no pope but only [a] poor monk."

◆

Guarding the ghetto of Rome is the Porticus Octavia, where one day almost two thousand years ago the ancient echoes of festive pomp heralded the start of the great triumphal march, led by Titus and the Emperor Vespasian in their purple robes and crowning laurel, to celebrate the destruction of Jerusalem. Now, on the rainy afternoon of October 15, 1943, a little bit of Jerusalem seemed once more poised at the abyss. But few of the Jews of Rome realized it.

The ghetto bustled with life in the usual pre-Sabbath rush. Kerchiefed housewives laden with umbrellas and shopping bags cried "Good Sabbath" to each other as they darted along the winding, cobblestone alleys from store to store, pushcart to pushcart, sometimes forced to wait in long lines for some precious item.

Although little food was available, such staples as spaghetti could go a long way, and tomorrow shops would distribute one egg to each ration-card holder. Even more important to some people, tomorrow the weekly tobacco ration would be sold—at least to those willing to spend half the night waiting in line to make sure the supply did not run out before they reached the counter.

Despite the hard times and gloomy weather, the atmosphere was cautiously cheerful. The payment of gold to the Germans about two weeks before had made the ghetto residents feel secure. And many of the Jews who, when the Nazis came, had gone to live with gentile friends to avoid forced labor were now drifting home.

Meanwhile, on that day, the conspirators fearfully waited to learn the results of their frenzied efforts to call off the roundup and thus save Pius from plunging in status to the level of the monk visualized by Weizsäcker, if indeed he survived at all.

The roundup was to take place the following day, and since Hitler had not yet triggered his kidnap plan, there was some reason to believe that he had at least acceded to the conspirators' tactic—blackmail. He would wait to see how the pope would react when the trucks jammed with Jews began rumbling past the papal apartments before deciding whether to set the kidnap plan in motion. Only a last-minute cancellation of the roundup order, it seemed, could make sure that the pope's lips would remain sealed publicly.

◆

Until now, General Wolff claimed, he had made about eight phone calls to Hitler stalling off an order to activate the kidnap plot with arguments that the communists were ready to rise up, or that preparations were not quite completed. Earlier, while in Germany, Wolff had twice met with Himmler on September 15, and must surely have discussed with him Hitler's kidnap order as well as the imminent roundup of Jews in Rome.

When in late September Wolff flew to Rome and then to Fasano, where he reluctantly prepared a kidnap plan, he also had one hundred policemen from an SS police battalion based in northern Italy join the *Waffen*-SS units that were to be used for the roundup operation Hitler was determined to execute. Wolff placed all these forces, numbering only 365, under the command of Kappler, who, he knew, was reluctant to carry out the operation, just as he himself was.

But Wolff had a plan of his own and needed to assure that Kappler cooperated. And by "coincidence" he suggested to Himmler, apparently when he had met with him in Germany on September 15, that Kappler be promoted and awarded the Iron Cross. Himmler, agreed. Was it because he, too, needed Kappler's cooperation—in sabotaging the roundup?

On October 6, when Wolff was on another trip to Germany, Kappler alerted him that Dannecker had arrived in Rome with orders to seize all Jews and ship them off "to the Reich." The following day, October 7, Wolff met with Hitler again in the Führer's East Prussian headquarters and apparently warned him once more that the operation could provoke the pope to speak out and cause trouble in the streets of Rome and other Italian cities.

But on October 11, Kaltenbrunner, reflecting Hitler's will, cabled Kappler to proceed with the roundup, referring to the arguments that had been made to cancel or suspend the operation:

> It is precisely the immediate and thorough eradication of the Jews in Italy which is the special interest of the present internal political situation and the general security in Italy. To postpone the expulsion of the Jews until the *carabinieri* and the Italian army officers have been removed can no more be considered than the idea mentioned of calling up the Jews in Italy for what would probably be very improductive [*sic*] labor under responsible direction by Italian authorities.
>
> The longer the delay, the more the Jews, who are doubtless reckoning on evacuation measures, have an opportunity by moving to the houses of pro-Jewish Italians, of disappearing completely.

The roundup would take place on October 16.

◆

The long-feared order had finally come. Tomorrow the pope might speak out and detonate the plot against the Vatican. As a witness before a Nuremberg court after the war, Wolff was reluctant to talk about the Holocaust, given his role as Himmler's chief aide, but he had hesitantly replied to a question about the deportation of the Roman Jews:

> I vaguely remember that—I believe in the summer of 1943, September, or it could have been October—at the very beginning, when

I was sent to Italy and not quite fully trained—an order came from Berlin, as a reminder from Himmler, that Jews in Italy were to be arrested and deported to the Reich.

In the days preceding the roundup, Wolff was busy in northern Italy looking for a suitable residence for Mussolini's rump republic and then flying off once more to Germany. He was, he would claim, unaware of the events in Rome.

But he was surely aware that his SS representative in Rome, Colonel Dollmann, was also at Hitler's headquarters serving as an interpreter at a meeting between the Führer and Mussolini's defense minister, Marshal Rodolfo Graziani. Dollmann was to discuss his notes, as well as a letter from the Duce, with the Nazi dictator that evening—a chance to try one more time.

Colonel Dollmann felt uneasy as he sat painstakingly translating the letter into German. It concerned the Allies' advance toward Rome after their landing at Salerno, pleading with the Führer to defend Rome street by street if necessary. And that included the streets of Vatican City.

Reports of Hitler's plan to kidnap the pope added to Mussolini's apprehension that the Führer expected to evacuate Rome soon. To the Duce, the abandonment of that city would be madness, since it was the heart and soul of the Italy he still claimed as his own.

Though Dollmann liked and admired the Duce and admitted that he had fallen under his spell, he unfortunately had to argue *against* his proposal. Dollmann could not agree with the Italian dictator that the Germans, for reasons of prestige, should, if necessary, let the city and the Vatican crumble in battle with all their treasures.

Dollmann had fallen in love with Rome long before the war had so inextricably linked his fate with that of the city. He had come as a student in the late 1920s to relive the Renaissance and weave the fantasy of a new united Europe dedicated to the cherished values that had stimulated such creative achievement under the old monarchs and popes.

Dollmann first eyed his own splendid world as a child, when his mother, a close friend of His Imperial and Royal Majesty Franz Josef I of Austria-Hungary, took him along on a visit to the emperor. While he listened to the low hum of conversation, he stared at the emperor as if he were God, and as remote. Yes, those had been regal days, days of gallantry and loyalty unto death.

And now he served Adolf Hitler.

Well, why not? It was a means to an end. And the end was to stay in Rome. For him, Rome was not simply there to be enjoyed; it implored him to accept its favors. He mingled with the social elite, the aristocracy, and the artistic personalities of the time.

Beautiful women vied for his attention, though he rather disdained women except as dispensers of gossip about the latest scandals. He found a perverse pleasure in throwing some of the more "snobbish" princesses and duchesses into jail—actually convents—for such minor "crimes" as listening to the BBC, and releasing them to wealthy relatives who would not only pay anything for their release but also happily invite him to their lavish parties.

In any event, all the doors of Rome, at least those that counted, were open to Dollmann. And General Wolff gave him the key to those that were closed. His principal function was to serve as liaison between Wolff and Field Marshal Kesselring, and between Kesselring and the Vatican. But he was also to keep his hand on the pulse of Roman society, whose influence on the Vatican was powerful and whose political loyalties, geared to survival, could be dangerous. And with his sparkling wit, elegantly effeminate manners, and genteel appearance—ash-blond hair, expressive eyes, tapered hands, rosy complexion—he was the perfect man for this task. Dollmann and the Roman elite understood each other; both wanted to keep what they had at almost any cost.

But if Dollmann relished his job in part because of his entree into Roman society, he had soared swiftly in the SS hierarchy because of his remarkable ability to exploit this entree. He had first joined the Nazi Party shortly after Hitler came to power in 1933 because for the German students in Rome that was the thing to do. Hitler was a crude, rather boorish man, and even a bit mad, but this seemed to be the traditional mark of the German despot. And he might eventually unite Europe—the first step back to the old glorious Europe Dollmann pined for.

His big break came in 1937 when he went to Germany as guide and interpreter for a group of Italian fascist youth and served as Hitler's personal interpreter. Charmed by Dollmann, Himmler enlisted him in the SS without the usual training; and with his intimate knowledge of the Italian scene, Dollmann proved so valuable to the Nazis that he soon strutted the streets of Rome as a lieutenant colonel, his finely tailored uniform decorated with almost as much braid as Emperor Franz Josef had displayed.

Now, Dollmann made clear to me, he was most urgently concerned that "if the pope spoke out against the killing of Jews and was kidnapped as a result," chaos might reign in the city, with only broken art treasures and champagne bottles to remind one of a once joyous life.

Yes, Dollmann loved Rome, and, as he prepared for his meeting with Hitler, he was quite persuaded that destiny had chosen him to save the city—and the Vatican.

◆

That evening of October 15, Dollmann, accompanied by Field Marshal Keitel, the German chief of staff, apprehensively sat down with Adolf Hitler. The colonel would later say that he felt he was "one of the very few people who came into close contact with the Führer without falling prey to his hypnotic influence." It was exerted, Dollmann explained, principally through the eyes, which remained fixed steadfastly on anybody to whom Hitler was talking. Those who could withstand this gaze were accepted, those who wilted under it were either pounced upon with devastating discourse or dismissed abruptly. They had the feeling they were going straight to an unpleasant death in Dachau, while those who were apparently indifferent to it roused in Hitler profound hostility, which sooner or later led to their downfall.

Dollmann was now determined to withstand his gaze, as he had done in the past, but never with the stakes so high.

"The field marshal," Hitler cordially said, his gaze, as expected, boring relentlessly into the tightly focused eyes of the colonel, "has told me that you are doubtful about the possibility of staying in Rome and that you would prefer to evacuate the city. Why does an old Roman like yourself see it this way?"

Dollmann replied carefully with brief explanations interspersed with flashes of history; a misstatement, he feared as others had, could consign him to Dachau. There were several reasons, he said. The Roman Resistance might cause trouble, as might the Vatican. The Allies, who had already bombed outlying areas of the city, might continue such attacks. Priceless works of art would be destroyed and the world would blame Germany for occupying the city. Furthermore, feeding Rome was a huge problem. Unless military factors dictated continued occupation, he concluded, the Germans could well lose more prestige than they gained by staying in Rome.

With a look of some surprise and curiosity, Dollmann would report, Hitler asked: "This evacuation which you advise, how do you suppose it can be carried out in practice? Undoubtedly you have thought about it. Or do you perhaps think that I should restitute Rome to the traitors from the south [where the king and his government had fled] as compensation for their violation of their agreements and their word of honor?"

The atmosphere was tense, and Dollmann noted the pulsating nerves in Keitel's face. There were two possibilities, Dollmann replied calmly, suppressing his own fear. One was to place the city under the International Red Cross. The colonel paused before the alternative suggestion, which could be the key to saving the Vatican and its pope.

The second possibility, he continued—knowing Hitler's venomous feeling toward the "treacherous" king—would be a way to deliver a grave blow to the monarchy: Extend the Vatican's control over the city. Hitler seemed stunned by this novel idea, which he knew would give Mussolini fits. Was there to be a return to the old papal states that had been demolished in 1870 in favor of temporal government?

"Have you spoken with Ambassador Weizsäcker about this?" he asked suspiciously.

This question did not bode well; Weizsäcker had a disturbing reputation as a "defeatist."

When Dollmann replied in the negative, the Führer quietly asserted: "We are in Rome now and I think we shall stay in Rome!"

As he departed, Dollmann realized that the blackmail test would play out to the end. He had done his best to serve General Wolff. But it was too late for Rome—and the Jews.

The following morning, October 16, Adolf Hitler flung his long-contemplated challenge at the pope in a momentous showdown that could determine who, after the war (which Hitler still expected to win), would reign as the greater power.

CHAPTER 17

"But They Promised Me"

Princess Enza Pignatelli Aragona was sound asleep in her modest home in Rome when the telephone rang at about five that rainy morning. She lifted the receiver, she told me, and heard an excited voice: "Princess, the Germans are arresting the Jews and taking them away in trucks!"

The princess, a tiny but dynamic woman, was shocked fully awake. She had hidden many Jewish friends in her house and in the homes of other Christian families, but she had never dreamed that the Germans would go this far.

"What can I do?" she asked the caller, a Christian friend who lived at the edge of the ghetto.

"You know the pope," was the answer. "Go and see him. Only he can save the Jews."

At first, Princess Pignatelli considered this suggestion entirely unrealistic. Yes, she did know the pope well. Of a noble Neapolitan family, she had been his student at a convent and her father had been a close friend. But even if the pope agreed to receive her at this hour, she could not get to the Vatican, for she did not have a car and there was no public transportation this early.

Then she remembered her friend, Gustav Wöllenweber, a diplomat in Ambassador Weizsäcker's embassy, who, like his boss, she knew, opposed his government's anti-Semitic policies. She telephoned him.

"Please come and pick me up immediately," the princess urged. "I must go to the Vatican. I'll explain later."

When Wöllenweber arrived and learned her mission, he drove her first to the ghetto to see if the report was true. The SS police stopped them at the edge of the quarter and refused to let even a German diplomat pass. However, the two saw people, many still clad in their pajamas, being marched down the street in the rain and thrown into black-canvassed trucks. They saw frightened children clinging to their mothers' skirts and old women begging for mercy. They heard screams, pathetic wails of prayer, and the slap of leather on cobblestones as some Jews tried to flee.

While they sped to the Vatican, Princess Pignatelli reflected on the irony of her desperate undertaking; a German diplomat was helping her to frustrate official German policy. On arriving at the Vatican, she pleaded with an official:

"Please take me immediately to His Holiness!"

The startled official glanced at his watch and wondered if she was mad—coming at this hour to demand an audience with the pope! But after she explained her mission, he guided her to the door of the papal chapel where the pope was attending Mass.

When Pius XII emerged, he greeted the princess with a surprised smile, remarking on the hour, and suggested that they walk together to his study.

"Your Holiness," the princess urged, "you must act immediately. The Germans are arresting the Jews and taking them away. Only you can stop them."

The pope halted and stared at the princess with a shocked expression. This was obviously the first word he had heard about the arrests.

"But they promised me not to touch the Jews in Rome!" he exclaimed.

Pius's shock might suggest why he did not warn the Jews of the roundup; he apparently did not know it was imminent. Who made the promise to him? Weizsäcker or one of the other anti-Hitler German diplomats? Dollmann or another military man acting on behalf of Wolff? Someone who was trying to head off preparation of a papal outcry against an action that could trigger the kidnap plan, but found himself unable to keep his vow?

Whatever the answer, this was a moment of dread for the pope, a moment when he must finally solve his excruciating dilemma. Should he speak out before it was too late, knowing the present Mass might be the last he would conduct—at least at the Vatican—while risking the victimization of even more people? Or should he quietly protest to Ambassador Weizsäcker and hope for the best?

After a pause, Pius escorted the nearly hysterical princess to his study, picked up the telephone, and called Cardinal Maglione. German troops are rounding up the Jews, he said. Call Ambassador Weizsäcker urgently and protest the action!

As the pope showed Princess Pignatelli to the door, he promised: "I'll do all I can."

◆

Later that morning, Ambassador Weizsäcker arrived at the Vatican for a meeting with Cardinal Maglione that both men knew could decide the fate of the pope, his place in history, and his prospects for serving as a peace negotiator. Never would Weizsäcker's diplomatic skills be so vigorously tested. His whole mission in Rome, as he conceived it, now teetered in the balance.

At the same time, he worried that during the roundup the Gestapo might learn that he had concealed a Jewish family in the Teutonic College in the Vatican. That could end his role in the Vatican and perhaps his hopes for arranging, with the pope, a negotiated peace.

Now that the roundup had already begun despite all his efforts to thwart it, the ambassador would not give up. He must keep Pius from protesting publicly. And despite his anxiety, he was still hopeful. The pope, after all, had not publicly protested against the deportations and reports of mass murder in most countries in Europe. And he would be dealing with a reasonable man in Cardinal Maglione, perhaps the only person who could persuade the pope to remain silent at this climactic moment. But would Maglione, knowing of Hitler's kidnap plot, instead feel compelled by moral concern or diplomatic pressure to advise the pope to speak out?

As Pius's secretary of state, the cardinal was a powerful influence indeed, in part because the two men complemented each other's temperament, personality, and diplomatic experience. Pius, hesitant and withdrawn, had dealt mainly with the Germans, and Maglione, decisive and worldly, principally with the French. Each had learned how to convince the other, at least occasionally, to change his opinion. As for the roundup, the cardinal was thought to favor a stronger statement protesting it.

In pressing for papal silence, Weizsäcker would have to persuade Maglione to overcome his alleged pro-Allied feelings, though as a prisoner of Pius's neutralist policy the cardinal did not share his knowledge of the Final Solution with anyone outside the Vatican, even the Catholic Resistance.

Maglione thus followed, often with frustration, the priorities set by Pius, especially in his conversations with the German bishops. He didn't mention the extermination camps but stressed the need to save the treasures of Rome and the Vatican. Why provoke a backlash? Why stir up a storm with Catholics who, intimidated by Hitler, might feel it necessary to declare their primary loyalty to him?

Many ambassadors to the Holy See thought that Maglione was of stronger fiber than Pius. They knew that the pope once told the cardinals, "I don't want collaborators. I want people who will do what I say." But they also knew that he often did what Maglione wished. At times, Maglione, who had known Pius for many years, frequently seemed to irk his superior by treating him as an equal, as he did when Pacelli was still a cardinal himself.

Maglione's interests were many and more varied than the pope's. He followed the military movements of World War II and commented expertly on the strategy of generals, sticking flags on a wall map to defend his views. Other walls in his study were plastered with maps of the Napoleonic campaigns. Yet, if the two men usually smoothed out their differences, their contrasting natures would not allow for a relationship as intimate as the one the Holy Father had with his two other assistants, Monsignor Tardini and Monsignor Montini.

Both men were strongly anti-Axis, but again, would they use their influence over the pope to end his public silence about the massacres and risk a violent Nazi attack? Tardini was a rotund, jolly, yet somewhat sardonic little man; his strong jaw was often in motion with spoutings of biting, even vulgar humor typical of the Roman little-educated underclass from which he came.

Tardini sometimes alarmed his fellow cardinals with his tendency to speak his mind with brutal, undiplomatic frankness. In his notes of a meeting with Myron Taylor, Tardini reported that when Taylor had urged that the pope protest the Jewish murders, he (Tardini) replied:

"The pope has already spoken."

"He can repeat," Taylor responded.

"And I could not but agree," the cardinal would write.

While Tardini's rather raucous personality contrasted sharply with Pius's milder manner, Montini had a quiet, kindly, persuasive disposition reflective of the professional diplomat, perhaps explaining why he had an especially close relationship with the diplomatically inclined pope. Foreign diplomats and Vatican journalists greatly appreciated Montini, especially when he brought them gifts of fish from the lake at Castel Gandolfo, the papal summer home, or baskets of fruit from its orchards.

But it was Maglione whom Weizsäcker would see now, and although he was not likely to leave with fish or fruit, he was praying for a gift that would save the pope and, perhaps in the end, Germany. Would subtle blackmail at this point work?

◆

On being ushered into Maglione's office, Weizsäcker was immediately greeted with a protest. The Holy See, Maglione said, had tried to avoid giving the German people the impression that it would do, or wish to do, anything that might hurt Germany. But the pope was profoundly distressed that poor and innocent people should have to suffer simply because they belonged to a particular race, especially "right here in Rome under the eyes of the Common Father."

He would "try to do something for these poor Jews," Weizsäcker replied. But, "what would the Holy See do," he asked, "if these things were to continue?"

"The Holy See would not want to be faced with the need to express its disapproval," the cardinal replied. And in emphasis, he added that "if the Holy See were forced to [protest], it would trust the consequences to divine Providence."

Weizsäcker listened attentively and was apparently shaken. This was the first hint that the worst could happen: The pope might speak out publicly if the roundup of Jews continued. The ambassador responded carefully:

"For more than four years I have followed and admired the attitude of the Holy See. It has succeeded in steering the boat amid all shapes and sizes of rocks without running aground and, even though it has had greater faith in the Allies, it has kept a perfect equilibrium. Now, just as the boat is about to reach port, is it worth it, I ask myself, to put it all at risk? I think of the consequences that a protest by the Holy See might precipitate."

The ambassador added, "The order for the action comes from the highest level. Will Your Eminence leave me free not to take account of this official conversation?"

When Maglione expressed surprise at this request, Weizsäcker said that he did not want to take responsibility for telling his superiors of a possible papal protest. He knew their mentality, he asserted, and they would react with even greater violence, not only against the Jews but against the Church.

Clearly, the word "kidnap" was on both their minds.

Maglione replied that he would say nothing about the conversation, which he described as "so friendly," and that Weizsacker was free to use his own judgment about whether to report on it.

The ambassador departed feeling that the cardinal's answer did little to relieve his fear of a papal protest. Had blackmail worked? Perhaps. But he knew that Maglione, unlike some of the prelates close to Pius, rejected fascism and favored the Allies, who were pressing the pope to speak out.

◆

Meanwhile, Secretary Kessel, Ambassador Weizsäcker's deputy, rushed in desperation to see Consul Möllhausen at the embassy in Rome to seek his help in stopping the roundup and imminent deportations. But Möllhausen was away in Fasano, and standing in for him was Gerhard Gumpert, the Rome embassy economic secretary, whose principal function was to obtain Italian goods for Germany. Kessel insisted that Gumpert act to stop the arrests and prevent the deportations, arguing that if his own embassy in the Vatican took such action, Hitler might react against the pope.

"But, Kessel," replied Gumpert, a frustrated lawyer suffering from an ulcer, "what can I do? If you asked me for some barrels of potatoes or sacks of grain, I could help you. But I don't know about these things."

"Well . . . well," Kessel stuttered in his strong nasal tone, "something must be done."

Finally, Gumpert argued that the only answer was to tap the Vatican's influence—indirectly. The two men then considered how to achieve this, and came up with a devious maze of intrigue. They wrote a letter to General Stahel, who was sympathetic to their cause, requesting that the arrests be halted. They then asked a "high Vatican official," Bishop Alois Hudal, rector of the German Catholic Church in Rome, Santa Maria dell'Anima, to sign it because he was reputed as being pro-Nazi and would have special credibility.

The two diplomats had Father Pankratius Pfeiffer, superior of the Salvatorian Order in Rome and the Holy See's liaison with the Germans, deliver the letter to General Stahel. It is not clear whether Pius knew of this ruse. The letter read:

> I must speak to you of a matter of great urgency. An authoritative Vatican dignitary, who is close to the Holy Father, has just told me that this morning a series of arrests of Jews of Italian nationality has been initiated. In the interest of the good relations that have existed until now between the Vatican and the high command of the German armed forces—above all thanks to the political wisdom and magnanimity of Your Excellency, which will one day go down in the history of Rome—I earnestly request that you order the immediate suspension of these arrests both in Rome and its environs.
>
> Otherwise, I fear that the pope *will take a position in public* as being against this action, one which would undoubtedly be used by the anti-German propagandists as a weapon against us Germans.

As soon as Father Pfeiffer had delivered the letter to General Stahel late that afternoon, Gumpert called at Stahel's office and, as planned, the general handed *him* the letter. Gumpert then cabled the contents to Berlin, pointing out that the letter had been addressed to Stahel but that the general had turned it over to him because it involved a diplomatic rather than a military matter. The general was thus cleared of any suspicion that he was involved in the rescue plan.

Several hours later, Weizsäcker, on learning of the scheme, sent a follow-up cable to Berlin:

> I can confirm that this represents the Vatican's reaction to deportation of the Jews of Rome. The curia is especially upset considering that the action took place, in a manner of speaking, under the pope's own window. The reaction could be dampened somewhat if the Jews were to be employed in labor service here in Italy. Hostile

circles in Rome are using this event as a means of pressuring the Vatican to drop its reserve.

It is being said that when analogous incidents took place in French cities, the bishops there took a clear stand. Thus, the pope, as the supreme leader of the Church and as Bishop of Rome, cannot but do the same. The pope is also being compared with his predecessor, Pius XI, a man of a more spontaneous temperament. Enemy propaganda abroad will certainly view this event in the same way, in order to disturb the friendly relations between the curia and ourselves.

Weizsäcker thus conveniently used the Hudal letter to convey the sense of Cardinal Maglione's warning hours earlier that the pope might feel compelled to speak out if the roundup continued—but without revealing that the cardinal himself had issued the warning to him. Hudal's unofficial message, he obviously hoped, would not be strong enough to provoke a violent reaction against the Vatican, but, coming from a Nazi sympathizer, might just give Berlin second thoughts about continuing the arrests and deporting those who had already been arrested.

◆

Late that night, Kappler cabled Himmler a nervously awaited message. Blackmail, it seemed, had worked, or at least contributed strongly to a great triumph. The pope, in his view, had blinked in this confrontation between two powerful rivals for the psyche and soul of much of mankind.

Action against Jews started and finished today in accordance with a plan worked out as well as possible by the office. All available [SS] forces employed. Participation of the Italian police was not possible in view of unreliability in this respect, as only possible by individual arrests in quick succession inside the twenty-six action districts.

To cordon off whole blocks of streets, in view both of [Rome's] character as an open city and of the insufficient number of German police, 365 in all, not practicable. In spite of this 1259 persons were arrested in Jewish homes and taken to assembly camp[s] of the military school here in the course of the action which lasted from 0530 to 1400 hours. After the release of those of mixed blood, of foreigners including a Vatican citizen, of the families in mixed marriages including a Jewish partner, and of the Aryan servants and lodgers, there remain 1002 Jews to be detained. . . .

Attitude of the Italian population was unequivocally one of passive resistance, which in a large number of individual cases has developed into active assistance. In one case, for example, the police were met at a house door by a fascist with an identity document and in a black shirt, who [claimed to have] taken over the Jewish home only an hour before and alleged it to be his own . . . [and some] even attempted to keep single policemen back from the Jews.

After two days of incarceration in a military college near the Vatican, the victims were taken to the city's main railroad station and herded into boxcars. On October 18, these cars pulled out of the Tiburtina suburban railway station packed with more than one thousand Jews, about 90 percent of them women and children. They were calm, resigned, unsuspecting, even as they were deprived of food, water, and toilet facilities. Five days later, on October 23, the boxcars ground to a halt in Auschwitz and dumped their human cargo into the gas chamber—all but the few whom Dr. Josef Mengele judged were fit for slave labor.

That same day, Ribbentrop leisurely referred the Rome cables to Adolf Eichmann, who in turn asked his superiors for instructions he was apparently never to receive.

In the rubbish left behind on the platform in Rome, a sweeper found a crumpled, unaddressed message, whose author, a well-known businessman, Lionello Alatri, apparently trusted that the finder would guess his identity and take it to his company:

We are going to Germany! I, my wife, my father-in-law, and Anita. Notify our traveling salesman Mieli. Give six hundred lire to my portiere at the end of every month and two hundred and fifty lire to Irma, whom you must also reimburse for the gas and electric bills. . . .

We face our departure with fortitude, though of course the presence of my father-in-law in his poor condition alarms me. Try to be brave, as we ourselves are. I embrace you all. Lionello.

Alatri scribbled the following pathetic postscript under his signature:

Tell the Baron that Ettore and Elda and her cousin are with us. Tell sales representative Riccardelli that his wife and children are with us and are fine. Notify the *portiere* at Via Po, n 42, that sister and sister-in-law with us and fine. Notify *portiere* Via Po 162 Lello and Silvia with us and fine. Notify *portiere* Via Vicenza 42 that furrier is with us and fine. Notify *portiere* Corso Italia 106 the Di Veroli family with us and fine. Raoul with us and fine. Notify the *portiere* Sicilia 154 Clara with us and fine.

Now the Jews who managed to elude the Nazi dragnet knew—even President Foa. Though his fascist friends may have helped to cross off his name from the list of targeted Jews, he no longer could trust them, and he fled to Livorno two days after the roundup.

Miraculously, it seemed, most of the eight thousand Jews of Rome had escaped. Some had gone into hiding earlier, including those few who had heeded warnings and left their homes just before the Germans could close their trap. Actually, the trap had not completely closed. Days after the main roundup, a limited number of arrests were made and no Jew was safe.

A few days later, on October 23, none of the relatives and friends whom Lionello Alatri had named were still fine. They were dead. Could they have survived if the pope had spoken out publicly? No one can be sure, but critics speculate that such a protest might have prompted the Germans to redirect the train to a conventional concentration camp like Mauthausen, or to have incited partisans to attack it and free the victims.

Aside from the estimated forty-three hundred crowded into Roman monasteries, churches, and convents, the Vatican itself welcomed some refugees, though a raid within the Vatican walls would menace the Church far more than one on a Vatican institution outside the walls. In any case, the danger of an invasion of the Vatican itself, it seemed, had subsided.

But had it? Not only Weizsäcker was uncertain; so was the pope. Yes, he had remained publicly silent. But how Hitler, with his mercurial temperament, might act at any moment was unpredictable. And the ambassador's concern grew when, on October 23, the envoy read in the Vatican newspaper, *L'Osservatore Romano:*

> Persistent and pitiful echoes of calamities . . . continue more than ever to reach the Holy Father. The august pontiff . . . has not desisted for one moment in employing all the means in his power to alleviate the suffering, which, whatever form it may take, is the consequence of universal and paternal charity . . . that knows neither boundaries nor nationality . . . neither religion nor race.

A master of subtlety himself, Weizsäcker viewed this complaint about the deportations, however veiled, as jeopardizing the Vatican, especially in light of Berlin's failure to answer the cables from Rome. This failure, he is said to have felt, showed that he had been right in the first place. If his superiors could regard the *threat* of a public papal protest as not even worthy of a reply, it was unlikely that an *actual* protest, even one as vague as that appearing in the Vatican organ that morning, would move them to call off the roundup—and could indeed spark a strike.

Weizsäcker, in any event, cabled Berlin a subtly worded message of his own, cleverly designed to assure Berlin in deceptive detail that no further roundups were needed:

> The pope, although under pressure from all sides, has not permitted himself to be pushed into a demonstrative censure of the deportation of the Jews of Rome. Although he must know that such an attitude will be used against him by our adversaries and will be exploited by Protestant circles in the Anglo-Saxon countries for the purposes of anti-Catholic propaganda, he has nonetheless done everything possible even in this delicate matter in order not to strain relations with the German government and the German authorities in Rome. As there apparently will be no further German action taken on the Jewish question here, it may be said that this matter, so unpleasant as it regards German-Vatican relations, has been liquidated.

On October 25, *L'Osservatore Romano* gave a papal version of the same picture in a semiofficial communiqué on the loving kindness of the pope, which is written in the circuitous and muddled style of this Vatican newspaper:

> The pope bestows his fatherly care on all people without regard to nationality or race. The manifold and growing activities of Pius XII have in recent times further increased because of the great sufferings of so many unfortunate people.

Weizsäcker told Berlin:

No objections need be raised against this statement, inasmuch as its text . . . will be understood by only a very few as alluding in any particular way to the Jewish question.

What effect did these apparent attempts to make the pope look "reasonable" in Nazi eyes actually have? Did it help the Jews by encouraging Berlin not to provoke the pope unnecessarily? Did it hurt them by making Berlin think the pope would not take a strong stand against the anti-Jewish moves? Or did it have no effect at all? No one could be sure.

An additional one thousand Roman Jews were deported in the next several months. They were captured, however, not in organized roundups but in individual arrests, mostly by Italian fascists seeking reward money for turning them in.

The pope was more trusted now in Nazi circles and less likely to be abducted; he had not only failed to publicly condemn the crime after it took place under his window, but, having survived the kidnap threat, at least temporarily, he could revert to his original enemy priority list. Even before the roundup, on October 14, Harold Tittmann cabled the State Department to say that the people "seemed preoccupied that in the absence of sufficient protection, irresponsible elements might commit violence in the city." And he asked the Germans to bring more police forces into the city.

After the roundup his fear grew and he further secured his position when he authorized Cardinal Maglione to accept Weizsäcker's request to publish in the *L'Osservatore Romano* on October 30 a communiqué expressing gratitude to the German troops for respecting the Vatican and the pope, the protector of all Romans—if the trucking of helpless civilians to death camps right outside the Vatican can be seen as a sign of respect. In return, the Germans promised to maintain the same respectful attitude in the future. The statement would read in part: "The Holy See, recognizing that the German troops have respected the Roman curia and Vatican City, has gladly taken note of the assurance given by the German ambassador as regards the future."

Blackmail, it seemed, had worked, for both the blackmailers and the blackmailed—as the German conspirators had hoped.

The communiqué appeared within a week after most of the captured Jews of Rome, among the most deeply rooted Romans, had been turned into ash in Nazi incinerators. So improved were Vatican-German relations that, on October 25, Tittmann could assure the Department of State:

> The anxiety displayed by Holy See with regard to possible violation of Vatican City neutrality during first days of German occupation of Rome would appear to have been progressively allayed to such an extent that at present moment atmosphere in Vatican can be described as optimistic.

On October 28, with almost all the captured Jews dead, Weizsäcker cabled Berlin that the danger of a papal protest was over. Blackmail, it seemed, had saved the pope and perhaps Germany as well. Only the captured Jews, it seemed, were losers.

On November 3, the British diplomat Osborne cabled the foreign office:

> Situation would now seem to be easier and the prospect of an invasion of the Vatican more remote. . . . There are indications that [the Germans] are attempting to ingratiate themselves with the population, that arrests are now infrequent and that there is less looting. The threatened house-to-house search of Rome has not materialized and the Gestapo are either less active or considerably reduced in number.

It is not clear whether Osborne knew that intelligence analysts back home had decoded cables exchanged between Berlin and German officials in Rome from July on and learned in advance that the Jews would be rounded up on October 16—yet did not warn them, or do anything to stop the crime with action or at least publicity.

In December, the relaxed mood in Berlin was reflected in a memorandum that Security Chief Ernst Kaltenbrunner sent to Ribbentrop stating that only Germany's euthanasia and sterilization policies, less explosive than the "Jewish problem," still disturbed the relationship with the Vatican—even though these policies had been suspended.

In his cable of October 25, Tittmann had written:

> The Holy See appeared to be satisfied with the treatment it had received from the German authorities in Rome. There were signs of increasing German warmth toward the Vatican, for which there was no adequate explanation.

As reflected in this remark, American officials in Washington and the Vatican, it appears, were never aware of the importance and real danger of Hitler's kidnap threat, with its blackmail implications, in determining the relationship between the pope and the Führer.

On the other hand, with Hitler's kidnap plot no longer as threatening, Pius felt freer to speak out, at least privately. In the summer of 1944, when the Jews in northern Italy faced deportation, he told Myron Taylor that "neither history nor his conscience would forgive him if he made no effort to save at this psychological juncture [more] threatened lives."

Hitler's attitude toward Pius had softened, though not necessarily reflecting greater respect for him. The pontiff, in his eyes, had blinked first in a momentous test of wills. But had he really?

CHAPTER 18

A Bargain in Blood

Absent from Italy on October 16, General Wolff was either at Hitler's or Himmler's headquarters. He told the Nuremberg court when appearing as a witness that he learned the roundup had taken place only when Kappler telegraphed a report to him in Germany marked "Urgent! Secret! Present Immediately!" on October 18, the day that the train crammed with Jews had chugged out of Rome for the death camp at Auschwitz.

This urgent message, Wolff said, proved that he knew nothing about the roundup until it was too late to do anything about it. But the prosecutor at his trial before a Munich court concluded that Wolff had arranged for the urgent telegram to be sent to him on October 18 because he was to have lunch with Hitler and Himmler the following day and wished to report that Kappler had described how efficiently orders had been carried out—without an outcry by the pope, at least, so far.

And there may well be truth in that. Especially since Wolff could use this "good news" to stress that it would be pointless to carry out the plot against the Vatican. But it seems unlikely that the general, who had a legendary devotion to detail about every aspect of his job, would not know almost minute by minute what was happening in Rome on October 16.

Though Colonel Kappler was authorized to order the roundup on his own, he was required to confer with Wolff, the SS commander in

Italy, before implementing it, with Theodore Dannecker's help. And the general had the authority to modify his instructions.

It is notable that only about one thousand of the eight thousand Jews in Rome were dragged away in the organized roundup on October 16 and sent to Auschwitz, where about half of them perished. Yes, most Jews did not leave their homes, unaware that the Nazis had a list of their addresses and convinced anyway by the gold extortion nightmare that they were now safe; though some, frantically notified by friends, made a last-minute escape to convents, monasteries, or neighboring homes.

It is also significant that only 365 SS soldiers and police were employed in the roundup. Wolff must have known that many more would be needed for an operation meant to snatch eight thousand victims, and could have told Berlin, if he had wished, that he must have more to succeed. Indeed, the original plan called for two thousand men.

Instead, enough men were used to grab only enough Jews to sate the Führer's blood lust—at least temporarily—but not enough to impel the pope to speak out against the deadly operation.

Although the Hudal letter and Weizsäcker's efforts may have helped to influence Hitler and Himmler, it appears that Wolff had persuaded the SS chief—who, like Wolff, was thinking of betraying Hitler anyway—to stop or limit the operation in their mutual interest. And that they had persuaded the Führer to compromise, arguing that it was not worth risking papal condemnation and enemy propaganda complications when a thousand Jews were already in hand. Himmler sealed the bargain with an order to Kappler: Stop the roundup at 2:00 P.M.

Anyway, it is clear that Wolff, who had once helped to facilitate the Final Solution, had the power, incentive, desire, and opportunity to limit for his own self-serving reasons the scale of the Rome roundup—and at least postpone Hitler's plot to kidnap Pius and plunder the Vatican. And so, in the end, with the pope and seven-eighths of the Jews saved, and with Hitler able to boast of so limited a catch in so symbolic and defining an operation, Hitler, too, blinked.

However inconclusive the showdown, Wolff could revel in his personal victory. He had probably helped to rescue the pope (and himself) with stalling and other deceptive measures. And he had abated Hitler's ravenous appetite by serving up at least a batch of new victims.

◆

In mid-December 1943, General Wolff, his courage buoyed by the pope's public silence, visited the Führer to report on, among other topics, his preparations for the raid on the Vatican. But he had also prepared words he had mulled over for months—words that he knew could catapult him into oblivion together with the pope. With a veneer of calm cloaking his anxiety, he quietly argued that the Church, the only indisputable authority in Italy, should not be molested; that the operation would lead to "extremely negative effects at home and at the front." On the other hand, the general said, the people could be "very useful for us in the future" in helping to establish the new order in Europe. Had the pope not shown his good will toward the Germans in the Jewish matter?

Wolff paused with a controlled air of composure as he waited for Hitler to proclaim his fate.

"All right, Wolff," the Führer finally replied. "Act as you, an expert, think best. But do not forget that I shall hold you responsible in case you fail to fulfill your optimistic guarantees."

Wolff departed with a sense of triumph, yet with trepidation. For if Pius should suddenly act against Hitler's interests, he, as well as the pope, would feel the Führer's whip of wrath.

Wolff still had one special concern; would Pius, who had been informed of his vow to foil the kidnap plot, show his gratitude when the time came for surrender to a vengeful enemy? He couldn't ask to see the pontiff without getting permission from Field Marshal

Kesselring, his superior in Italy, who himself had never been invited to a papal audience or been given Berlin's approval to seek one. And the pope, already criticized by the Allies for not speaking out publicly against the Jewish roundup, was not likely to welcome the top SS officer in Italy and further strain his relations with the United States and Britain. Wolff would simply have to wait for a propitious time to pry open the Vatican door.

Several months later, with the pope once more in danger, the time seemed ripe.

CHAPTER 19

The Mathematics
of Murder

In October 1943, hardly had the Nazis piled Jews into trucks headed for oblivion when two Italian students joined the Patriotic Action Group (GAP), the activist arm of the Communist Party, the arm that wielded the bomb and the gun. Rosario Bentivegna, the son of a fascist diplomat, and Carla Capponi, a Florentine contessa, found a passion for revolution in their common contempt for the privileged society that had bred them.

They had both discovered Marxism by themselves but knew little about the ideology, except that it promised to wash away every trace of fascist inequity. Like many other idealistic students, they had not been won over by Communist Party propaganda; they had sought out the party. They figured that as soon as the Nazis were forced to flee and before Allied troops arrived, leftists like themselves would have the opportunity to take over the government.

Bentivegna was chosen to lead one of four GAP groups operating in Rome, and Carla was to assist him. Their task at first was to terrorize only the fascists and to discourage their collaboration with the Nazi occupiers. Thus, only days after the October roundup, Bentivegna killed a fascist policeman. And on March 1, 1944, while Rosario stood by covering her, Carla would shoot a German soldier in the back. She heard a loud gasp, and the man crumpled to the ground. Grabbing his leather bag, Carla dashed away, weeping as she ran. Now she was ready to kill others. And there would be many others.

Comrades of Carla and Rosario had committed similar acts of terrorism. The Germans and fascists, however, had reacted not with wild reprisals, but with cool, cruel, silent efficiency, arresting and torturing individual partisan leaders without substantially raising the public temperature. As more and more Resistance leaders were being captured, the chances for insurrection when the Allies finally arrived dwindled. The Romans appeared more apathetic than ever.

The Romans, the GAP had calculated, had to be roused to the boiling point of revolt. For their own good, some would have to die.

◆

Via Rasella seemed the ideal place for a bombing that would at once seriously wound the enemy occupiers and detonate a reaction powerful enough to set off a rebellion. It was a narrow street near Piazza Barberini in the center of Rome's shopping area that echoed with the tramp of heavy boots and the rhythm of marching songs every day at about 2:00 P.M. The sounds came from the men of the 11th Company, 3rd Battalion, SS *Polizeiregiment Bozen,* mostly over-age recruits from South Tyrol who had just been brought to Rome to help wipe out the Resistance.

Because the street was narrow, the troops had to march in close files and the partisans could more easily bomb them. And as the route led up a hill, the marchers had to slow their pace, making them still easier targets.

The possibility for a massive assault at just the right psychological moment—during the celebration of fascism's twenty-fifth anniversary—was simply too good to pass up.

◆

"You better be careful," said the street cleaner to one of his colleagues, who had parked his rubbish cart in front of Tittoni Palace on Via Rasella. "An inspector from the Sanitation Department is checking around here. Get busy or you may be fined."

The man who had been warned nodded and started sweeping the area around him, but when his fellow street cleaner had gone away, he stopped his work and looked at his watch. Almost 3:30 P.M., an hour and a half late. Would those Germans never come?

A youth casually sauntered by and mumbled as he passed the sweeper. "Give them ten minutes more. Then leave."

The sweeper—Rosario Bentivegna—was disgusted. He had dragged his rubbish cart, which resembled a baby stroller, halfway across Rome, and now, if the Germans didn't come, he would have to drag it all the way back—together with the forty pounds of TNT it contained.

At the top of Via Rasella, which ended at Viadelle Quattro Fontane, Carla Capponi, whose long titian hair had been cut and dyed black, waited in front of Barberini Palace. Nervous and apprehensive, she had already bungled one aspect of the plan. She was to have waited in front of the *Il Messaggero* building, down the hill around the corner from Via Rasella; then, on receiving a signal from another partisan that the troops were approaching, she was to have turned up Via Rasella and walked past Bentivegna to the top. Her advance would be the signal to Rosario that the Germans were coming. However, she had misinterpreted the signal she had received and had moved ahead prematurely, giving a false alarm.

Now she could not return from Barberini Palace to *Il Messaggero* because two fascist policemen guarding the newspaper building had already become suspicious and had followed her, keeping about a block behind her. She would simply wait in front of Barberini Palace and cover Bentivegna when he headed up the hill after lighting the fuse. Another partisan, Guglielmo Blasi, was supposed to be there, but he had disappeared. Carla would have to cover Rosario's escape alone.

Suddenly, she was horrified to see several children playing in the garden behind the gates of the palace.

"Go home, children," she urged. "Hurry!"

But they simply moved farther into the garden.

Finally, the sound of marching men could be heard, the pounding of their boots on the cobbles almost drowning out the vigorous military rhythm of more than 150 singing voices. The Germans were coming up Via Rasella! Carla waited, and, as she would later recall in a poem:

> Long pain marked the minutes,
> Quivering like struck blades of steel about to descend on us,
> We who were trapped on the street
> Our hearts compressed in our breast . . .
> Under the pounding heels,
> A cadence sounded on the pavement.
> Echoing in the heart (only the brain left the vow intact) . . .
> Eyes upon us at every corner
> Watching, waiting . . .

Franco Calamandrei, who stood near the bottom of Via Rasella, walked across the street in front of the troops and lifted his cap. With this signal, Rosario lit a long fuse snaking from the rubbish cart and placed his own cap on the cart, the signal that everything was in order.

He walked up the hill to Via Quattro Fontane and turned the corner to the right, where he met Carla. As the two of them started running down the street, the earth shook under a tremendous explosion, then three more from shells hurled by partisans from behind the troops.

> And it passed, swept away with fear,
> The timidity of youth,
> Of our twenty years . . .

"Revenge! Revenge for my poor *Kameraden!*"

General Kurt Mälzer, the commandant of Rome, was beside himself with rage and grief when he arrived at Via Rasella shortly after the explosions. And the extraordinary quantity of alcohol he had consumed at lunch with Colonel Kappler fed his wild, incoherent emotionalism as he saw the bodies of German soldiers, many of them dismembered, lying in pools of blood amid the wreckage and listened to the groans and cries of the wounded.

"I am going to blow up the entire block of houses!" he raved. "I have already issued the necessary order. I'm going to blow the whole thing up. I swear it, and nobody is going to stop me!"

Dollmann and Möllhausen, who had arrived shortly after Mälzer, tried their best to stop him. Soldiers were already breaking into every house along the street, dragging out men, women, and children, and lining them up in front of Barberini Palace.

"*Herr* General," Möllhausen pleaded, "I beg you not to do it. Try to calm yourself. This is a matter of Germany's good name as well as your own. Since it is we who have been attacked, we have a psychological advantage."

Mälzer started to weep. "My soldiers!" he sobbed. "My poor soldiers! I'm going to blow up the whole neighborhood, with whoever might be in the houses. And you, Möllhausen, with your face of a Byzantine Christ, I'm going to dump you into jail at once!"

Mälzer then ordered an aide to contact Field Marshal Kesselring. "Explain the situation. Tell him that I request full powers and tell him also that the *Herr Konsul* disagrees with my orders."

"Wait a minute," Möllhausen told the officer. "If you use my name, tell the field marshal why I disagree."

"I remind you again," Mälzer shouted to the consul, "this is my business and I am the commander here. Anyway, no one asked you to come here!"

With a mocking salute, Mälzer walked away, and Möllhausen angrily jumped into his car. The consul was driving toward his embassy, hoping to call Kesselring before Mälzer did, when suddenly he saw Kappler's car speeding toward Via Rasella. Möllhausen and Kappler stopped their vehicles, got out, and discussed the situation.

"That fool Mälzer wants to blow up all the houses here," Möllhausen cried. "He must be stopped at any cost!"

After some minutes, Kappler returned to his car and continued on to Via Rasella, where Dollmann confronted him and repeated what the consul had said, but in a calmer manner. Both men knew that a decision would have to be made immediately.

Dollmann seldom went out of his way to commit evil, but he was usually willing to go along with it. He was, after all, enjoying the fruit of that collaboration. Kappler did not collaborate with evil; he was part of the machinery. This distinction in commitment and role created friction between them, and the friction was exacerbated by social differences. Dollmann's aristocratic snobbery clashed sharply with Kappler's small-town policeman's mentality.

Recently, relations between them had improved because Kappler's estranged wife attempted to use Dollmann to damage her husband's reputation in revenge for his flagrant infidelity. *Frau* Kappler had offered Dollmann copies of embarrassing reports that Kappler had made about him to his superiors. Dollmann informed Kappler of his wife's machinations—thus putting the Gestapo chief in Dollmann's debt. As it turned out, Kappler's wife solicited help from high-placed friends and might have had the colonel recalled from Rome if he had not been decorated during the Jewish roundup crisis.

Kappler could not afford any more scandals. He was an ambitious man. He had even adopted a son through the *Lebensborn* society for fatherless SS children because he knew he would not go much further in the SS if he remained childless, and he was prepared to carry out the orders of his superiors to the last comma.

But Dollmann remained a threat. He knew many deleterious details about Kappler's private life aside from what his wife had told him—for example, that Kappler was having an affair with a mysterious Dutch girl whom Dollmann deeply distrusted. And Dollmann was a protégé of Himmler and Wolff.

"You see, Kappler, what they have done to my boys," Mälzer said bitterly when the Gestapo chief arrived at the scene. "Now I am going to blow up all these houses."

Kappler stared at the bodies that the survivors had laid out in a row along the street, then quietly persuaded Mälzer to return to his headquarters, promising to take care of everything. Mälzer, glancing at the civilians lined up in front of Barberini Palace, issued one more order:

"They are all to be shot!"

But the cold and methodical Kappler decided to defy Mälzer's unstable show of authority. Although technically Mälzer, as the commandant of Rome, was his superior, Kappler had really to obey only his SS bosses.

Consul Möllhausen arrived at the German Embassy about an hour after the incident, still in a state of fury. He kicked aside a chair in his path, picked up the telephone, and called Kesselring, only to learn that he was at the front and could not be reached. He then spoke with Kesselring's chief of operations, Colonel Dietrich Beelitz, who immediately called Hitler's headquarters in East Prussia. An aide to Hitler, General Treusch von Buttlar, went to report the Via Rasella incident to the Führer and returned to the telephone half an hour later, at about 4:30 P.M. He told Beelitz:

"He is in an uproar and wants an entire quarter of the city blown up together with all those who live there, and he wants an exceptionally high number of Italians to be shot. For every German policeman shot he wants from thirty to fifty Italians shot"—though the figure was finally reduced to ten.

That night Möllhausen, after learning of Hitler's order from Beelitz, rushed to see Kappler at Via Tasso; and a scene then took place reminiscent of their encounter months before when an order had come to round up the Jews for deportation.

The pope could be persuaded to remain silent when that roundup took place, the consul said. No one could be sure where they were being sent. But how could he remain silent when hundreds of Italian hostages were actually murdered before his very eyes? Hitler's kidnap plan could well be revived, which could result in widespread civil violence.

"I do not have to tell you," the consul told me he said, "that I would do nothing to aid or favor the enemy. I do not forget that we are at war. But what you plan to do goes beyond war and the Fatherland."

Kappler listened patiently, his small, lead-gray eyes expressionless. He had made up his mind.

"All those picked," he calmly replied, "will be or already have been sentenced to death. Or else they are guilty of at least being *Todeskandidaten* [candidates for death]. For each name that I write, I shall think three times."

Kappler would do considerable thinking that night, for he would have to compile a death list of 320 men—ten names for each of the thirty-two Germans killed on Via Rasella. General Eberhard von Mackensen, the commander of the Fourteenth Army, to whom Mälzer was responsible, first set that figure on his own in discussing a reprisal with Kappler. Mackensen also approved the idea of executing only persons already in prison and condemned to death or life imprisonment and detainees who had not yet been judged of crimes punishable by death.

What if there were not enough Italians in these categories to make up the full required list? Never mind, said Mackensen, the full figure could be publicized even if fewer were actually shot. Now all that was needed was the approval of Kesselring and Hitler.

When the field marshal returned from the front that evening and learned with shock what had happened, he agreed to the plan and telephoned Hitler's headquarters. The chief of staff, General Alfred Jodl, after conferring with the Führer, relayed final approval. The reprisal, Hitler ordered, must be carried out within twenty-four hours. Kesselring was relieved. After all, people who deserved to die would die. He did not question Kappler's apparent assurances that only men in the prescribed categories would be shot—though he was aware that there were too few such men. The less he knew about the details of the operation, the better.

But the details *did* greatly interest Kappler, who had to compose the list of men who would die. Only four prisoners were actually sentenced to death. He would thus have to add many "less guilty" people to the list.

Kappler, however, did not dare tell anyone, especially not Dollmann, who might resort to blackmail and would certainly ask General Wolff to order him to cut down the list. Wolff had already ordered Kappler to delay all reprisal plans until he, Wolff, arrived from Fasano the following day, March 24. But Kappler would go ahead anyway, as Hitler had commanded.

After working through the night, Kappler found that he could not complete his list even though he included the vaguest suspects in hand. But his immediate SS superior, General Wilhelm Harster, telephoned a helpful suggestion from his headquarters in Verona: "If you can't reach the right figure, take as many Jews as you need."

Kappler was concerned, as he had been when ordered to round up the Jews several months earlier, that the mass killing would feed a popular rebellion, but since Hitler had given him a direct order, he would carry it out to the letter. The problem, however, was that he did not have enough Jews to make up the required number. He would have to collect a new batch.

And he did, grabbing a few more scattered Jews as well as victims at random out of Via Tasso and other prisons. In fact, the final count of his quarry exceeded the required number by five, but since they were already in his hands, it was common sense to throw them in with the others.

When the shooting in the Ardeatine Caves, the execution site, finally started, Kappler's main concern was the morale of his men. For they soon got tired and despondent, sloppy in their shooting. It was one thing to machine-gun a mass of people, but quite another to extend the suffering of the victims by making them wait while the soldiers shot one after the other at close range.

A man, even an SS man, could be disturbed when he had time to note that he was murdering another human being. Kappler tried to explain the rationale for the killing, putting his arm around each one as he entered the caves in the manner of telling the facts of life to an adolescent son. The challenge was reflected in an article that appeared in the *Il Messaggero* on March 26, 1944:

> On the afternoon of March 23, 1944, criminal elements executed a bomb attack against a column of German police in transit through Via Rasella. As a result of this ambush, thirty-two men of the German police were killed and several wounded. The vile ambush was carried out by communists and Badoglio supporters. An investigation is still being made to clarify the extent to which this criminal deed is attributable to Anglo-American involvement.
>
> The German Command has decided to terminate the activities of these villainous bandits. No one will be allowed to sabotage with impunity the newly affirmed Italo-German cooperation. The German Command has therefore ordered that for every murdered German, ten Communist-Badogliani criminals be shot. This order has already been executed.

The communiqué understated the extent of reprisal by declaring that thirty-two Germans had been killed on Via Rasella, thereby implying that only 320 Italians were shot in retaliation although, in reality, 335 were executed. Not only did the Germans wish to hide the fact that Kappler had killed by mistake five more men than the ten-to-one ratio order required, but Kappler's colleagues, looking to possible postwar repercussions, were far from sure that it was "legal" to shoot the ten extra hostages shot for the German who died *after* the order was issued. A German noncommissioned officer would afterwards describe the massacre:

> The prisoners had their hands bound behind their backs. Their feet too were tied so that they could move only with very short steps or

jumps. They were picked up and thrown into the lorries like baggage. Many of them had signs of ill treatment on their faces and some had lost their teeth.

Out of curiosity, I went into the caves and watched the execution of about sixty hostages. They were made to kneel in a row of from five to ten, one behind the other. SS men, stepping behind the rows, discharged their guns into the necks of the victims. They died quietly, some crying "Long live Italy!" Most of them were praying . . . an old man, whom I learned to be General Simoni, was speaking words of encouragement to all the rest. . . . I came away because I felt I was going to be sick.

Two priests who later visited the crime scene would report they "found a tunnel about fifty yards long with corpses piled four deep and stuck together with some unrecognizable adhesive substance so that it was impossible to remove one from another." They continued:

Of the six corpses examined in detail, one was of a distinguished old man with gold-rimmed spectacles. The others were all young men. One young man whose right hand was visible [had] three fingers that had been twisted [with] the flesh removed in torture. Another, with his hands tied, was pressed against the wall in an obvious effort to get out, this proving that he had not been dead when the grave was sealed.

General Wolff was enraged when he learned on his arrival in Rome from his headquarters in Fasano on March 24 that the Ardeatine massacre was in progress. Not because he disapproved of the action but because Kappler had proceeded without waiting for his approval.

Colonel Dollmann claims in his memoirs that he was also irate, but for a different reason. He had surmised that Kappler was planning some kind of reprisal for Via Rasella, but had not been informed of the details and felt sure that the Gestapo chief would not act before Wolff, whom he considered a reasonable man, tried to prevent such killings.

Dollmann would say that he had a plan of his own: Fly the families of the men killed on Via Rasella to Rome and parade them through the streets in a solemn funeral procession to win the sympathy of the Romans. Simultaneously, the Germans would threaten drastic action if terrorism continued.

According to Dollmann, he had discussed this plan as a substitute for reprisals with Father Pfeiffer. If the pope pressured the German leaders to accept this plan, many lives might be saved.

The colonel had begun to explain his idea to Wolff on the way from the airport to Monte Soratte to see Field Marshal Kesselring when suddenly someone fired at their car from some roadside bushes. The general, infuriated, shouted:

"Do you see? There is humanity for you! Himmler is right. We need to set an example here!"

But did he really mean this, or was it simply an emotional outburst after this close escape?

Wolff was further enraged on learning that Kappler had begun to set an example without conferring with him. He rushed into Kesselring's office for an explanation, and the field marshal reported on the series of conversations between Rome and Berlin that led to the reprisal. After all, he pointed out, Hitler himself had ordered it—and it had to be completed within twenty-four hours.

Kesselring's report calmed Wolff, who, in any event, had a much bigger operation in mind than the killing of a few hundred Romans. Himmler, he told Kesselring (apparently on Hitler's order), wanted all communists and suspect elements driven from Rome. He was to immediately send all eighteen of the forty-five-year-olds, and their families, from the most dangerous sections of Rome to the north of Italy.

Dollmann would claim that he was stunned. In his view, such mass deportation would exceed in horror even the punishment the barbarians had meted out to the ancient Romans. And for Kessel-ring, the plan didn't make military sense. Where would he get the troops for such a massive operation? But Wolff, still shaky from his own brush with death that day, said to the surprise of the others that it was a fine idea.

Aside from the few hundred Romans who were killed, the Romans should consider themselves fortunate, he apparently felt. The non-Jews would simply be relocated; the Jews would have been ec-static to settle for such a fate. And while he distrusted the Italians in general for condoning or even supporting the terrorists, who were a threat to his own men, he harbored little hatred for the Jews, even though he felt they were an inferior people.

Hadn't he saved most of the Roman Jews—and what if he did hope to ultimately save himself in the process? Anyway, the Jews never really threatened him and he even liked some of them. Of course, that didn't mean he should react emotionally to their des-tiny. He was simply doing his job, trying to please his boss and earn a promotion, just as any other soldier would do.

On the other hand, Wolff now appeared to lust for revenge on the political terrorists and the masses who shielded them. If he had helped Himmler carry out Hitler's policy toward the Jews, and peo-ple who had not notably harmed him or his men, did it make sense to be soft on non-Jews who killed Germans? At the least, they should be banished from Rome, if only to make it a safer base for his troops.

He hadn't felt such fury since he rounded up the ill-fated residents of Lidice, Czechoslovakia, after the assassination of Wolff's close friend, Reinhard Heydrich, the man who made sure the gas cham-bers kept humming.

But then Dollmann reminded Wolff how Pius might react. His public silence during the deportation of the Jews had helped to save him from Nazi abduction. Wouldn't the pontiff feel more compelled to speak out against the Nazis when action was taken not just against a few thousand Jews but against a huge part of the population of

Rome? And would not such a reaction reactivate Hitler's kidnap plot and perhaps tighten the noose around their respective necks if the Allies won the war, as now seemed virtually inevitable?

Was Wolff convinced? Not quite, it seemed. But his sense of realism struggled to trump his vanity and ego and gradually calmed his Nazi fury. After successfully defying the Führer's kidnap order to improve his chances of postwar survival, was it rational for him to jeopardize that effort by brutally forcing an evacuation? Or did his bluster simply veil a perceived new opportunity?

As Wolff pondered whether to go through with the mass evictions, he wasn't at all sure that he could convince Hitler again that so drastic an act would harm German interests and once more risk a papal condemnation. Could he—and the pope—survive another such dangerous game? On the other hand, by saving the Romans from catastrophe, most of them this time, he would place Pius even more in his debt.

CHAPTER 20

The Path to the Vatican

With the killings on Via Rasella, the pope's worst forebodings seemed to be coming true. As he had predicted a few months earlier to Harold Tittmann, "irresponsible elements," in his view, now threatened Rome with chaos and communism. The communists apparently sought to provoke a reaction that would stir the Romans to revolt, and this fear consumed Pius. It turned into a new tormenting dilemma when he learned of the massacre that took place in the Ardeatine Caves the day after Via Rasella, apparently before he had a chance to protest.

Already accused by many of "letting" the Nazis deport the Jews, Pius might this time be accused of standing silently by while the Nazis vengefully slaughtered hundreds of other Romans as well, including some Jews who had survived the roundup. And if he spoke out strongly now, it would be said that he was biased in selecting the victims he would save. Should he protest after the fact? If he did, a livid Hitler might use papal intervention as an excuse to revive the kidnap plot.

Pius finally decided to speak, but softly, through the *L'Osservatore Romano*. He would take a neutralist approach and carefully link the Ardeatine reprisal to the provocation on Via Rasella; with this strategy, he hoped to avoid setting in motion Hitler's dormant plot against him. Blackmail, it seemed, still worked. In any case, what was done was done, he apparently felt. The article would read:

We call upon the irresponsible elements to respect human life, which they can never have the right to sacrifice, to respect the innocence of those who are their fatal victims; from the responsible elements we ask for an awareness of their responsibility toward themselves, toward the lives they seek to safeguard, toward history and civilization.

The day after this article appeared, expressing equivalence of blame for the tit-for-tat killings, the Germans replied with a grateful gift; they agreed to turn Rome into an open city, and in fact they removed some troops and equipment from the city.

Pius had at once appeased the Nazis and the Romans, justifying in his eyes the Vatican's neutralist policy and saving the Vatican and the papacy once more from Hitler's madness. And he mourned the Roman victims, though many of them were communists, people who would gladly replace the Nazis as the destroyers of the Vatican and potentially of Christianity. In any case, Pius didn't know yet of the Führer's order to drive thousands of Romans out of their city.

❖

On the night of the Via Rasella reprisal, Wolff, Kappler, Möllhausen, and Dollmann met in the general's hotel suite to discuss the executions and Hitler's drastic order for mass deportations. When Kappler, his eyes flaming in dark sockets, his face gray and haggard, reported in a final account on the killings in the caves, Wolff, according to Möllhausen, said that the Romans did not "merit favored treatment." They must suffer more.

Wolff detailed plans for deporting them, though Dollmann argued that the pope would almost surely denounce such action, and the Ardeatine killings as well. And such a protest would probably revive the kidnap plot, for Hitler was still reluctant to let the pope fall under Allied control.

At about one in the morning of March 25, Dollmann telephoned Himmler. He had persuaded Wolff to have Ambassador Weizsäcker ask the pope not to publicly condemn the deportations. Himmler who, like Wolff, was still thinking of his own future, agreed that the deportations could be postponed if, "in the judgment of the influential people in Rome, it is absolutely essential."

The next day, Wolff and Dollmann went back to see Kesselring, who, after listening to all the arguments, seemed more opposed to the plan than ever. Möllhausen would report that he had visited the field marshal that morning and had drawn a verbal picture for him: "Hundreds of thousands of persons marching north on foot . . . carrying their possessions, with the weaker ones falling along the way. . . . The supply roads blocked, the troops endangered."

Most persuasive of all was the unsentimental military rationale of General Mackensen. His Fourteenth Army was planning a new drive to throw the Allied forces at Anzio into the sea, and he could not spare troops for a nonmilitary purpose. And the Tenth Army was at that moment fighting off an Allied assault on Monte Cassino.

Wolff now advised Himmler that he would hold off on the deportation plan until the Fourteenth Army could spare the troops needed—presumably after the new attack on the Anzio beachhead (the planned attack, in the end, was canceled). Wolff welcomed the delay; perhaps the operation would be unwise, as Dollmann argued. Karl Wolff had to think of his own future.

And his future could still lie in the hands of the pope, whom he had helped to save months earlier but who was now in danger again. If most Romans were forced to flee their homes, the pontiff would have little choice this time but to speak out. In fact, it might be time to start collecting on the pope's debt. He would try to meet secretly with Pius and subtly claim his gratitude.

At the same time, knowing from Weizsäcker that Pius might be interested in mediating a negotiated peace, Wolff thought, perhaps he could help the pontiff achieve one. Pius might like to see Hitler out of power, but he was a friend of Germany who did not wish to see it destroyed—a shared view that could further tighten the bond between them.

More than physical survival compelled Wolff to seek true ties with the pope. As he would tell a German court after the war, he would "never forget" the massacre in Minsk in 1941, the sight of one human being after another jumping into a hole atop those already shot dead until the hole was filled to the top. Although his physical sickness from the scene gradually dissipated, the images in his mind apparently did not.

Wolff could keep books on genocide—such as the number of people jammed into a boxcar—and that was like counting money in the bank where he once worked. But when the statistics turned into real people, the images froze. It wasn't easy operating a human slaughterhouse.

A meeting between Wolff and Pius would have to be secret since only Weizsäcker was authorized to meet with the pope without Berlin's approval, and Hitler would not trust a military leader to conduct talks with the hated pontiff. Even Field Marshal Kesselring, the top military leader in Italy, had never visited him and would never do so without first consulting Berlin.

So how, Wolff—and Dollmann—wondered, could an audience with Pius be arranged? Surely the pope, to whom neutralism was almost a biblical imperative, would be reluctant to sit down with the SS leader in Italy and a confidant of Heinrich Himmler, especially since the pontiff was already under attack by the Allies for not publicly and specifically condemning SS atrocities.

Wolff decided he must first win the trust of a high dignitary in the Vatican and went to see Weizsäcker, whom he knew felt similarly about a negotiated peace and had close connections with the Vatican. The ambassador, who needed all the support he could muster in his own effort to save Germany from annihilation, gladly agreed to arrange for him a meeting with Dr. Ivo Zeiger, a Jesuit priest and the rector of the German Theological College at the Vatican.

The general was delighted, especially since he had always admired the rules and discipline of Zeiger's order, the Society of Jesus, and had helped, with Himmler, to integrate some of its bureaucratic regulations into the SS rule book. Accompanied by Weizsäcker and Dollmann, Wolff went to see the priest, who was shocked that Himmler's adjutant would want to see a man whose Jesuit order was on Hitler's blacklist.

When Zeiger broached the subject of the "horrible measures" that were taken by German officials behind the frontline, implying that Wolff, as a top SS leader, was involved in the horrors taking place in the concentration camps, the general was confronted, apparently for the first time, with a veiled charge he knew could result ultimately in his execution. It was a moment of final decision: He would betray Adolf Hitler to save his skin and to live a lie that he apparently rationalized into an ersatz reality.

But until the Third Reich finally came crashing down, he would pose as a loyal soldier, and, to make sure his grandchildren would remember him, perhaps win the German Gold Cross for his role in fighting the partisans and helping to direct the war in Italy. A medal he would indeed receive later, in December 1944, shortly before he would completely betray his mad, trusting benefactor.

Brushing away the countless ghosts of the Chosen People he ordered into cattle cars bound for oblivion, Wolff replied to the Jesuit priest: "Yes, these things are very sad. I thank fate—or if you will, the Lord God—that I had nothing to do with those ugly things."

Zeiger would later say that these words "stuck in his memory even more" because the general "made some sharp critical comments" in the presence of the ambassador and Dollmann "which according to the way the system worked at the time . . . could have been dangerous." Wolff, the pragmatist, had in fact abandoned the system.

"As the German police chief in Italy with the top responsibility," the general told Zeiger, he firmly intended "to avoid all unnecessary difficulties for the Holy See, the Church, and other institutions." Wouldn't it be useful for him to meet His Holiness?

The priest expressed skepticism, pointing to the arrest of a religious leader who had been sentenced to death even though he had done "nothing wrong politically."

Several days later, the cleric was released from prison; Wolff had passed the test. But when no word of an audience with the pope came, Dollmann, who hoped to survive by clinging to his boss's coattails, decided that someone else must come to the rescue. And rescue, he was convinced, meant a personal tie with Pius XII.

Who else could make the contact? A particular woman suddenly came to mind. Though Dollmann was known to view most women as devious and duplicitous, he did trust this one. Indeed, she might be the only person who could bring together Pius, the Vicar of Christ, and Wolff, the protégé of Hitler and Himmler.

Dollmann thus went to see his old friend, Donna Virginia Agnelli, the forty-four-year-old widow of Edoardo Agnelli, the Turin Fiat heir. Wearing a Venetian-lace bed jacket, Virginia greeted him from her bed in the clinic where she lay ill—under police guard. And by coincidence, she had just written him asking for his help.

In early January 1943, two fascist policemen in mufti had come to Virginia's magnificent old mansion, Villa del Bosco Parrasio, at the foot of Janiculum Hill in Trastevere, and asked to see her. Though she was in bed suffering from a sore throat and fever, she came downstairs and was whisked away to San Gregorio Convent, which the fascists had converted into a relatively comfortable prison for ladies of rank and breeding who harbored dangerous political inclinations. The Fiat heiress had been accused of some minor misdemeanor.

Virginia, whose mother was American (and whose son, Giovanni, or Giani, would become the president of Fiat), was largely apolitical, as befitted members of industrial families that could never be sure who their customers might be in the future. She had entertained Crown Prince Humbert, Colonel Dollmann, and many fascist figures in her stunningly furnished drawing rooms in past years.

But her heart was with the British, and she was not at all unhappy when Mussolini was overthrown. Nor did she keep these sentiments to herself. She often conducted her cocktail chatter and telephone conversations in English rather than in Italian, providing considerable material for fascist police diaries. Virginia's arrest followed.

When even the most important fascist generals and diplomats failed to obtain her release, Virginia remembered Colonel Dollmann, who had secured the freedom of other socially prominent prisoners. Dollmann had always treated Virginia with great deference, and his charm and wit had brightened many of her soirees during the golden days of fascism.

Dollmann recalls in his memoirs that he had joked about her Anglophile tendencies and offered friendly warnings that she speak Italian rather than English to avoid arousing police suspicions. She had smiled and asked Dollmann, he relates, if he had suddenly joined the neo-fascists.

It was while under detention that Virginia wrote to Dollmann asking for his help. He would recall that shortly after the Germans had occupied Rome, she expressed concern over champagne cocktails that when the Germans eventually left—and she gently pointed out that international opinion was predicting they would—Rome might be destroyed in battle or by sabotage. Unaware that the pope himself was in grave danger, Virginia had felt that only his influence could save her beloved city.

Now here was Virginia, who knew Pius well, requesting Dollmann's help—at the very moment he was trying to arrange a papal audience for Wolff. The colonel came up with an ingenious plan. He asked Virginia to pretend to prison authorities that her sore throat had developed into a serious infection. She fell gravely "ill" at once and was switched to a clinic; her Italian doctor then falsely reported that she had tonsillitis, intending to simulate a tonsillectomy and thus give his patient time to "recover" from the "operation."

But with a German doctor and nurse looking on at the operating table and fascist guards standing outside the room, the surgeon had little choice; he would have to remove Virginia's tonsils even though they were in fine condition. And he did, while her sister, Princess San Faustino—who did not know of Dollmann's role in the plot— stood by dressed as a nurse to silence her sibling if she protested.

Colonel Dollmann visited Virginia in the recovery room to tell her how she could help save Rome—while apparently keeping secret even from her that she could help save the Vatican and its pope as well. Would she please try to arrange a secret meeting between the pope and General Wolff?

Virginia's recovery period gave Dollmann a chance to drop in on Kesselring and shortly return to the clinic with the field marshal's own medical officer. Awed by the sight of the beribboned visitor, the police, sympathizing with Virginia anyway, permitted the two Germans to leave with the patient. Still attired in lace, and with a silk scarf tied around her neck, Virginia found herself some minutes later in a suite of the Excelsior Hotel, German military headquarters.

She and Dollmann now solicited the help of Father Pfeiffer, the Vatican liaison with the Germans, who in turn interested Cardinal Caccia Dominioni in their endeavor. Thus, in early May 1944, the cardinal arranged a papal audience for Virginia and she went to see Pius to request an audience for Wolff. General Wolff, the SS leader in Italy!? The pope had heard that the general had been instrumental in foiling the kidnap plot and helping to save the Vatican.

But if Pius was surprised by the request, he immediately agreed to it, even though he knew he would be engaged in a highly dangerous gamble—just as would Wolff. He was already under tremendous pressure from the Allies and some of his own priests to speak out publicly against the genocide conducted by Himmler's SS. And he would now invite a top SS leader to an audience! But even someone committing the worst offenses deserved a chance to redeem himself, especially Karl Wolff.

Pius didn't appear to realize, or wish to know, that the general, as Himmler's chief aide, had helped to cram Jews into boxcars and submit others to deadly medical experimentation. But the pontiff did know that Wolff had the power to abduct him and steal the Vatican's incalculably valuable files and sacred treasures collected over the centuries, and yet had not exercised this power. He had helped to save the Vatican at great risk to himself. However unsavory his past, Vatican officials aver even today, there had to be some good in him.

But the pope apparently viewed the audience as more than an expression of gratitude. He saw it as an opportunity to win assurances that the Vatican and Rome were now fully secure.

And so Pius would welcome the SS general.

Dollmann decided to break the good news to Wolff at a dinner party to be held on May 9 during one of the general's visits to Rome. A papal audience had been scheduled for the following day. The general arrived at the party in good humor, his fair Aryan face alight, a mood perhaps brightened by the company of an attractive blond woman who accompanied him. When Dollmann informed him of the audience, he was as startled as he was delighted. The pope had actually agreed to meet with the SS chief in Italy!

Wolff would now have the opportunity to seal his bond with a godly patron who could attest to his humanitarianism and his efforts to save Vatican treasures and the pope himself.

CHAPTER 21

The Odd Couple

Wolff's tall, muscular physique almost burst the seams of the ill-fitting civilian suit he had borrowed from the smaller Dollmann to wear for his secret audience with Pope Pius XII on May 10, 1944. Only the pope and his closest aides were to know of this meeting, and a general's uniform would not go unnoticed by others. Wolff feared the consequences if the Führer learned of the audience, and the pope wanted no new altercations with the Allies.

After stealing into the Vatican, Wolff sat facing Pius and listened to him with all the reverential attention he usually reserved for the Führer. The pope subtly remarked in his excellent German that he had heard rumors of certain goings-on at Via Tasso, the Gestapo torture house, and asked that Wolff do something about it. In particular, he requested the release of a socialist activist, Giuliano Vassalli, who was the son of a conservative friend. The general promised to speak to Colonel Kappler.

The ice was broken. Wolff had shown his good faith.

True to his philosophy of neutralist silence, Pius did not specifically urge Wolff to use his influence to stop the murder of millions, though the general was known to be especially close to the man directing the genocide. Could he stir the perilous waters with the fate of the Church at stake? Or save a single Jew if word reached Hitler of his direct plea?

Pius, however, did ask his guest to use his influence to achieve peace—without German humiliation. They agreed that the war would best end in an alliance of the Allies and Germany to halt the Soviet advance beyond its own borders. If Germany compromised, the pope said, maybe the Allies would, too. The Allied call for unconditional surrender, he added, was, at best, likely to prolong the war.

Wolff suggested that the pope himself would be an appropriate mediator. The pontiff expressed appreciation. Here was the kind of German officer needed to achieve peace. He would, the general promised, do his utmost to help terminate the war.

Pius then urged Wolff to do what he could to cancel a reported plan to evacuate most of the people of his beloved Rome. Wolff's growing doubt about the wisdom of such an operation suddenly dissolved in total submission to a new idol.

Of course he would, Wolff replied, as if in thanks for granting him a new lease on life after the war. He must now somehow convince the Führer once again—as he would—how extreme action could rebound disastrously against German interests.

But Pius was apparently concerned that Hitler might overrule Wolff. Couldn't this lead to revival of the kidnap plot?

"Whatever happens," the pope said to the man who had been ordered to abduct him, as he had to Weizsäcker and others in the past, "I will not leave Rome voluntarily. My place is here and I will fight to the end for the Christian commandments of humanity and peace."

Wolff assured the pope that he would try to frustrate any plot and to avoid fighting, bloodshed, and sabotage in Rome. Clearly Rome would be an open city.

Pius felt safer than he had for months. Here was the kind of leader needed to save Germany from destruction and save Europe from Soviet enslavement. With deep feeling, he told Wolff: "How many injustices, how many crimes, how many offenses against the Christian spirit of love for his fellow men, how many misunderstandings could have been avoided if you had come to me first of all?"

But the pope, consistent with his subtle, obscure style of communication, apparently did not directly thank Wolff for his role in saving him and the Vatican from Hitler's possibly lethal fury. Did not the very fact that he received in audience the SS chief in Italy, an intimate of Heinrich Himmler—at the risk of condemnation by critics already hounding him to speak out against Hitler—express his gratitude more precisely than any words could? Anyway, why make a point of Wolff's betrayal of the man he served, even if it was totally justified? Pius seemed to amplify his appreciation with a heartfelt benediction:

"You have a hard road to travel, General Wolff. Will you allow me to give you my blessing as you tread this perilous road—you and the members of your family?"

Pius could now relax a bit knowing that the SS chief in Italy was on his side and that he had promised to protect him and the Vatican—if he could. But what if he couldn't and Hitler learned of their conversation? Despite the pontiff's greater sense of safety, the Church would not really be free from danger until the Nazis left Rome—without the communists in control.

Wolff, for his part, was overwhelmed. On the one hand, Hitler regarded him as an exemplary Nazi poster boy for enslaving the world, and on the other, Pius, apparently, as a man who could help *save* the world. He would now be serving the Antichrist (for a while) and the Vicar of Christ simultaneously, an incredible interworld feat perhaps unique in history.

His decision to sabotage Hitler's kidnap plot was, it seemed, turning out just as he had hoped. He had not experienced so thrilling a moment since the Führer had shaken his hand and praised him as the ideal Nazi when, years earlier, he had caught the wayward staff of a prancing drum major and saved many people from injury or death.

As Wolff would state almost nostalgically to an Allied interrogator after the war:

"I am still convinced today, just as I was at the time, that my way of handling politics—without bloodshed and with a light hand—

was of the greatest advantage to both sides. Well, as I said, I was on very good terms with the pope—he did not try to win me over to the Catholic Church, and I didn't try to win him over to the Reich—we understood each other and always got on well."

After the papal blessing, Wolff rose, clicked his heels together— and stiffly raised his arm in the Nazi salute!

Father Pfeiffer, who was waiting at the open door, could hardly believe his eyes. But the pope smiled forbearingly, apparently relieved that Wolff had not cried, "Heil Hitler!" In his enthrallment, especially with his seeming salvation from the gallows, the general had simply confused his gods. It wasn't easy juggling them.

As suggested by the reflexive salute, Wolff's joy was tainted by a disturbing thought. He could not wrench from his mind the oath he had taken as a Nazi officer: "I swear before God to give my unconditional obedience to Adolf Hitler, Führer of the Reich and of the German people, Supreme Commander of the Wehrmacht, and I pledge my word as a brave soldier to observe the oath always, even at the peril of my life."

The Führer had supported him at every turn, in every controversy with other leaders. Wolff owed his whole career to the man. Yet he had betrayed him once again. He had helped to sabotage the papal kidnap plan and now secretly promised the pope to work toward a peace that would doom his benefactor. Was there no way to ease his angst?

As the war neared an end, Wolff would find out.

CHAPTER 22

Meeting a
New Conqueror

Less than a month after the papal audience, the day came—June 4, 1944. As Allied forces under General Mark Clark surged toward Rome, Colonel Kappler and other Nazi and fascist leaders left in such a hurry that Ambassador Rahn in Fasano compared them to "rats abandoning a sinking ship."

Among the most reluctant to leave was Colonel Dollmann, who had a double attachment to Rome: the power and glory it had conferred on him and the artistic beauty it had seduced him with. Escorted by his Roman chauffeur, Mario, and his German shepherd, Dollmann drove up to the peak of Monte Soratte, the hill celebrated in verse by Horace and Virgil, to bid goodbye to Field Marshal Kesselring. As he gazed upon Rome for the last time, he recalled that the youthful Emperor Otto III, son of the Greek Empress Theophano, had died at the foot of the hill. He had also been making his way north after being driven out of Rome.

By noon that day, only one important German military leader remained in Rome—General Mälzer. Kesselring, who would stay at his headquarters on Monte Soratte until eight that night, had ignored Weizsäcker's suggestion that the Germans contact the Allies directly to arrange for the unobstructed departure of all German troops. But Mälzer, thinking he might still be needed as the German contact man, informed Kesselring's headquarters that he intended to stay in Rome "as long as possible." He then proceeded to drink away his fear and sorrow.

◆

Mälzer did not have much time to get drunk. Guided by partisans, the main Allied forces began entering Rome late that afternoon after fierce fighting in some areas. As they advanced, hundreds of people rushed from their homes and, throwing themselves upon their liberators with shrieks of joy, grabbed hands, arms, and legs, and almost dragged the Americans out of their jeeps and tanks. A new conqueror had driven out the old, and the cynical Romans were happy because the new one could hardly be worse than the old one.

In other parts of Rome, people demonstrated in parades, some led by partisans wearing either the red, white, and green armbands of the moderate leftists or the red hammer-and-sickle ones of the Communist Party or the Red Flag Party, whose members roved around lustily singing the party anthem, *Bandiera Rossa*.

Many pro-Allied Italians were missing; almost ten thousand had been executed during the nine months of German occupation. The partisans played an important, though hardly a decisive, role in the capture of Rome, taking many Germans and fascists prisoner after bloody local battles and picking off fascist sharpshooters perched on the roofs of key buildings. Some smashed into fascist headquarters situated in stores and apartments, making arrests, and wrecking everything in sight.

Carla Capponi and Rosario Bentivegna had rushed to Rome to take part in an insurrection, but they ended up occupying a fascist newspaper building so that the first "above ground" issue of *Unita* could be published immediately. The revolution that the pope had feared never materialized.

◆

Ambassador Weizsäcker and his wife, out of sheer curiosity, emerged from their embassy for a stroll on the morning of June 5. They had spent the previous night glued to the radio listening for news of the Allied arrival. At about 9:30 P.M. they had heard calls and shouts and applause from the direction of Via 20 Settembre, and they knew the moment had come. Although the outcome had long been inevitable, their hearts sank, and their depression deepened as their proud soldiers retreated like desperate, wounded animals.

They themselves, along with other members of the German mission to the Vatican and their families, would remain in Rome, enjoying diplomatic immunity, as Allied diplomats to the Vatican had done when the Germans first occupied the city. But they would move into the Vatican as soon as possible.

Now, on the first morning under enemy rule, the Weizsäckers wandered through the streets, watching the parades, the flutter of enemy flags, the Italian girls walking arm-in-arm with enemy soldiers. The day before, Romans had at least feigned friendship with the Germans. Today, they loved the Americans and British. They shifted their affection as easily as they changed their clothes. After all, while the Germans had nothing to offer them, Allied trucks were bulging with cigarettes, food, medicines. Well, it was no secret, the Weizsäckers felt, that the Italians lacked the sturdy character of the Germans.

But the ambassador perhaps questioned the sturdiness of his own character, too. For as the Germans were fleeing Rome and the SS troops were about to search the Teutonic College, he agonizingly turned in the Jewish family he was hiding there. If he had not and the soldiers had found them, his mission would surely have ended, as might his life.

As the couple approached their embassy after their stroll, they saw several boys pull the swastika from a flagpole and then drag it down the street to lead a new parade. On entering, the couple learned from the diplomats gathered there that two men were missing; Ludwig Wemmer and Albrecht von Kessel had been arrested despite their diplomatic immunity. Weizsäcker was almost thankful that Wemmer, whom he knew had been sent by Martin Bormann to observe him, was at least temporarily out of the way, especially since he suspected that Wemmer hoped to replace him after Rome's fall. Weizsäcker felt that now, more than ever, he was needed in Rome to exert an influence on the pope.

And so was Kessel, the one man he could trust completely. It was likely that Kessel, an anti-Hitler conspirator, told Weizsäcker about the suspended plot to assassinate the Führer in 1939, and if so, this knowledge would have increased the ambassador's concern about his friend's arrest. Kessel was needed to play his role in a later plot.

If it succeeded, Weizsäcker's own diplomatic efforts in Rome might be amply rewarded. He was in a position to obtain the immediate cooperation of the pope in mediating a negotiated peace between a post-Hitler Germany and the Anglo-Americans. And his moment of destiny might come even before the Russians set foot in Europe.

Nor did the "miracle" of Rome's salvation fail to comfort the ambassador. Without any agreement, the two sides had spared the city, and, aside from the railroad yards, about 95 percent of it had survived the nightmare unscathed. He liked to think that Rome's salvation had paved the way for the salvation of Germany.

But what mattered more to Weizsäcker was his role in saving the pope from a horrible fate that would have forever blemished Germany's reputation. Yes, thank heaven he had helped to keep the pope from speaking out against the Jewish mass killings, thereby thwarting the plot against him and the Church, and negating his possible role as a neutralist qualified to mediate a desirable peace.

He still could not admit what many of his colleagues now knew—that, as Allied intelligence would report, "the Anglo-Saxons would never permit the question of peace negotiations with Germany to originate and develop in the Vatican, since it would add too much prestige to the Catholic Church. Even the Vatican diplomats openly admit this. It is possible that England may eventually consent to discuss extraordinary proposals made by the Vatican, but this is doubtful."

At 5:00 P.M. that day, the great bell of St. Peter's pealed and a roar of acclamation greeted the appearance of the slender, white-robed figure behind the ceremonial drapery decorating the parapet of the basilica's central balcony. People waved and applauded and held their children up and cried, *"Viva Papa!"*

Many carried flags—Italian, American, British, French, even the red flag—while an American Piper Cub overhead showered the area with flowers.

Pope Pius XII gazed down with smiling benevolence upon his children; a half million people formed a massive mosaic of color, including large patches of khaki, as they stood bathed in the glow of sunset. Twice in the morning people had gathered in St. Peter's Square to cheer him, and once he had appeared to extend his blessing.

But the pope had been piqued by the sight of an armored car at the edge of the square. He had telephoned his secretary of state three times to demand that the car be sent away, but as soon as that one left, another appeared. If the Germans could respect Vatican neutrality, why not the Allies? The war was not yet over—nor was the chance of his mediating peace.

Now he was in a subdued mood. The people of Rome still loved him. They knew that he had helped to save their sacred city, the center and symbol of Christian civilization. He raised his hand and his listeners grew quiet as he began to speak: "We must give thanks to God for the favors we have received. Rome has been spared. This day will go down in the annals of Rome."

After further references to Rome's salvation, the pope, frequently interrupted by applause, concluded his brief talk and blessed the kneeling crowd. Even after he had left the balcony, the throngs continued to acclaim him. Then, while the military departed in their jeeps and trucks, the Italians, without public transportation because of the lack of fuel and electricity, walked back to their homes. It didn't matter. Rome was saved.

Actually, it seemed to many at the moment more important that Rome had been *liberated*—though the pope had not mentioned liberation and *L'Osservatore Romano* had, in fact, neglected so far even to report that the Allies had arrived. But the people, however aroused by their sudden freedom, understood the pope because they were Romans.

Conquerors and liberators had come and gone for centuries. They were but men, who eventually died, the good and evil alike, their deeds obscured in the infinity of history. But Rome—and the Church—were eternal. And did not the pope have the duty to make sure they remained so, whatever the price?

◆

Three days later, on June 8, the two most powerful men in Rome met. General Clark and his staff, wearing battle dress, drove in jeeps to the Vatican and were escorted to the pope's chambers by Swiss guards in their colorful uniforms. Pius had only reluctantly granted Clark an audience, fearing that the invitation would disqualify him as a potential peacemaker in German eyes.

Besides, Clark represented an alliance that was insisting on unconditional surrender in partnership with the Soviet Union. And although the pope's people were celebrating their "liberation," how long would this liberation last if an Allied victory brought the Russians into Europe? With the Germans no longer a threat to the Vatican and himself, it was time to renew his furious attacks on Stalin.

Yes, he had enthusiastically welcomed General Wolff, but he had heard that the SS chief had helped to sabotage Hitler's kidnap plan, and that he could be a useful friend of the Vatican. But Clark, on the contrary, could ruin his peace dream just by visiting him, though he realized he had little choice but to greet him.

Pius invited Clark to talk with him in private before meeting with his other guests. It was not a particularly happy moment for either man, each churning with mixed emotions. Clark had realized his dream by having the Fifth Army beat General Sir Harold Alexander's British Eighth Army into Rome—but at huge human cost (many experts thought that Clark should have bypassed Rome and trapped Kesselring's forces instead at much lower cost). And he had joyously wallowed in the glory reflected in eye-popping headlines around the world—but only for one day. Clark's name was suddenly buried in the obscurity of the inside pages, for on June 5, the day after his triumph, the headlines were trumpeting a much more important moment: D-Day.

The pope, for his part, was deeply relieved that he and the Vatican were now sealed off from Hitler's madness. But the D-Day landings probably meant the Allies would not stop their advance until Germany was forced to surrender unconditionally—and that he would never be called to mediate a peace that could keep the Red Army from lunging into Europe.

Even so, he had to maintain his neutralist stance to save what he could of the Church and its refugee-packed institutions in Europe. And who knew, perhaps some miracle could still catapult him to the peace table.

"I understand your headquarters are now in Rome," the pope said. "How long will you be here? I am fearful that your presence may bring retaliation from the Germans."

The Germans were in no position to retaliate, Clark replied. Anyway, he would be in Rome only a few days longer.

Did he have any contact with the Russians? the pope asked, expressing fear about the prospective shadow of communism over Europe.

It was almost déjà vu, with much of the conversation sounding like that which the pope had often conducted with the Germans, though the language was no longer German. But he realized that this was a historic moment. He was meeting for the first time with the latest conqueror of Rome. Not yet the liberator, not with the red flag shimmering in the wind under his window.

But if the pope had miscalculated in his fear that the communists might seize Rome and the Vatican as the Germans departed, Hitler had miscalculated in *his* fear that the pope might speak out publicly about the genocide once he fell into Allied hands. He didn't. Not, he argued, while the Church was still hiding hundreds of thousands of people in its institutions all over Nazi Europe who could suffer the consequences.

In any event, Pius felt enormous relief that the communist thrust for power had been at least temporarily thwarted—and that he would no longer have to search German eyes, with terror in his heart, for some hint of his fate and that of the Vatican he had spent most of his life regenerating into a spiritual home worthy of God.

CHAPTER 23

Saved from the Noose

It was after Germany's humiliating defeat in the Ardennes offensive in January 1945 that Wolff first glimpsed his destiny. There would be no compromise "peace" in which he could help lead a united German-Allied force against the barbarian hordes of the Soviet Union. There were no secret weapons that he had hoped would finally turn the tide against the relentlessly advancing enemy. Nothing could turn the tide, and Germany seemed doomed. But did that mean he was, too?

Wolff decided to take a gamble that might save him—if the pope's support could not. With the future so bleak, he had little to lose. Hitler had always seriously considered every proposal he had ever made. Now he would offer him one that could mean either delivery or death—for Germany as well as himself. He would ask Hitler to let him seek ways to make peace before the enemy demolished the Fatherland. He could do this without his consent, but why not try to honor the oath of loyalty that weighed so heavily on him?

According to Wolff, Himmler warned him that this effort "might cost [him his head] . . . but I explained to him that there were only two ways open to me: Either to lose my life fighting and to leave my troops to the same fate, or to face the Führer like a man and try to do my duty. I'd probably lose my head whatever I did."

Himmler was reluctant to have Wolff see Hitler because he himself was hoping to be the peacemaker and win the Allied sympathy that could save him from the fate to which he had condemned millions. Wolff would thus say after the war that Himmler "wanted to prevent me from carrying out my plans. He had plans of his own which later came to nothing." But the general, who knew of his boss's plans, was sure that Himmler, who knew he knew, wouldn't dare try to stop him and risk exposure of his unauthorized talks with the enemy. And so Wolff, accompanied by Ribbentrop, called on Hitler in his Berlin bunker.

Wolff was frightened as he sat across from the Führer on February 6, 1945, staring him straight in the eye as he had routinely done after years of working with him as his liaison with Himmler. And he came quickly to the point. Could he seek some way to end the war before it was too late?

The general half-expected an explosion. But Hitler was not the same man he had once been. Once ramrod stiff, he was now hunched, his cheeks drawn, his eyes droopy. Explosive? He actually seemed calm. According to Wolff, he told Hitler: "My Führer, the situation is critical. We should find some discreet way out, and some trustworthy people, and try to do something in the political line."

Wolff claimed he "told the Führer everything, and represented to him . . . that an increasing number of feelers were being put out . . . to [him] from the Allies." He added: "I suggested to him that . . . the offer should not be turned down. . . . One should listen to what they had to offer."

Then, knowing that Hitler was placing his hopes on a split between the Anglo-Americans and the Russians that would permit Germany to join in battle against Russia, Wolff continued:

My Führer, I know, it is obvious from interrogations for one thing and from evidence I have from my particular field, that there are naturally differences among these unnatural Allies, but please do not be offended if I say that I do not believe the alliance will split up of itself without our own active intervention. Before that happens

we shall be dead or beaten to the ground, and that must not happen—
we must do something first.

The Führer replied, "A step of that kind would have a bad effect
on morale."

Wolff said later that Hitler was "very pleasant and didn't actually
say 'no.' He accepted my views in principle, but he did not actually
give me permission to do anything."

That, however, was enough for Wolff. He could now have peace
of mind while pursuing a larger peace.

In March 1945, Wolff sent Dollmann to Switzerland to make
contact with Allen Dulles and tell him that he (Wolff) was prepared to negotiate the surrender of all German troops in Italy.
Shortly thereafter, the general himself went to Switzerland, convinced Dulles that he was serious, and agreed to surrender the
troops unconditionally.

When Wolff returned to Italy, and while talks were still ongoing, an
angry Himmler called him. Ernst Kaltenbrunner, the security chief, he
bellowed, had informed him about the general's secret meeting.

"This was imprudent of you," Himmler told his longtime comrade-
in-genocide. "And I have taken the liberty of correcting the situation. Your wife and your children are now under my protection."

Wolff froze. He knew Himmler intimately. He could kill a child
clutching a teddy bear.

Some weeks later, Himmler called again and ordered him to come
to Berlin immediately.

"I want to talk to you personally," he ordered.

Wolff had no choice. He had to go—and probably would never return. He sent a verbal message to Dulles through one of his agents:
"I am going to Berlin because I believe that by making this dangerous trip there may be a chance of accomplishing something for the
entire German people. I shall be back in Italy in a day or two."

Dulles was depressed. Wolff had worked his charm on him, as he
had on Hitler and the pope, and the OSS chief trusted him com-

pletely, though before meeting him he could not even imagine dealing with any member of the criminal SS, much less a top leader. But without him, Dulles believed, chances for a deal "seemed slim indeed."

The agent also handed Dulles a letter from Wolff:

In case I should lose my command . . . and the action with which I have associated myself should not succeed, I request that the German people and the German troops in Italy should not suffer the consequences. If, after my death, my honor be assailed, I request Mr. Dulles to rehabilitate my name, publicizing my true, humane intentions; to make known that I acted not out of egotism or betrayal, but solely out of the conviction and hope of saving, as far as possible, the German people.

After my death, ask Mr. Dulles, in the name of the ideas for which I shall have fallen, to try to obtain for the German and Italian troops honorable terms of surrender.

I request Mr. Dulles to protect, after my death, if this is possible, my two families, in order that they not be destroyed.

Missing from this possible good-bye letter was any sign of regret for having helped manage history's greatest crime.

Now, as he met his superior in this crime, Wolff coolly listened as Himmler ranted about the general's virtually "treasonous" behavior. Kaltenbrunner, who, like the other two, was seeking contacts who could turn him into a peacemaker, presented to Himmler evidence bolstering his case.

The charge was false, Wolff asserted. He had no secret meeting with Dulles! Let the three of them go to the Führer and let him decide whether it was true!

The accusers suddenly mellowed.

Himmler agreed to arrange the visit, but refused to accompany him, apparently still fearing exposure of his own connections with the Resistance, and most recently with Count Folke Bernadotte of Sweden, a prospective "peace contact."

Go with Kaltenbrunner, Himmler said.

Kaltenbrunner also seemed reluctant; he, too, was secretly dick-ering with a "peace contact," but agreed to go.

When Wolff and Kaltenbrunner arrived at Hitler's bunker, Wolff, realizing he might not leave there alive, stopped the security chief and warned him: If he accused Karl Wolff of secretly negotiating or showed the Führer those "phony" agents' reports, he, Wolff, would tell the Führer that both Kaltenbrunner and Himmler had learned of the contacts earlier but deliberately kept this information from the Führer. As Allen Dulles would later comment: "If Wolff was going to the gallows, he would see to it that Kaltenbrunner would swing next to him."

What Wolff apparently did not know was that Kaltenbrunner had already told Hitler of Wolff's contacts with the enemy.

As the two visitors sat down with Hitler, the Führer, with shoul-ders hunched, cheeks drawn, saliva trickling from his lips, con-fronted Wolff with that charge, snapping that his behavior was "a colossal disregard of authority." But if Wolff began to feel the noose tightening around his neck, he underestimated the power of his ex-traordinary charisma and air of authenticity. Hitler treated Wolff as a father might a mischievous child. He didn't accuse him of treaso-nous action but only of using bad judgment in making the contacts without knowing what plans Hitler had on his mind.

Wolff saw his opening. Without flinching as eye met eye and speaking with the frankness of a master actor, he reminded Hitler that he acted only after his Führer did not forbid him to approach the enemy when the idea was broached at their last meeting.

Why didn't Wolff consult him before he went to see Dulles, Hitler asked.

Wolff explained: Because he wanted to give his Führer the possi-bility of placing the blame on him (Wolff) in case the peace effort failed. He was glad to have opened a channel to the enemy if his Führer ever wanted to use it. He was only trying to give his Führer an additional option.

After a moment of tense silence, Hitler benignly said that yes, he understood Wolff's argument. And to the general's joyous relief, the Führer asked what terms of surrender the enemy was demanding. The question was no longer whether Hitler would surrender, but on what terms. Wolff now spoke the words he never imagined he could utter to the Führer: The enemy demanded unconditional surrender—with the possibility of some mitigation if the Germans demonstrated good will toward the Italians.

Hitler, in shock, got up and left the room.

At another meeting later in the day, Hitler, appearing now befuddled and incoherent, spoke of a new plan: Turn the Allies against the Red Army and then join the side that offered him the most or came to him first. And he added: "I cannot allow myself to be softened. . . . For the man who is to make the final decision must not let himself be moved by the misery and the horror that the war brings to every individual on the front and in the homeland."

Hitler then ordered Wolff: Dig in and defend! If his people could not do so, they would have forfeited their right to survive. And they would simply have to go down heroically before the Russians, who, he snarled sarcastically, had turned out to be the superior race.

But he concluded: "Go back to Italy; maintain your contacts with the Americans, but see that you get better terms. Stall a bit, because to capitulate unconditionally on the basis of such vague promises would be preposterous. Before we come to an agreement with the Americans, we've got to get much better conditions."

As Hitler departed, he said he appreciated the conscientious manner in which Wolff had acted.

Wolff was aglow. Coming from the Führer, who almost never complimented anyone, that remark amounted to a blessing. A blessing first from the pope, and now from the Führer. Truly incredible! Ever since his decision to sabotage Hitler's order to kidnap the pope and ravage the Vatican, his "disloyalty" had gnawed at his psyche, but now that subtle torment dissolved into the greater pain of moral ambivalence.

Hitler's "blessing" seemed to ease his sense of dishonor for having violated a sacred oath, but was he now extending this dishonor to treachery by submitting to the Allied demand for unconditional surrender against the specific orders of the Führer? Was this his repayment for all that Hitler had done for him, for the faith the man had placed in him?

Dulles would later write of Wolff's state of mind:

He seemed to have been somewhat infected by the paralysis of the Berlin bunker atmosphere, or perhaps a deep-set conflict of loyalties had been awakened, despite Hitler's confused and senseless plans. Hitler had, after all, extracted a kind of promise from Wolff, and Wolff had Hitler to thank, in a sense, that neither Himmler nor Kaltenbrunner had been able to "eliminate" him.

In any case, . . . Wolff after returning from Berlin seemed unwilling to act on Sunrise [the code name for the surrender talks]. At best, he sounded as if he were trying to find some compromise between Hitler's request that he hold out and the promises that had been made to us to deliver the surrender of Italy as soon as possible.

After returning to Fasano, Wolff asked an OSS agent to deliver this message to Dulles: "Under the circumstances I cannot negotiate at the moment. I consider this tragic, but I have no other course now. Tell him I will resume contact with him as promptly as possible in order to carry out the original plan."

With Hitler's suicide on April 30, Wolff finally conquered his qualms of treachery and again pursued a final agreement. All he needed now was the support of Field Marshal Kesselring, his military superior. But Kesselring was reluctant to agree, still feeling bound by his oath despite Hitler's death.

According to Wolff, he furiously replied to the field marshal: "If you don't act now, then I want you to realize that you are one of the biggest and worst war criminals of all time."

Kesselring finally agreed; he would approve the peace terms. And on May 2, 1945, Wolff surrendered all German forces in Italy to the Allies. Six days later, the war ended in all Europe. If this had happened before the surrender in Italy, history would probably never have noted Wolff's achievement—and neither would the courts that would judge whether he should hang.

The momentous struggle between his two idols for power in the world thus ended—and it was Pius who survived.

◆

With the last bullet fired, Karl Wolff could relax in the palace in Bonzano and celebrate his good fortune at a sumptuous birthday party that symbolized his rebirth. He had escaped the noose and now didn't even need the pope's intervention on his behalf.

Gradually, Hitler's bittersweet image would recede into some dark recess of Wolff's long-captive mind as he pondered the Führer's parting remark that Germany did not deserve to survive. He could finally say, as if suddenly awakened from an evil, dope-induced dream: "The Führer lacked all sense of reality, and would not listen to advice. I felt that we [had been] lied to. It was a devilishly difficult situation for me. There was my honor as an officer, loyalty, my oath. . . . But it was wrong that loyalty should be demanded of us. We had been shown no loyalty at all. . . . He sacrificed the nation quite unnecessarily."

At any rate, now he could look forward, he felt, to the comfortably normal life every human being deserved. He had only to will away the pesky ghosts of those human beings he had crammed into cattle cars heading for an oblivion his mind was reluctant to define. Meanwhile, he would indulge in the memory of his exquisite conquests over a proxy from heaven and another from hell.

Epilogue

When the European war ended, the pope, humble as he was, surely exulted in his final triumph in the race with Adolf Hitler for spiritual control of much of mankind. Perhaps no modern spiritual leader before him had ever wielded such power over so many. With Hitler gone, the great consolidated Church edifice he had so skillfully built as Cardinal Pacelli was no longer subject to demolition by a psychopath who had held the massive structure hostage.

The pope probably stood up to Hitler to the degree beyond which the edifice might have collapsed, together with its eminent supervisor. He had cherished power in the service of God, and, to protect what he had gained, apparently felt he had little choice but to keep public condemnation of the genocide largely muted.

The crucial question now was: Should preservation of the Church's power have warranted moral priority over an attempt to save millions of lives, even if the effort might fail and result in the destruction of the holy edifice with still more loss of life? Was this not what Godly morality was all about?

However well-intentioned this diplomatic pope may have been, it was further asked, should not his sensitivity and understanding have overcome the diplomat's instinctive pursuit of "realistic" solutions? At least for genocide, did not morality trump realism as a sacred value and require him to speak out publicly at any cost?

Supporters of the pope reply pragmatically that it was simply common sense to avoid provoking an utterly irrational criminal to augment his crime and kill not only more Jews but more Christians.

This controversy barely simmered within diplomatic and ecclesiastic circles after the war until 1963, five years after the death of Pius XII, when Rolf Hochhuth's play *The Deputy,* which showed the pope in an almost evil light, created a sensation around the world. And the controversy has continued ever since, but before this book little notice had been given to the importance of Hitler's plot against the Vatican and the related roundup of Roman Jews in shaping the pope's wartime attitudes and policies.

At this writing, it is unclear whether the Church will approve a proposal to beatify Pius XII, a step toward sainthood. Research of the pope's background has been completed, and, Church officials say, the process is "on course." But some leading Catholics and Jewish groups argue that they cannot support beatification until the Vatican archives for the World War II period are opened so that Pius's policies during the Holocaust can be examined. Church authorities, while reluctant to offend Jewish sensitivities, respond that this cannot be done until all the research material is catalogued, a process that could take years.

◆

Largely due to Allen Dulles's influence, General Wolff would avoid war criminal charges at Nuremberg. But just as an American general ignored Dulles's wish and, after the surrender, whisked Wolff from a prisoner's paradise at war's end to a prison cell, so did other brass also see little reason to go easy on a Nazi general, even without knowing at the time that he had been an intimate of the "monster" Himmler or why Dulles wanted him treated more like an ally than as a war criminal.

When Dulles didn't insist that his promise to Wolff be honored, Wolff, as he languished in jail, felt that his American "savior" had "betrayed" him, especially since his family was left to rely on friends to stave off hunger. The pope had blessed him, and Hitler, in a sense, had too. But Dulles? He may have saved Wolff's life, but what about compensation for his confiscated furniture? Even the treasured medals awarded him by the Führer had disappeared.

Why did Allen Dulles "lie" to him? The answer, Wolff apparently didn't realize, was that the OSS chief was hoping to head a new CIA, and that his brother, John Foster Dulles, might become secretary of state. Could Allen press his superiors to coddle an apparent war criminal, whatever his role in the surrender? Better to let history judge Wolff.

In any case, though Dulles felt obliged to help the general, he could not jeopardize the well-being of his own family. In the end, he was saved from Wolff's continued embarrassing demands when the Americans turned the general over to the British, who felt no obligation to him.

Wolff thus languished in a British prison for two years; upon his release, he entered a most inhospitable new world in which he had to sell his personal belongings, including his treasured beribboned uniforms, to provide for his family. In 1958, with new information about his past surfacing, a German court in Munich tried and convicted him for crimes against humanity.

Sentenced now to a fifteen-year prison term, Wolff was released after five years for health reasons and once again sank into a quicksand of impoverishment. He sold whatever swastika-decorated mementos he still possessed to a collector and squeezed out a living as an aide to a journalist who needed an expert on Nazi history.

Wolff perhaps found his greatest pleasure talking over old times with his friends from the SS, whom he still viewed as proud German elitists like himself, especially with Eugen Dollmann. This comrade had "escaped" from an American internment camp in Rimini, Italy—with the help of Dulles's OSS officers. As Wolff's chief aide, he, too, had been promised freedom after the war, and permitting him to get away would relieve Dulles of the need to plead still another case of an SS leader.

Barred from Germany, Dollmann drifted from country to country and was frequently attacked by communist groups for alleged engagement in neo-Nazi activities. He was forced to flee from Italy to Spain after one such attack in 1952 almost cost him his life. Several years later he finally managed to settle down in Munich.

I asked Wolff at his modest home in Darmstadt whether he would join the SS again if he could relive his life. He replied wistfully: "I lived a very good life. I was so young and I was a general. I had everything I wanted."

Wolff died in 1984 without anything he wanted.

As the war ground to an end, SS leader Himmler found his path to salvation far more difficult than did his protégé Wolff. For while the general could use his virtual anonymity to make a deal with American intelligence agents, Himmler was only too well known to them. His only chance, Himmler now felt, was to do what Wolff had been far less reluctant to do—to betray Hitler. He must convince General Dwight D. Eisenhower himself that with his support he could succeed Hitler and help turn back the Soviet surge toward Europe.

So he stopped killing people, and in April 1945 he even met with a representative of the World Jewish Congress for talks mediated by Dr. Kersten in which Himmler promised to release all surviving Jewish prisoners. He then met with Count Bernadotte and pressed him, unsuccessfully, to arrange a meeting with Eisenhower. But word soon leaked of this "treachery," and Hitler, bursting into a rage in his Berlin bunker, cried, "A traitor must never succeed me as Führer," and ordered the SS chief's arrest.

Later, Himmler, his mustache shaved off and a black patch covering an eye, sought to flee Allied forces but was arrested at a British control point. While being interrogated by British officers, he admitted that he was Himmler, pulled off his eye patch, and fatally crunched a poison pill lodged in his mouth to go the way of the millions he had poisoned to death.

Wolff told his American interrogator that Himmler "had a bad conscience because of the concentration camps." As Himmler's chief aide, he was no doubt reflecting his own inner turmoil as well. But he was at least comforted by the thought that Hitler had died before a final accord for unconditional surrender was reached. The Führer might never have agreed to it, and Wolff, who was determined to sign it regardless, would have had to live with the shame of betrayal.

How great must have been Himmler's suffering in his last moments, Wolff surely felt, for having killed all those millions to please the Führer and pave the way to a new reign of Heinrich I—only to meet, ironically, so ignominious an end. All the while, Wolff himself denied that he knew of the genocide.

Colonel Kappler reached a more fortunate end. He was convicted in 1948 of murder in connection with the Ardeatine massacre and of extortion for his Jewish gold-gathering scheme. But he did not serve his life sentence, escaping from an Italian prison in 1977 and fleeing to Germany. He died at his home in Stuttgart a year later.

◆

After the war, the Allies arrested Ambassador Weizsäcker and tried him before a Nuremberg court for instigating war, taking part in the plunder of France, and participating in SS crimes, including the deportation of Jews. In his final plea he stood before the court a broken man, though with his usual haughty, defiant bearing, and asserted: "What does a sailor do when the weather and the captain have brought the ship into danger? Does he set to do all he can to help, with all the strength and all the means at his disposal? I did not attempt to leave the danger spot but tried to stick it out and fight, which was my decision. My goal was peace."

Weizsäcker was convicted and sent to prison in 1948. He was released in 1950 and died the following year.

◆

The Jewish community in Rome continued to suffer under the curse of the Holocaust long after the war was over. Israel Zolli, after being returned by Allied authorities to his position of chief rabbi, presided over a largely hostile congregation. He remained a source of division within the community, and even his supporters began to think that he should resign.

Zolli was deeply depressed—until Yom Kippur, the Day of Atonement, in autumn 1944. While conducting services in the temple on that holiest of Jewish holy days, he recounts in his memoirs:

> I felt so far withdrawn from the ritual that I let others recite the prayers and sing. I was conscious of neither joy nor sorrow. I was devoid of thought and feeling. My heart lay as though dead in my breast. And just then I saw with my mind's eye a meadow sweeping upward, with bright grass but with no flower. In this meadow I saw Jesus Christ clad in white mantle, and beyond His head the blue sky. I experienced the greatest interior peace.
>
> If I were to give an image of the state of my soul at that moment, I should say: a crystal-clear lake amid high mountains. Within my heart I found the words:
>
> "You are here for the last time."
>
> I considered them with the greatest serenity of soul and without any particular emotion. The reply of my heart was: So it is, so it shall be, so it must be.

That evening at home, his wife, according to Zolli, told him: "Today while you were before the Ark of the Torah, it seemed to me as if the white figure of Jesus put His hands on your head as if He were blessing you."

Zolli writes that he was "amazed but still very calm." He adds: "I pretended not to have understood." Then his youngest daughter, Miriam, called him to her room, he claims—though Miriam told me that she does not recall this episode—and said: "You are talking about Jesus Christ. You know, Papa, tonight I have been dreaming I saw a very tall, white Jesus, but I don't remember what came next."

What came next was that Zolli secretly began to take Catholic instruction while remaining in his position of chief rabbi. Under pressure from fellow Jewish leaders—who did not, however, suspect his plans—he resigned on February 1, 1945, and rejected an offer to head the Rabbinical College. Nevertheless, he continued to perform the duties of the rabbi—even presiding at divorce cases between sessions of Catholic instruction.

Finally, on February 13, Israel Zolli and his wife received the sacrament of baptism in the Basilica of Santa Maria degli Amgeli and entered the Catholic Church.

The Jews were shocked and incredulous on reading in the newspapers about what they termed Zolli's "treachery" and "deceit," convinced that he had converted not out of conviction but out of sheer spite. Otherwise, they asked, why would he keep his intention a secret? Why would he perform rabbinical functions until the very last day? Whatever the answers, Catholic priests who knew him insisted that he was sincere.

Zolli, who changed his first name from "Israel" to "Eugenio" in honor of the pope, began working for a small salary in the Vatican Library (the Jewish community refused to pay him the pension he claimed). He had finally been welcomed into the Vatican and now met the pope as he had been unable to do as a rabbi.

At least one Jewish official concedes that during the reign of Pope John XXIII, Zolli helped influence the historic revision of certain passages in the New Testament that had reflected unfavorably on the Jews. If this report is true, Zolli, ironically, performed as a Christian a service for the Jews far more important than any he might have performed as a Jew.

The former rabbi died in 1956 a lonely and impoverished man. The Jews despised him and, despite the Church's ill-concealed pleasure over its extraordinary conquest, many Catholics did not quite accept him. Zolli told visitors on his deathbed that a feeling of peace had at last filled his soul. But no one will ever know the feeling that filled his heart.

Bitterly hostile toward the Jewish community for what she regarded as its unfair treatment of her father, Miriam Zolli converted to Catholicism shortly after her parents had. She told me that she is only a nominal Catholic, having failed to find the satisfaction her father found in their new religion. But she nevertheless brought her children up as Catholics. Zolli's elder daughter, Dora, remained Jewish.

Shortly before he died, Zolli wrote in his memoirs that the pope "measured and foretold the greatness of the tragedy ... and took into his heart the pain of all the sufferers." But the former chief rabbi denied speculation that he converted because he was grateful to Pius XII for the Jews he had saved during the war. Even so, it was believed by some in the Vatican that Zolli's conversion helped show that Pius's role in dealing with the Holocaust was virtuous.

In any event, largely unknown to the public until now, the Hitlerian threat to the Vatican, which began before Eugenio Pacelli became pope and climaxed with the kidnap plot, primarily drove papal policy in the last years of World War II—most agonizingly when Pius found himself facing the greatest crime in history.

Notes

Prologue

1–4 **Wolff and his birthday party:** Interviews with Eugen Dollmann and Karl Wolff; Dollmann, *Call Me Coward,* pp. 11–20; *New York Times,* May 16, 1945.

Chapter 1: Prelude to Madness

5–7 **Hitler calls meeting after Mussolini ousted:** Interview with Rudolf Rahn; Louis P. Lochner, *The Goebbels Diaries, 1942–1943,* pp. 405–408.

8–10 **The king and the premier escape:** Interviews with Giacomo Carboni, Giuseppe Cosmelli, Peter Tompkins; Pietro Bagdoglio, *Italy in the Second World War;* Carboni, *Pi che il dovere;* Melvin Davis, *Who Defends Rome?;* Tompkins, *Italy Betrayed;* R. Zangrandi, *1943: 25 luglio–8 settembre* (dialogue involving the king, Mussolini, and Badoglio); "The Guilty Victor Emmanuel III," *Collier's,* June 10, 1944.

Chapter 2: Wolff in the Wolf's Lair

11–16 **Hitler orders Wolff to kidnap the pope:** Interviews with Wolff, Dollmann, Rahn; Wolff's notes on meeting with Hitler.

16–17 **Wolff as witness at Nuremberg:** *Trials of War Criminals Before the Nuremberg Military Tribunals,* vol. 5, pp. 771–778.

Chapter 3: The Plotters

19–22 **Himmler's background:** Interviews with Richard Breitman, Dollmann, Rahn, Wolff; Breitman, *The Architect of Genocide;* Willi Frischauer, *Himmler;* Felix Kersten, *The Kersten Memoirs, 1940–1945;* Jochen von Lang, *Top Nazi;* Roger Manvell and Heinrich Fraenkel, *Himmler;* Peter

Padfield, *Himmler;* Gerald Reitlinger, *The Final Solution;* H. R. Trevor-Roper, *The Last Days of Hitler.*

21 **The Madagascar project:** Reitlinger, pp. 76–78; Kersten, pp. 160–163.

23 **Heydrich and massacre at Lidice:** Frischauer, pp. 193–196.

23–24 **Massacre at Minsk:** Wolff trial file, *Staatsarchiv,* Munich.

25–26 **Medical experiments:** Ibid., pp. 177–182; *Trials of War Criminals,* vol. 5, pp. 771–778.

26–27 **Himmler letter to SS man with Jewish blood:** Manvell and Fraenkel, pp. 58–59.

27 **Heydrich and his Jewish ancestry:** Ibid., p. 82; some sources believe that only Sarah's husband was Jewish.

27–28 **Himmler and the Jewish girl:** Frischauer, pp. 72–73.

28 **Wolff and Eichmann:** Interview with Wolff; von Lang, *Top Nazi,* pp. 118–119.

28 **Wolff accused of courting Jewess:** Ibid., pp. 61–62.

28–29 **Himmler and Rothschild:** Frischauer, pp. 108–110.

31 **Wolff's letter to his wife re Hitler:** Wolff trial file, *Staatsarchiv,* Munich.

33–34 **Wolff catches drum major's baton:** Interview with Wolff; von Lang, *Top Nazi,* pp. 69–70.

34 **Wolff claims he sometimes opposed Himmler:** Interview with Wolff.

34–35 **Himmler, his marital problems, and his appointment of Wolff as his eventual successor:** Ibid., p. 187.

36 **Himmler and Aryan physical standards:** Ibid.; Frischauer, pp. 74–75.

36–37 **Care of Wolff and Himmler for each other's interests:** Interview with Wolff, Dollmann; Frischauer, pp. 74–75.

37–38 **Himmler as "reincarnation" of Heinrich I:** Interviews with Wolff, Dollmann; Frischauer, pp. 85–88; Kersten, p. 238.

38 **The path of Genghis Kahn:** Interview with Wolff; Trevor-Roper, p. 47; Hugh Thomas, *The Strange Death of Heinrich Himmler,* p. 15.

Chapter 4: Flirting with Treason

39–41 **Himmler, Hitler, and Wolff's divorce problems:** Interview with Dollmann; Wolff trial file, *Statsarchiv,* Munich; von Lang, *Top Nazi,* pp. 202–207.

40–41 **Himmler and *Lebensborn:*** von Lang, *Top Nazi,* pp. 97–100; Frischauer, pp. 138–139.

41 **Wolff's illness, conflict with Himmler, and transfer to Italy:** Interview with Wolff.

42–44 **Himmler, Wolff, and Schellenberg:** Reinhard R. Doerries, *Hitler's Last Chief of Intelligence* (Allied interrogations of Walter Schellenberg), pp. 115–116.

44–46 Himmler and religion: Kersten, pp. 150–151.
46 Birth ceremony for Wolff's son: Interview with Dollmann.

Chapter 5: Fighting for Hitler's Ear

49–50 Wolff plans attack on Vatican: Interview with Wolff.

50–51 Wolff meets with Kesselring: Interviews with Dollmann, Rahn, Wolff.

51–52 Rahn and Möllhausen: Interviews with both.

52–53 The conspiracy to save the pope: Interviews with Dollmann, Albrecht von Kessel, Möllhausen, Rahn, Wolff.

53–62 Rahn meets with Hitler and other top Nazis: Interview with Rahn (including Hitler's statements).

56–58 Himmler, Wolff, Popitz, and Langbehn: Interview with Wolff; Sefton Delmer, *Black Boomerang*, pp. 216–217.

58–60 Bormann and Christianity: Interview with Rahn; Jochen von Lang, *The Secretary*, pp. 125–137.

Chapter 6: The Only Way to Save Germany

63–73 Weizsäcker's background: Interviews with his wife, Marianne von Weizsäcker, his son, Richard, and Leonidas Hill; Weizsäcker, *Memoirs; Journal of Contemporary History* (January 1968); Hill, "Three Crises, 1938–39," *Journal of Modern History* (June 1967); Hill, *The Vatican Embassy of Ernst von Weizsäcker, 1943–1945; Rundbriefe aus Rom* (collection of unpublished letters sent by Weizsäcker from Rome to his family, furnished me by his wife, Marianne); Official Record, United States Military Tribunals, Nuremberg (Case No. 11, Tribunal IV [IVA], U.S. vs. Ernst von Weizsäcker et al., vol. 28), 1948; pistol story from a defense affidavit written by Weizsäcker's daughter-in-law, Gundalena, to whom he told it.

64–66 Weizsäcker and the Jews: Weizsäcker, pp. 270–271.

69–71 The pope supports a military coup: Interviews with Father Peter Gumpel, Father Angelo Sodano, and other Vatican officials; Harold C. Deutsch, *The Conspiracy Against Hitler in the Twilight War*, pp. 102–128. Comment on the pope's daring "akin to foolhardiness," p. 121. Osborne cable to foreign office, London (date unknown).

72 Leonidas Hill's comment: "Three Crises, 1938–39," *Journal of Contemporary History* (January 1968).

Chapter 7: Closer to Himmler than to *Himmel*

74 The pope's reaction to Project Pontiff: Interview with anonymous Vatican official.

74 **Ciano plan to oust the pope:** Interview with Father Robert Graham; *Domenica del Corriere* (Rome), March 14, 1972.

75 **Vatican officials fear Nazi strike:** Interview with Father Robert Graham; David Alvarez and Graham, *Nothing Sacred,* p. 84; *New York Herald Tribune,* March 22, 1963 (interview with Archbishop Egidio Vagnozzi).

75 **Choosing successor to Pius:** Interview with anonymous Vatican official.

75 **Weizsäcker cable to Berlin:** August 4, September 10, 1943.

75–76 **Weizsäcker meets with Kessel:** Interview with Kessel; Eric Bentley, *Storm Over the Deputy* (Kessel contribution, including quote), pp. 74–75.

76 **Tittmann and Warsaw ghetto massacre:** Interview with Harold Tittmann; Tittmann, *Inside the Vatican of Pius XII,* p. 120.

76 **Fahrener warns Jews of roundup:** Interview with Kessel.

77 **Himmler cables Kappler re roundup:** Robert Katz, *Black Sabbath,* pp. 222–223.

77 **SS report on occupation of St. Peter's Square:** Pinchas Lapide, *Three Popes and the Jews,* p. 235. OSS reports, U.S. National Archives.

78 **Weizsäcker cables Ribbentrop re Vatican sovereignty:** September 18, 1943.

78–79 **Ribbentrop cables Weizsäcker re Roosevelt comment:** October 4, 1943.

80–81 **Himmler sends second message to Kappler; Möllhausen reads it and replies:** Interview with Möllhausen.

Chapter 8: A Wandering Dog

82–86 **Zolli urges Jewish leaders to warn congregation and flees:** Interviews with Renzo Levi, Goffredo Roccas, and Eugenio (Israel) Zolli's daughter Miriam; E. Zolli, *Before the Dawn,* pp. 141–151 (including dialogue).

86–88 **Fascism and the Jews:** De Felice, *Storia degli ebrei italiani sotto il fascismo;* Lochner, *The Goebbels Diaries;* Attilio Milano, *Il ghetto di Roma* and *Storia degli ebrei in Italia;* Cecil Roth, *The History of the Jews of Italy; On the Jewish Question in Fascist Italy,* Yad Vashem Studies, vol. 4; Marcel Grilli, "The Role of the Jews in Modern Italy," *The Menorah Journal* (Winter 1940).

Chapter 9: A Prisoner of Sorts

89–90 **British black radio broadcasts and the pope's reaction:** Sefton Delmer, *Black Boomerang,* p. 119; Mella Di Santella, *Instantaneo inedite degli ultimi 4 papi.*

90 **Vatican informed that the pope would be safe:** Interview with Dollmann.

90–93 **Weizsäcker visits the pope, October 9:** Interview with Albrecht von Kessel; Weizsäcker, *Memoirs,* pp. 286–287; Weizsäcker's cable to Ribbentrop, October 9, 1943.

93–94 **The pope's family background:** Constantine, *The Pope;* Alden Hatch and Seamus Walsh, *Crown of Glory;* John N. McKnight, *The Papacy;* Margherita Marchione, *Man of Peace: Pope Pius XII.*

Chapter 10: Out of Fear of Men

95–104 **Pacelli, the Concordat, and German Catholics:** Interview with Graham; Hitler's comment was in *Voelkischer Beobachter,* February 22, 1929, as was quote from Italian expert; varied views from Marchione, *Pope Pius XII;* Guenter Lewy, *The Catholic Church and Nazi Germany;* Klaus Scholder, *The Churches and the Third Reich,* vol. 1; and Gordon C. Zahn, *German Catholics and Hitler's Wars.*

Chapter 11: Living with God and the Devil

105–113 **Choice of evils—Nazism or communism:** Interview with Graham; "Informal Notes by Monsignor Domenico Tardini, May 30, 1943," British National Archives; letter from Osborne, British minister to the Holy See, to Anthony Eden, foreign office, London, April 26, 1943, British National Archives; Tardini memo to Myron Taylor, September 1942, U.S. National Archives.

105–106 **Menshausen on Russian and German threats to Church:** German diplomatic records, U.S. National Archives.

106–107 **Tardini, the British, and Taylor:** Owen Chadwick, *Britain and the Vatican During World War II,* pp. 213–214.

109 **The pope's remark to visitor re Nazi danger:** Interview with Graham.

109–111 **The pope and the communist parties:** Interviews with Giorgio Amendola, Rosario Bentivegna, Carla Capponi, Giorgio Caputo, Mario Fiorentini, Pietro Griffoni, Carlo Salinari, Antonello Trombadorf; *Foreign Relations of the United States, 1943,* vol. 2 (Tittmann audience, October 19); Amendola, *Il sole e sorto a Roma;* Roberto Battaglia, *The Story of the Italian Resistance;* Daniel Blackmer, *Unity in Diversity;* Benedetto, Croce, *The King and the Allies;* Robert Katz, *Death in Rome;* Luigi Longo, *Un popolo alla macchia;* Renato Perrone Capano, *La Resistenza in Roma;* E. Piscitelli, *Storia della Resistenza romana;* Carlo Trabucco, *La prigionia di roma;* thesis on history of Italian communism by Joan B. Urban, Catholic University, Washington, D.C.; OSS reports; Herbert L. Matthews, "A

New Chapter in Eternal Rome," *New York Times Magazine,* June 18, 1944.

111–113 **The pope and the moderate anti-Nazi parties:** Interviews with Luigi Barzini, Ugo La Malfa, Pietro Nenni, Sandro Pertini, Giuliano Vassalli; C.F.D. Delzell, *Mussolini's Enemies: The Italian Anti-Fascist Resistance;* Max Salvadori, *Brief History of the Patriot Movement in Italy, 1943–1945.*

113–114 **The torture chambers:** Interviews with Dollmann and Möllhausen; Goffredo Roccas's collection of material on fascist criminals, Rome.

Chapter 12: A Blueprint for Massacre

115 **Bormann sends Wemmer to Rome:** Interview with Kessel.

115 **Diplomats burn their papers:** Interview with Tittman.

116 **Kessel comments on papal abduction plan:** Interview with Kessel.

116–118 **Operation Rabat:** *Alcuni documenti "riservatissimi" della RSI,* Annali di storia moderna e contemporanea, by Professor Anna Lisa Carlotti, who discovered the letter involving the two fascist leaders in a Milan University archive.

118–119 **Plan for the pope's escape:** Interview with Marchione, anonymous Vatican official; Marchione, *Pope Pius XII,* pp. 79–80.

Chapter 13: An Agonizing Dilemma

121 **The pope calls genocide reports exaggerated:** Foreign Relations, 1943, vol. 2 (Tittmann report).

122 **The pope doesn't explicitly condemn atrocities:** Tittmann, p. 122.

122 **Kessel on the pope's policy:** Bentley, p. 71 (Kessel contribution).

122–123 **Osborne writes of morality and neutralism:** Osborne's diary, January 5, 1943 (Chadwick, p. 213).

123 **The pope fears blame for German defeat:** Interview with Tittmann; Tittmann, p. 122.

123 **The fate of Dutch Jews:** Joseph Bottum and David G. Dalin, *The Pius Wars* (Dalin contribution), p. 20; Margherita Marchione, *Consensus & Controversy,* p. 30.

124–125 **Orsenigo fails in talk with Hitler:** From report made available by Vatican official.

127 **The pope meets with Ribbentrop:** Interview with Graham; John Cornwell, *Hitler's Pope,* pp. 238–239; Dalin (contribution to *The Pius War*), p. 18; *New York Times,* March 14, 1943.

127–128 **The pope's Jewish schoolmate:** Interview with Marchione; Marchione, *Pope Pius XII,* pp. 24–25.

128 Letter describes revolutionary events in 1918 Germany: Cornwell, pp. 74–75.

129 Osborne and "policy of silence": Chadwick, p. 213.

130 The pope burns his protest: Interview with Marchione; Marchione, *Pope Pius XII*, p. 79.

130–131 Encyclical *With Burning Concern:* Ernst Christian Helmreich, *The German Churches Under Hitler*, p. 281; Pinchas Lapide, *Three Popes and the Jews*, p. 111; Marchione, *Consensus and Controversy*, pp. 30–31; Zahn, p. 76.

133 Rabbi Dalin quotes the Talmud: Bottum and Dalin (Dalin contribution), p. 20.

Chapter 14: The Art of Examining Walls

135–140 Zolli's mission to the Vatican: Interview with M. Zolli; E. Zolli, *Before the Dawn*, pp. 159–161 (including dialogue).

140–142 Kappler meets with Foa and Almansi: Dante Almansi report *(Prima relazione al governo italiano circa le persecuzioni nazi-fasciste degli ebrei in roma [settembre 1943–giugno 1944])*; Ugo Foa, *Relazione del presidente della comunite israelitica di Roma Foa Ugo circa le misure razziali adottate in Roma dopo 18 settembre a diretta opera delle autorite tedesche di occupazione,* November 15, 1943, and June 20, 1944 (booklet); testimony, Herbert Kappler trial (Foa, June 11, 1948; Kappler, June 1, 11, 1948).

143–144 Jews bring gold for the Germans: Interviews with Levi, Roccas, M. Zolli; Katz, *The Battle for Rome*, pp. 74–76; Giacomo Debenedetti, *16 ottobre 1943;* Renzo de Felice, *Storia degli ebrei italiano soto il fascismo;* C. Lizzani, *L'oro di Roma;* "Perche non si difesero," *L'Expresso* (Rome), December 3, 1961.

Chapter 15: A Question of Priority

147 Karski and the Warsaw Ghetto fighters: Jan Karski, *Story of a Secret State* (including dialogue).

148 Ben-Gurion and the Holocaust: Dan Kurzman, *Ben-Gurion: Prophet of Fire*, pp. 236–237; Gruenbaum quote, *Haboker* (Israel), December 7, 1942.

149–151 The pope and the bombing of Lorenzo: Interviews with Vatican officials and bombing survivors, including Angela Maria Romano; Hatch and Walshe, *Crown of Glory* (including dialogue); Nazareno Padellaro, *Portrait of Pius XII;* Myron C. Taylor, *Wartime Correspondence Between President Roosevelt and Pius XII,* vol. 2, *Foreign Relations of the United States, 1943* (Tittmann audience with the pope, October 19).

151–152 **Osborne: "The more I think of it . . . ":** Chadwick, p. 216.

152 **Tittmann: The pope threatens public protest against bombing:** Taylor, *Foreign Relations of the United States*, vol. 1, p. 911.

152–153 **A petition "favoring" the Jews:** Guenter Lewy, *The Catholic Church and Nazi Germany*, pp. 291–292.

154 **Tittmann feels Pius chose "better path":** Tittmann, pp. 122–123.

155 **Pacelli confronts communists in 1919:** Cornwell, pp. 76–77; Pasqualina Lehnert, *Ich durfte Ihm dienen: Erinnerungen an Papst Pius XII,* p. 15.

156–159 **Finding the gold:** Interview with M. Zolli; E. Zolli, *Before the Dawn,* pp. 159–161 (including dialogue).

157–158 **Levi, Foa, and the gold:** Interview with Levi.

159 **Kessel asks Fahrener to warn Jews to hide:** Interview with Kessel (including quote).

Chapter 16: Eve of Desperation

160 **The cancelled coup:** OSS records, U.S. National Archives.

161–162 **Delmer and his Himmler campaign:** Delmer, p. 216–221.

162–166 **Möllhausen, Stahel, Kappler, Kesselring discuss Himmler's message:** Interviews with Kessel, Möllhausen, Rahn; German Embassy, Rome, diplomatic dispatches.

166–168 **Möllhausen and his messages to Berlin:** Interviews with Kessel, Möllhausen, Rahn; German Embassy, Rome, diplomatic dispatches.

171 **Wolff meets with Hitler on October 7:** Interviews with Dollmann, Wolff.

171 **Kaltenbrunner cables Kappler on October 11:** OSS records, U.S. National Archives.

171–172 **Wolff testifies re Himmler's order to deport Jews:** *Trials of War Criminals Before the Nuremberg Military Tribunals,* vol. 5, pp. 771–778.

172–176 **Dollmann meets with Hitler:** Interview with Dollmann; Dollmann, *The Interpreter,* pp. 282–284, and *Roma Nazista* (dialogue).

Chapter 17: "But They Promised Me"

177–179 **Princess Pignatelli pleads with the pope to save Jews:** Interview with the princess.

179–183 **Weizsäcker-Maglione meeting:** Interviews with Graham, Kessel, Father Burkhart Schneider, and other Church officials; memorandum written by Maglione after meeting.

183–185 **German diplomats plot to save Jews:** Interviews with Gerhard Gumpert, Kessel, Möllhausen, Rahn. Vatican officials claim that the pope's nephew, Carlo Pacelli, initiated the Hudal protest, though Kessel and Gumpert told me in separate interviews that it was *they* who did so.

185–186 **Kappler cables Himmler on results of roundup:** OSS records, U.S. National Archives.

187–188 **Deportation of Jews:** Interviews with Levi, Ravenna; S. Bertoldi, *I tedeschi in Italia;* Debenedetti, *16 ottobre 1943;* Katz, *Black Sabbath;* S. Sorani's diary.

188–189 **Weizsäcker misleads Berlin re the pope's attitude:** His cable to Berlin, October 17, 1943.

191 **Kaltenbrunner on euthanasia:** Memorandum to Ribbentrop.

Chapter 18: A Bargain in Blood

193–195 **Wolff on October 16:** Interviews with Dollmann, Rahn, Wolff; *Trials of War Criminals Before the Nuremberg Military Tribunals,* vol. 5, pp. 771–778; Wolff trial file, *Staatsarchiv,* Munich.

195–196 **Hitler calls off kidnap plan:** Ibid.

Chapter 19: The Mathematics of Murder

198–200 **Communists attack Germans on Via Rasella:** Interviews with Giorgio Amendola, Rosario Bentivegna, Carla Capponi, Georgio Caputo, Mario Fiorentini, Pietro Griffoni, Carlo Salinari, and Antonello Trombadori; Amendola, *Il sole è sorto a Roma;* Katz, *Death in Rome;* Luigi Longo, *Un popolo alla macchia;* Renato Perrone Capano, *La Resistenza in Roma;* E. Piscitelli, *Storia della Resistenza romana;* Carlo Trabucco, *La prigionia di Roma;* thesis on history of Italian communism by Joan B. Urban, Catholic University, Washington, DC; OSS records, U.S. National Archives; Herbert L. Matthews, "A New Chapter in Eternal Rome," *New York Times Magazine,* June 18, 1944.

201–211 **Germans retaliate:** See above note; interviews with Dollmann, Kessel, Möllhausen, and Wolff (each whenever he is involved); Dollmann, *Roma Nazista;* Möllhausen (dialogue); Paolo Monelli, *Roma 1943;* Ardeatine Caves Commission, inquest (*Sommario dell'incidente del 23 marzo 1944* [Rome]); Kappler's testimony, Italian trial record (dialogue when Möllhausen not present); *Il Messaggero,* March 25, 1944; *L'Osservatore Romano,* March 24, 1944.

Chapter 20: The Path to the Vatican

211–213 **Resistance to Roman deportation plan and effort to keep the pope silent about executions:** Interviews with Dollmann, Möllhausen; Möllhausen (dialogue).

213–216 **Wolff seeks meeting with the pope, sees Zeiger:** Interview with Dollmann.

216–218 **Dollmann and Virginia Agnelli:** Ibid.; interviews with Giovanni Agnelli, Jolanda Berardi, Carla Colli, Susana Agnelli (Contessa Pattazzi), Lydia Redmond (Princess San Faustino).

218–219 **The pope agrees to see Wolff:** Interviews with Dollmann and Wolff.

Chapter 21: The Odd Couple

220–223 **Pius-Wolff meeting:** Interviews with Dollmann and Wolff.

Chapter 22: Meeting a New Conqueror

224–227 **Nazis and fascists flee Rome:** Interviews with Dollmann, Rahn; Dollmann, *The Interpreter* and *Roma Nazista*; Albert Kesselring, *A Soldier's Story*; Peter Tompkins, *A Spy in Rome*; U.S. Tenth Army records.

225 **Carla, Rosario, and the "revolution":** Interview with both.

227–229 **Roman celebrations:** Interviews with many Romans; Eric Severeid, *Not So Wild a Dream*; *New York Herald-Tribune*, June 5, 1944 (article by Homer Bigart); *New York Times*, June 6, 1944; Daniel Lang, "Letter from Rome," *New Yorker*, June 17 and 24, 1944; *Stars and Stripes* (Rome), June 5 to 12, 1944 (varied articles on Allied welcome).

226–228 **Weizsäcker and the Allies' arrival:** Interview with Marianne von Weizsäcker; her diary; Weizsäcker, *Memoirs*, p. 292, and *Rundbriefe aus Rom*; OSS report, A-42208, 1943, U.S. National Archives (Weizsäcker concealed Jewish family).

227–228 **Anglo-Americans "oppose" papal peace mediation:** OSS report, A-42208, 1943, U.S. National Archives.

228 **The pope speaks to Romans:** Interviews with many Romans; *New York Herald-Tribune*, *New York Times*, and *Stars and Stripes*, June 6, 1944.

229–230 **Clark meets the pope:** Interview with Mark Clark; Clark, *Calculated Risk* (dialogue).

Chapter 23: Saved from the Noose

232–239 **Wolff's role in peace deal with Dulles:** Interviews with Dollmann, Rahn, Wolff; Allen Dulles, *The Secret Surrender*, pp. 130–177; Wolff interrogation reports and secret prison recordings of Wolff conversations with other war criminals, British National Archives; OSS reports on Operation Sunrise, U.S. National Archives.

Epilogue

242–243 **Wolff enters new world:** Interview with Wolff; von Lang, *Top Nazi,* pp. 361–365.

242–243 **Dollmann "escapes" from prison:** Interview with Dollmann; interrogation by OSS intelligence, U.S. National Archives.

243 **Himmler and the poison pill:** Frischauer; Manvell and Fraenkel.

244 **Weizsäcker sentenced to prison:** Interview with Marianne von Weizsäcker; her diary; Weizsäcker, *Memoirs,* pp. 310–312 (quote, p. 310).

245–247 **Zolli converts to Christianity:** Interview with Levi, Roccas, M. Zolli; E. Zolli, *Before the Dawn,* pp. 177–184 (including dialogue).

Bibliography

Books

Alfieri, Dino. *Dictators Face to Face*. London: Elek, 1954.

Algardi, Z. *Processi ai fascisti*. Florence: Parenti, 1958.

Alvarez, David J., and Robert A. Graham. *Nothing Sacred*. London and Portland, OR: F. Cass, 1997.

Aly, Gotz, *Endlösung: Völkerverschiebung und der Mord an den europäischen Juden*, Frankfurt am Main, 1995.

Anfuso, Filippo. *Roma Berlino Salo*. Milan: Garzanti, 1950.

Arendt, Hannah. *Eichmann in Jerusalem*. New York: Viking, 1965.

Ascarelli, A. *Le fosse ardeatine*. Rome: Palombi, 1945.

Bacino, Ezio. *Roma prima e dopo*. Rome: Atlantica, 1950.

Badoglio, Marshal Pietro. *Italy in the Second World War*. New York: Oxford, 1948.

Bandiera Rossa. N.d.

Barkai, M., ed. *The Fighting Ghettos*. Philadelphia: Lippincott, 1962.

Bartoli, Domenico. *La fine della monarchia*. Milan: Mondadori, 1947.

Battaglia, Roberto. *The Story of the Italian Resistance*. London: Odhams, 1956.

Bedarida, Guido. *Ebrei d'Italia*. Leghorn: Terrona, 1950.

Bentley, Eric, ed. *The Storm over the Deputy*. New York: Grove, 1964.

Berliner, Abraham. *Geschichte der Juden in Rom*. Frankfurt: Kauffmann, 1893.

Blet, Pierre. *Pius XII and the Second World War*. New York: Paulist Press, 1999.

Blustein, G. *Storia, degli ebrei in Roma*. Rome: Maglione and Stromo, 1921.

Bolla, Nino. *Dieci mesi di governo Badoglio*. Rome: Nuova Epoca, 1945.

Bottum, Joseph, and David G. Dalin, eds., *The Pius War*. New York: Lexington Books, 2004.

Breitman, Richard, Norman J. W. Goda, Timothy Naftali, and Robert Wolfe. *U.S. Intelligence and the Nazis*. National Archives Trust Fund Board: Washington, DC, n.d.

_____. *The Architect of Genocide*. New York: Knopf, 1991.

Bruce, David Kirkpatrick Este. *OSS Against the Reich*. Kent, Ohio: Kent State University Press, 1991.

Buckley, Christopher. *The Road to Rome*. London: Hodder & Stoughton, 1945.

Bull, George Anthony. *Inside the Vatican*. London: Hutchinson, 1982.

Bullock, Alan. *Hitler: A Study in Tyranny*. New York: Harper, 1953.

Burleigh, Michael. *Sacred Causes*. New York: HarperCollins, 2007.

Capano, Renato Perrone. *La Resistenza in Roma*. 2 vols. Naples: Macchiaroli, 1963.

Carboni, Giacomo. *Italia tradita dall'armistizie all pace*. Rome: EDA, 1947.

_____. *L'armistizio e la difesa di Roma*. Rome: De Luigi, 1945.

Carli-Bollola, R. *Storia della resisstenza*. Milan: Avanti, 1957.

Carpi, Daniel. *The Catholic Church and Italian Jewry Under the Fascists* (Yad Vashem Studies IV). Jerusalem: Yad Vashem, 1960.

Carroll, James. *Constantine's Sword*. Boston: Houghton Mifflin, 2001.

Carroll-Abbing, J. Patrick. *But for the Grace of God*. New York: Delacorte, 1965.

Chadwick, Owen. *Britain and the Vatican During the Second World War*. Cambridge and New York: Cambridge University Press, 1986.

Cianferro, Camille. *The Vatican and the War*. New York: Dutton, 1954.

Ciano, Galeazzo. *Ciano's Hidden Diary, 1937–1938*. New York: Dutton, 1953.

_____. *The Ciano Diaries, 1939–1943*. New York: Doubleday, 1946.

Clark, Mark W. *Calculated Risk*. New York: Harper, 1950.

Colvin, Ian. *Chief of Intelligence*. London: Gollancz, 1951.

Consiglio, Alberto. *Vita de Vittorio Emanuele III*. Milan: Rizzoli, 1950.

Constantine, Prince of Bavaria. *The Pope*. New York: Roy, 1956.

Conway, John S. *Nazi Persecution of the Churches. 1933–1945*. New York: Basic Books, 1969.

Cornwell, John. *Hitler's Pope*. Viking: 1999.

Crankshaw, Edward. *Gestapo*. New York: Viking, 1956.

Croce, Benedetto. *The King and the Allies*. London: Allen and Unwin, 1950.

Dalin, David. *The Myth of "Hitler's Pope."* Chicago: Regnary, 2006.

Davis, Melton. *Who Defends Rome?* New York: Dial, 1972.

Deakin, F. W. *The Brutal Friendship*. London: Weidenfeld & Nicolson, 1962.

Debenedetti, Giacomo. *16 ottobre 1943*. Rome: O.E.T., 1944. (Originally printed in *Mercurio* [Rome], December 1944.)

De Felice, Renzo. *Storia degli ebrei italiani sotto il fascismo*. Turin: Einaudi, 1961.

Delmer, Sefton. *Black Boomerang*. New York: Viking, 1962.

Delzell, Charles F. *Mussolini's Enemies*. Princeton, NJ: Princeton University Press, 1961.

Deutsch, Harold C. *The Conspiracy Against Hitler in the Twilight War*. Minneapolis: University of Minnesota Press, 1968.

Dineen, Joseph F. *Pius XII, Pope of Peace*. New York: McBride, 1951.

Di Santella, Mella. *Istantaneo inedite degli ultimi 4 papi, roma*. N.d.

Doerries, Reinhard R. *Hitler's Last Chief of Foreign Intelligence*. London and Portland, OR: F. Cass, 2003.

Dollmann, Eugen. *Call Me Coward*. London: Kimber, 1956.

_____. *The Interpreter*. London: Hutchinson, 1967.

_____. *Roma Nazista*. Milan: Longanesi, 1949.

Doyle, Charles Hugo. *Life of Pius XII*. New York: Didier, 1945.

Duclos, Paul. *Le Vatican et la seconde guerre mondiale*. Paris: Pedone, 1955.

Dulles, Allen. *Germany's Underground*. New York: Macmillan, 1947.

_____. *The Secret Surrender*. New York: Harper & Row, 1966.

Ebrei in Italia durante il fascismo. Milan: 1962.

Falconi, Carlo. *The Silence of Pius XII*. Boston: Little, Brown, 1970.

Farago, Ladislas. *Aftermath*. New York: Simon & Schuster, 1974.

Fisher, Desmond. *Pope Pius XII and the Jews*. New York: Paulist Press, 1963.

Foa, Ugo. *Relazione del presidente della comunita israelitica di Roma Foa Ugo circa le misure razziali adottate in Roma dopo 18 settembre a diretta opera delle autorita tedesche di occupazione*. Rome: Nov. 15, 1943, and June 20, 1944 (booklet).

Fogarty, Gerald P. *The Vatican and the American Hierarchy from 1870 to 1965*. Stuttgart: Hierseman, 1982.

Foreign Relations of the United States. 1943, vol. 2; 1944, vols. 2, 4. Washington, DC: GPO, 1943, 1944.

Friedlander, Saul. *Pius XII and the Third Reich*. New York: Knopf, 1966.

Frischauer, Willi. *Himmler, the Evil Genius of the Third Reich*. London: Odhams, 1953.

Gabrieli, Giuseppe. *Italia Judaica*. Rome: Fond, Leonardo, 1924.

Gilbert, Martin. *Auschwitz and the Allies*. New York: Holt, Rinehart and Winston, 1985.

_____. *The Righteous: The Unsung Heroes of the Holocaust*. New York: Henry Holt, 2003.

Graham, Robert A. *Vatican Diplomacy*. Princeton, NJ: Princeton University Press, 1959.

_____. *Pius XII's Defense of Jews and Others, 1944–45*. Milwaukee, WI: Catholic League Publications, 1987.

Gregorovius, F. *The Ghetto and the Jews of Rome*. New York: Schocken, 1948.

Halecki, Oscar. *Pius XII: Eugenio Pacelli, Pope of Peace*. New York: Farrar, Straus and Giroux, 1954.

Halperin, S. W. *Mussolini and Italian Fascism*. Princeton, NJ: Princeton University Press, 1970.

Hassell, Ulrich von. *The von Hassell Diaries*. Boulder, CO: Westview Press, 1994.

Heideking, J., and M. Frey, eds. *American Intelligence and the German Resistance to Hitler*. Boulder, CO: Westview Press, 1996.

_____. *Hitler Directs His Army*. Germany: *Wehrmacht, Oberkommando*, n.d.

Hochhuth, Rolf. "Sidelights on History" (appendix to *The Deputy*). New York: Grove, 1964.

International Military Tribunal. *Trials of the Major War Criminals Before the International Military Tribunals, Nuremberg, November 1945–April 1949.* Nuremberg: The Tribunal, 1949–1953; Washington, DC: GPO, 1949 and 1953.

Katz, Robert. *Black Sabbath.* New York: Macmillan, 1969.

_____. *Death in Rome.* New York: Macmillan, 1969.

_____. *The Battle for Rome.* New York & London: Simon & Schuster, 2003.

Keitel, Wilhelm. *The Memoirs of Field Marshal Keitel.* New York: Stein and Day, 1966.

Kershaw, Ian. *Hitler: 1936–1945: Nemesis.* New York: Norton, 2000.

Kersten, Felix. *The Kersten Memoirs, 1940–1945.* New York: Macmillan, 1957.

Kesselring, Albert. *A Soldier's Story.* New York: Morrow, 1954.

Kilzer, Louis C. *Hitler's Traitor.* Novato, CA: Presidio Press, 2000.

Kirkpatrick, Ivone. *Mussolini: A Study in Power.* Englewood Cliffs, NJ: Hawthorn, 1964.

Klemperer, Klemens von. *German Resistance Against Hitler.* Oxford: Clarendon Press; New York: Oxford University Press, 1992.

Konstantine, Prince of Bavaria. *The Pope: A Portrait from Life.* London: Wingate, 1954.

Lamb, Richard. *War in Italy, 1943–1945.* London: John Murray, 1993.

Lang, Jochen von. *Top Nazi.* New York: Enigma Books, 2005.

_____. *The Secretary.* New York: Random House, 1979.

Lapide, Pinchas. *Three Popes and the Jews.* New York: Hawthorne Books, 1967.

Lawler, Justus George. *Popes and Politics.* New York: Continuum, 2002.

Lehnert, Pascalina. *Pio XII, Ich durfte Ihm dienen: Erinnerungen an Papst Pius XII.* Wurzburg: 1982 (German).

Lettres de Pie XII aux Eveques Allemands, 1939–1944. Rome: Libreria Editrice Vaticana, 1966 (French).

Lewy, Gunther. *The Catholic Church and Nazi Germany.* New York: McGraw-Hill, 1964.

Lichten, Joseph. *A Question of Judgment.* Washington, DC: National Catholic Welfare Conference, 1963.

Linklater, Eric. *The Campaign in Italy.* London: HMSO, 1951.

Lochner, Louis P., ed., *The Goebbels Diaries, 1942–43.* Garden City, NY: Doubleday, 1948.

Macksey, Kenneth. *Kesselring.* London: Greenhill Books, 2000; Mechanicsburg, PA: Stackpole Books, 2000.

Manvell, Roger, and Heinrich Fraenkel. *Himmler.* New York: Putnam, 1965.

Marchione, Margherita. *Yours Is a Precious Witness.* New York: Paulist Press, 1997.

_____. *Pope Pius XII, Architect of Peace.* New York: Paulist Press, 2000.

_____. *Consensus & Controversy.* New York: Paulist Press, 2002.

_____. *Man of Peace: Pope Pius XII.* New York: Paulist Press, 2003.

_____. *Pope Pius XII.* Milan: Ancora Editrice, 2003.

McDermitt, Thomas. *Keeper of the Keys: Life of Pope Pius XII*. Milwaukee, WI: Bruce, 1946.

McKnight, John P. *The Papacy*. London: McGraw-Hill, 1953.

Mellini Ponce de Leon, A. *Guerra diplomatica a Salo*. Bologna: Cappeli.

Michaelis, Meir. *On the Jewish Question in Fascist Italy* (Yad Vashem Studies IV). Jerusalem: Yad Vashem, 1960.

Milano, Attilio. *Storia degli ebrei in Italia*. Turin: Einaudi, 1963.

Möllhausen, Eitel. *La carta pendente*. Rome: Sestante, 1948.

Newman, Louis I. *A "Chief Rabbi" of Rome Becomes a Catholic*. New York: Renaissance Press, 1945.

Norton-Taylor, Richard. *Nuremberg: The War Crimes Trial*. London: Nick Hern Books, 1997.

Official Record, United States Military Tribunals, Nuremberg. Case No. 11, Tribunal IV (IVA), U.S. vs. Ernst von Weizsäcker et al., vol. 28, 1948.

Padellaro, Nazareno. *Portrait of Pius XII*. London: Dent, 1956.

Padfield, Peter. *Himmler*. New York: MJF Books, 1990.

Pallenberg, Corrado. *Inside the Vatican*. Englewood Cliffs, NJ: Hawthorn, 1960.

Peterson, Neal H., ed. *From Hitler's Doorstep: The Wartime Intelligence Reports of Allen Dulles, 1942–1945*. University Park: Pennsylvania State University Press, 1996.

Phayer, Michael. *The Catholic Church and the Holocaust, 1930–1965*. Bloomington: Indiana University Press, 2001.

Pichon, Charles. *The Vatican and Its Role in World Affairs*. New York: Dutton, 1950.

Pietra, I. and R. Muratore. *La Resistance Italienne*. Milan: Archivio storico del C.V.I., 1949 (Italian).

Pisano, G. *Mussolini e gli ebrei*. Milan: FPE, 1967.

Poliakov, Leon. *Il nazismo e la sterminio degli ebrei*. Turin: Einaudi, 1955.

Rahn, Rudolf. *Ruheloses Leben*. Dusseldorf: Diedenrichs, 1949.

Ramati, Alexander. *The Assisi Underground: The Priests Who Rescued Jews*. New York: Stein and Day, 1978.

Reese, Thomas J. *Inside the Vatican*. Cambridge, MA: Harvard University Press, 1996.

Reitlinger, Gerald. *The Final Solution*. New York: Beechhurst, 1953.

Reynolds, Robert L. *Story of the Pope*. New York: Dell, 1957.

Ribbentrop, Joachim von. *The Ribbentrop Memoirs*. London: Weidenfeld & Nicolson, 1954.

Ripa di Meana, Fulvia. *Roma clandestina*. Rome: O.E.T., 1945 (Italian).

Roth, Cecil. *The History of the Jews of Italy*. Philadelphia: Jewish Publication Society of America, 1946.

Rychlak, Ronald J. *Righteous Gentiles*. Dallas, TX: Spence Publishing, 2005.

Salvadori, Max. *Brief History of the Patriot Movement in Italy, 1943–1945*. Chicago: Clemente, 1954.

Sanchez, Jose M. *Pius XII and the Holocaust*. Washington, DC: Catholic University of American Press, 2002.

Scaroni, Silvio. *Con Vittorio Emanuele III*. Milan: Mondadori, 1954.

Schellenberg, Walter. *The Labyrinth*. New York: Harper, 1956.

_____. *The Schellenberg Memoirs*. London: A. Deutsch, 1956.

Schotland, A. P. *Der Fall Kesselring*. Bonn: Leellen, 1952.

Scrivener, Jane. *Inside Rome with the Germans*. New York: Macmillan, 1945 (German and English).

Skorzeny, Otto. *Skorzeny's Secret Missions*. New York: Dutton, 1950.

Stehlin, Stewart A. *Weimar and the Vatican 1919–1933*. Princeton, NJ: Princeton University Press, 1983.

Stendardo, Guido. *Via Tasso*. Rome: privately printed, 1965.

Tardini, Domenico. *Memories of Pius XII*. London: Newman, 1961.

Taylor, Myron C. *Wartime Correspondence Between President Roosevelt and Pius XII*. New York: Macmillan, 1947.

Tittmann, Harold H. *Inside the Vatican of Pius XII*. New York: Doubleday, 2004.

Tompkins, Peter. *A Spy in Rome*. New York: Simon and Schuster, 1962.

_____. *Italy Betrayed*. New York: Simon and Schuster, 1966.

Trevor-Roper, H. R. *The Last Days of Hitler*. London: Macmillan, 1972.

_____, ed. *Hitler's Table Talk, 1941–1944*. New York: Enigma, 2001.

Trials of War Criminals Before the Nuremberg Military Tribunals, Nuremberg, October 1946–April 1949. Washington, DC: GPO, 1949–1953.

Valabrega, G., ed. *Gli ebrei in Italia durante il fascismo*. Milan: Centrodi Documentazione Ebraoca Contemporanea, 1963.

Warlimont, Walter. *Inside Hitler's Headquarters*. New York: Praeger, 1964.

Weizsäcker, Ernst von. *Memoirs*. Washington, DC: Regnery, 1951.

Westphal, Siegfried. *German Army in the West*. London: Cassel, 1951.

Wheeler-Bennett, J. W. *The Nemesis of Power*. London: Macmillan, 1953.

Wills, Garry G. *Papal Sin*. New York: Doubleday, 2000.

Zahn, Gordon C. *German Catholics and Hitler's Wars*. Notre Dame, IN: University of Notre Dame Press, 1962.

Zolli, Eugenio (Israel). *Antisemitismo*. Rome: A.V.E., 1945.

_____. *Before the Dawn*. New York: Sheed and Ward, 1954.

Zuccotti, Susan. *Under His Very Windows*. New Haven, CT: Yale University Press, 2001.

Newspapers and Periodicals

Annali dell Istituto storico italo-germanico, Monografia 18, germania e Santa Sede (Bologna)

Annali di storia moderna e contemporanea (Rome), 4th edition, 1998

Christian Science Monitor Magazine—October 9, 1943

The Churchman—June 1, 1945
La Civilta cattolica—March 4, 1961, 1972 (vol. 1)
Collier's—June 10, 1944
Commentary—November 1950
Commonweal—December 17, 1943, June 8, 1945
The Congress Weekly—March 2, 1945
Contemporary History—January 1968
Domenica del Corriere (Rome)—March 14, 1972
Il Giornali (Milan)—July 5, 1998
Harper's—July, August 1966
Incom (Rome)—March 1959
Inside the Vatican—March 2002
Israel (Rome)—February 14, 1945
The Jerusalem Post—October 10, 1958
The Jewish Chronicle—October 17, 1958
Jewish Journal of Sociology (London)—November 1960
The Journal of Ecclesiastical History—April 1977
The Journal of Modern History—June 1967
Il Messaggero (Rome)—March 25, 1944
The New Republic—March 8, 1943
The New York Herald-Tribune—March 21, 1964
The New York Times—April 17, 1916; June 27, September 5, 14, 15, 21, 22, October 12, 14, 15, 17, 30, 1943; March 23, May 3, 7, 16, 1945; January 23, 1962; May 22, July 7, 8, 14, 16, 21, 1964; July 17, 1984; July 21, 1991
Oggi Illustrato (Rome)—September 19, 1963
Osservatore Romano (Rome)—October 25, 26, 1943, March 26, 1944
La Rassegna Mensile di Israel (Rome)—January 1957
Scientific American—March 1957
Stern (Hamburg)—April 16, 1972
Il Tempo (Milan)—February, March 1951; March 1995
30 Days—Number 8, 2006

Unpublished Documents

Almansi, Dante. *Prima reazione al governo italiano circa e persecuzioni nazi-fasciste degli ebrei in Roma [settembre 1943–guigno 1944]*. Report to Italian government, Rome, August 15, 1944.
Almansi, Renato J. "Notes on Dante Almansi." New York.
Ardeatine Caves Commission. Inquest, sommario dell'incidente del 23 marzo 1944, Rome.
German World War II records (microfilm). National Archives, Maryland.
Graham, Robert A. Lecture: "Pius XII and the Axis in World War II." Rome.

Hitler, Adolf. Instructions for Karl Wolff on his assignment to Italy, September 10, 1943.

Kesselring, Albert K. *Operations from the Start of the Major Allied Attack up to the Evacuation of Rome; Special Report of the Events in Italy Between 25 July and 8 September 1943.*

Neufeld, Maurice. Collection of material on Zolli, copies in Library of Congress.

Notre Dame de Sion. Convent diary, entries during German occupation, Rome.

Office of Strategic Services, research and analysis branch, N. 2993. *The Contributions of the Italian Partisans to the Allied War Effort.* Library of Congress.

OSS/London (microfilm). Special Operations Branch and Secret Intelligence Branch war diaries.

Pacelli, Eugenio (Pope Pius XII). Letter to his superior denouncing Nazis, November 14, 1923. *Archivio Nunziatura Monaco, protocollo numero 28961, busta 396, fascicolo 7, foglio 6r–7v.*

Trial records of Karl Wolff. Staatsarchiv, Munich.

Urban, Joan B. Thesis on history of Italian communism. Catholic University, Washington, DC.

Weizsäcker, Ernst von. *Rundbriefe aus Rom.* Collection of letters to his family from Rome, made available to the author by Frau Marianne von Weizsäcker.

Weizsäcker, Marianne von. Personal diary from period of German occupation of Rome.

Wolff, Karl. Notes he read to author on his meetings with Hitler.

Archives and Libraries Used

Archivio Centrale della Stato (Rome)
Associazione Nazionale Partigiani d'Italia (Rome)
Bundesarchiv (Berlin)
Centro di Documentazione Ebraica Contemporanea (Milan)
Columbia University Library
Imperial War Museum (London)
Library of Congress
Il Messaggero archives (Rome)
National Archives (London)
National Archives (Maryland)
New York Public Library
Staatsarchiv (Munich)
University of California Library (Berkeley)
Via Tasso Library (Rome)

Index

About the Author

Dan Kurzman, a former foreign correspondent for the *Washington Post,* has written sixteen previous books, including the best-selling *Fatal Voyage: The Sinking of the USS* Indianapolis and *Genesis 1948: The First Arab-Israeli War.* He has won the George Polk Memorial Award, the Overseas Press Club's Cornelius Ryan Award for the Best Book on Foreign Affairs (twice), the National Jewish Book Award, and the Newspaper Guild's Front Page Award for Best Foreign Reporting.

Mr. Kurzman has reported from almost every country in Europe, Asia, Africa, the Middle East, and Latin America. Before joining the *Washington Post,* he served as Jerusalem correspondent for NBC News and as Asian bureau chief of the McGraw Hill News Service.